So Others
May Live

An amphibious HH-3F helicopter flies over the Statue of Liberty in New York Harbor from Air Station Brooklyn, circa 1970s. USCG CWO J. MACKEY

SO OTHERS MAY LIVE

Coast Guard Rescue Swimmers: Saving Lives, Defying Death

MARTHA LaGUARDIA-KOTITE

FOREWORD BY TOM RIDGE

THE LYONS PRESS
Guilford, Connecticut
An imprint of the Globe Pequot Press

The Lyons Press is an imprint of The Globe Pequot Press.

Quotations in this book were obtained from case files, awards documentation, and personal interviews with the individuals involved in each rescue, conducted from 2002 to 2005 by the author. Used with permission.

ISBN 978-1-59921-159-6

10 9 8 7 6 5 4 3

Printed in the United States of America

The Library of Congress has previously cataloged an earlier (hardcover) edition as follows:

LaGuardia-Kotite, Martha J.
   So others may live / Martha J. LaGuardia-Kotite.
      p. cm.
   ISBN-13: 978-1-59228-931-8
   ISBN-10: 1-59228-931-2
   1. United States. Coast Guard—Search and rescue operations—History. I. Title.
VG53.L34 2006
363.28'60973—dc22
                                        2006009665

DEDICATION

This book is for my family,
Peter J. Kotite, Aaron E. Bruner, and John P. Kotite;
for my brothers Charles, David, and Mark LaGuardia;
and for our mother and father,
Martha M. and Charles J. LaGuardia

CONTENTS

FOREWORD

So Others May Live captures the unsung heroism of the helicopter rescue swimmers of the U.S. Coast Guard. This book is an overdue and fitting tribute to those whose primary mission is to risk their lives to save others.

As the first secretary of the U.S. Department of Homeland Security, I was honored to serve as secretary of the United States Coast Guard. On behalf of our country, this service performs many demanding tasks at home and around the world. They do so with an unrelenting sense of duty that requires great sacrifice and courage.

By shining light on the selfless acts of these rescue swimmers, Commander LaGuardia defines and celebrates a very talented and patriotic group of Americans.

Simultaneously, she also acknowledges and celebrates the exemplary human and professional qualities of all the men and women who proudly serve their country as "Coasties"!

Governor Tom Ridge
April 2006

ACKNOWLEDGMENTS

Thanks to Master Chief Scott Dyer, Coast Guard Rescue Swimmer program manager, and to all rescue swimmers, flight mechanics, and pilots I spoke with and to their families, as well as to the survivors who helped me tell these stories and the profession's history. Thanks also to Ellie Roy and Patti Gross, the Coast Guard Foundation, John "Bear" Moseley, George Krietemeyer, and the Ancient Order of Pterodactyls for believing in my initiative and sharing their history files, to Glenn Grossman for his dramatic pictures, to Tom Cutler "DGUTS" for his support and encouragement. My appreciation as well to my husband Peter and my sons Aaron and John, to my writing group members Trish Marx and Lucy Barrett, to Governor Tom Ridge for his foreword, and to my editor Tom McCarthy and his talented team at The Lyons Press.

INTRODUCTION

When I was eighteen, I learned how short and fragile life can be. I was determined to help others and if I could, in some way, save lives.

Of all the military services, the Coast Guard's everyday mission of saving lives drew my interest. I applied to the Coast Guard Academy and was accepted. The amazing people I met, including Admiral Paul A. Yost, Jr. were encouraging and inspiring. Four years later, I graduated with the class of 1989 and was assigned to my first ship—the Coast Guard Cutter *Resolute*, home ported in Astoria, Oregon—as an ensign. It was during our patrol in Prince William Sound, following the *Exxon Valdez* oil spill, that I realized I had a liking and talent for telling the Coast Guard's story while serving as the ship's public affairs officer. I was helping people understand what had just happened and what was being done to help them. Following assignments included executive officer aboard the 110-foot patrol boat *Padre*, based in Key West, assistant operations officer for Coast Guard Group Key West, District 13 public affairs officer in Seattle, Washington, and assistant surface operations officer for activities in New York.

While living on Bainbridge Island and working in Seattle, I heard about rescue swimmer Tristan Heaton. The year before I moved to the Pacific Northwest, he had a near-death experience saving a teenager in an Oregon cave. His story of risk and self-sacrifice resonated and remained with me. Here was a person who went farther than I could have ever imagined to save a stranger's life. Why would he bring his own life so close to death's door for someone he did not know and would probably never hear from again?

By 1999, I left active duty and moved into Manhattan to work at a technology public relations firm. My long-time desire to write about Tristan and other amazing heroes who served in the Coast Guard was made possible a few years later. With the help of another rescue swimmer, Eric Mueller, I was able to call Tristan, who had left the Coast Guard years before. I asked Tristan and he agreed to let me tell his story. He trusted and believed in me the way I believed in him. Over the next couple of years, other rescue swimmers, pilots, and flight mechanics and those they rescued agreed to share their soulful stories with me. It has been a tremendous honor. May their stories inspire you and make a difference in your life.

I

SO OTHERS MAY LIVE

I do not believe that a greater act of heroism is recorded than that of Dailey and his crew on this momentous occasion. These poor, plain men, dwellers upon the lonely sands of Hatteras, took their lives in their hands and, at the most imminent risk, crossed the most tumultuous sea that any boat within the memory of living men had ever attempted on that bleak coast, and all for what? That others might live to see home and friends. The thought of reward or mercenary appeal never once entered their minds. Duty, their sense of obligation, and the credit of the Service impelled them to do their mighty best. The names of Benjamin B. Dailey and his comrades in this magnificent feat should never be forgotten. As long as the Life-Saving Service has the good fortune to number among its keepers and crews such men as these, no fear need ever be entertained for its good name or purposes.

(Excerpt from an officer's report of the rescue by Cape Hatteras Life Saving Station, North Carolina, of survivors of the wreck of the barkentine *Ephraim Williams* on December 22, 1884, from the U.S. Life Saving Service History Web site, www.LifeSavingService.org. The LSS joined the Revenue Cutter Service to form the U.S. Coast Guard in 1915.)

THE CULMINATION OF TWO TRAGIC incidents in the early 1980s with significant loss of life focused congressional and public attention on the need for search and rescue capabilities to assist incapacitated people in cold water. The National Transportation Safety Board (NTSB) investigated the Air Florida flight 90 crash into the Washington, DC, 14th Street Bridge on January 13, 1982.

Only one year later, the U.S. Coast Guard convened a Marine Board of Investigation to analyze the circumstances surrounding the SS *Marine Electric*'s capsizing and sinking on February 13, 1983, off the Atlantic Coast, thirty nautical miles east of Chincoteague, Virginia.

It was determined that search and rescue requirements and capabilities at that time were not required or able to assist hypothermic or injured people or, for that matter, anyone in the water who was unable to climb into a rescue basket lowered by a helicopter. A decade before, pioneers within U.S. Coast Guard aviation had created ways to train personnel in rescuing people in the water using helicopters, "that others might live." Limited by modest funding for equipment and lukewarm command support, these motivated individuals took steps to forge ahead. Their initiatives never caught on in the Coast Guard, so they were not be able to see their vision sustained beyond their own dedicated service.

Air Florida's Boeing 737 crashed into the 14th Street Bridge as rush-hour commuters tried to get home ahead of a major storm. According to the NTSB report, seventy-four passengers, including three infants and five crew members, were on board. The flight's scheduled departure was delayed almost two hours because of heavy snowfall that closed the airport. Snow and ice stuck to the aircraft, which took off from the runway in poor visibility. At about 4:01 P.M., according to the NTSB report, "the aircraft crashed into the barrier wall of the northbound span of the 14th Street Bridge which connects the District of Columbia with Arlington County and plunged into the ice-covered Potomac River. It came to rest on the west side of the bridge 0.75 nautical miles from the departure end of runway 36."

Close to the Pentagon, the aircraft struck the bridge and seven occupied vehicles. Then it "tore away a section of the bridge barrier wall and bridge railing. Four persons in the vehicles were killed and four were injured," summarized the NTSB report. "Four passengers and one crewmember survived the crash."

Emergency vehicles traveled on icy roads and into traffic that had begun backing up earlier that afternoon when local businesses released their employees so they could avoid getting stranded in the heavy snowstorm.

Twenty minutes after the plane crashed into the river, a U.S. Park Police Bell JetRanger helicopter dropped life rings and looped ropes to the few survivors. Some were able to hold on long enough to be dragged to shore while others were too frozen and incapacitated to even use floating debris to keep themselves above the surface. Only one life vest was located by a survivor, which she passed to another more critically injured one. "The life vest was packaged in plastic and was difficult to open. The survivors had to chew on the package and tear it open with their teeth," according to the NTSB. "When the rescue helicopter arrived, three of the survivors were still able to function sufficiently to help themselves into the life ring or held onto loops tied into rescue ropes. The other two survivors required hands-on rescue; one was pulled aboard the helicopter skid by the helicopter crewman, the other was rescued by a civilian bystander who swam out and pulled her ashore."

The bystander, Lenny Skutnik, twenty-eight, had just crossed the bridge on his way home from work. The *Washington Post* preserved his heroic moment in an interview by Chip Brown and Blaine Harden, which appeared in the paper the following day, January 14, 1982: "I felt so helpless," said Skutnik, who worked for the congressional Budget Office. "She was screaming 'Would somebody please help me!' It looked like she had passed out. I jerked off my boots and coat and jumped in the water."

Skutnik became a national hero.

"The Coast Guard inadvertently got bad press on that," recalled retired ASM (aviation survivalman) Master Chief Petty Officer Larry Farmer, manager of the Coast Guard's Helicopter Rescue Swimmer Standardization (STAN) Team from 1984 to 1991. "We launched a helicopter out of Elizabeth City, North Carolina, but because of weather could not get there."

One of the worst blizzards to ever hit Washington, DC, closed airports, schools, and businesses and prevented the Coast Guard from assisting with the rescue. Coast Guard Reserve Unit Station Washington was the closest unit in the area of the accident because the CGC *Capstan*, an ice-breaking harbor tug, was downriver working another search and rescue case. "We had to rely on Station Washington reservists from Maryland because the 14th Street Bridge was knocked out by the crash," said Lieutenant Jim Begis, the unit's commanding officer, in an article written by CWO3 Paul A. Powers for *Coast Guard* magazine. The unit recalled members to travel through icy conditions and bad roads to the boathouse in Maryland to respond. When they arrived, the thirty-foot utility boat was frozen "inside and out." It took a Navy tug and the CGC *Capstan* to cut a channel from the boathouse to the crash site where the reservists recovered bodies and debris the following day.

According to the report, the survivors had been in water that was thirty-four degrees Fahrenheit for twenty-two to thirty-five minutes at the time of rescue. "At least fifty percent of survivors should have lost consciousness during that time period.

"The Safety Board does not believe the various emergency response organizations were adequately equipped for this emergency. Undoubtedly, had there been a large number of persons surviving the impact forces, many would have drowned in the icy water before they could have been rescued."

In the Federal Aviation Administration's (FAA) response to recommendations from the NTSB, one of its many amendments to procedures and practices for air carriers and airports stipulated that they

> Provide for essential equipment and increased personnel training to improve the water rescue capabilities at the Washington National Airport in all anticipated weather conditions and provide necessary funding for surrounding communities and jurisdictions which will be called on to support the airport's rescue response.

THE FOLLOWING YEAR, ON FEBRUARY 12, 1983, the SS *Marine Electric* capsized and sank in gale force conditions just off the Virginia coast. The fully loaded coal collier was en route from Norfolk, Virginia, to Brayton Point, Massachusetts. The following information was obtained from the U.S. Coast Guard Marine Board of Investigation and the Coast Guard Marine Casualty Report on the accident.

The SS *Marine Electric* departed about 11:45 P.M., February 11, with a cargo of steam coal. A winter storm continued to build as she departed Chesapeake Bay. The winds were from the northeast from thirty-five to fifty-five knots and the seas built to twenty to forty feet in the Atlantic Ocean.

Around 4 P.M. on the afternoon of February 12, the U.S.-flagged ship sighted the fishing vessel *Theodora*. The fishing vessel requested assistance, reporting to the Coast Guard it was taking on water. As a result of the severe weather conditions, the *Marine Electric* had only traveled ninety-five miles from Chesapeake Bay. It located the fishing vessel and passed its position to the U.S. Coast Guard. The Coast Guard had asked the 588-foot vessel to stand by the *Theodora* and escort it toward Chincoteague. By 6:25 P.M. the *Marine Electric* had resumed its course to Massachusetts, having been released by the Coast Guard from its watch. The Coast Guard's patrol boat *Point Highland* was on scene to escort the fishing vessel, while a Coast Guard helicopter from Elizabeth City, North Carolina, returned from aerial surveillance of the vessel.

The *Marine Electric*'s master, Captain Phillip H. Corl, reported to the Coast Guard in Ocean City, Maryland, that it seemed his vessel was taking on water and going down by the head at 2:51 A.M.

The investigation recorded the final hours in part from testimony by the three survivors, Chief Mate Robert M. Cusick, Third Mate Eugene F. Kelly, and Able Seaman Paul C. Dewey:

> At about 0300, the crew was awakened and mustered at the starboard lifeboat, and the vessel altered course to 000 degrees True. Trim by the bow continued to increase but no list was reported until 0350, when a 5-degree starboard list was reported. The list increased to 10 degrees by 0410. With most of the 34 crewmembers on the starboard boat deck, the ship took a sudden roll to starboard, throwing the crewmembers into the 37 degree F. water before the lifeboat was lowered.

> Three men survived and were rescued by a Coast Guard helicopter, which arrived on scene at 0520. Twenty-four bodies were recovered, most of whom died due to hypothermia. Seven bodies remained unrecovered, including that of the relief Master, Captain Corl.

Prior to the ship's sinking, the Coast Guard Fifth District Operations Center coordinated rescue efforts. The district directed two 82-foot patrol boats, *Point Arena* and *Point Highland*, to head for the SS *Marine Electric* by 3:30 that morning. The CGC *Cherokee*, a 205-foot medium-endurance cutter, was diverted to the scene from a law enforcement patrol cruising near the mouth of the Chesapeake Bay.

Air Station Elizabeth City was directed to launch the ready helicopter, tail number CG 1471. The Sikorsky HH-3F Pelican had flown numerous sorties for the *Theodora* case. Because of severe turbulence, the air station requested that a Coast Guard C-130 Hercules aircraft, used for patrols, search and rescue, and logistical support, fly cover for the helicopter. Prior to taking off at 4:13 A.M. the aircrew off-loaded pumps to enable the aircraft to carry more passengers in the rescue effort.

A U.S. Navy duty officer, on the watch for the commander in chief of the Atlantic fleet, received details of the distress call from the U.S. Coast Guard. The USS *Jack Williams* and the USS *Seattle* were about seventy miles from the *Marine Electric* and would be diverted to assist.

At 3:44 A.M. the Coast Guard District Operations Center requested the assistance of a Navy helicopter from Naval Air Station Oceana, Virginia.

A second Coast Guard helicopter, CG 1434, launched from Elizabeth City. The first helicopter, CG 1471, arrived on the scene at 5:20 A.M. The pilots reported to the district operations center that survivors were not actually in the lifeboats as expected.

According to the Coast Guard district chief of search and rescue, Captain Blankett, "transmissions the Coast Guard had received from the *Marine Electric* . . . led us to believe that it was a fairly sequenced event; that they did have boats and rafts; all the crew were in life jackets and that they would take to their boats and rafts . . . As soon as the aircraft got on scene, we knew right away that that was not the case."

The Coast Guard helicopter searched for survivors among a great number of strobe lights that were attached to the life vests and a few empty life rafts scattered in the Atlantic Ocean. Two individuals were recovered alive.

The Navy's rescue helicopter arrived on scene at 6:05 A.M. and transferred its rescue swimmer, Petty Officer James McCann, to CG 1471. McCann urgently searched the water for survivors among the dead. He recovered deceased crew using the rescue basket. At 7 A.M. one survivor in a lifeboat was located and rescued before the helicopter departed for Peninsula General Hospital with a total of three survivors and three deceased on board.

Two merchant ships, the *Tropic Sun* and *Berganger*, had responded to the urgent marine information broadcast over VHF channel 22A (157.1 MHz) and arrived to assist with the search. Their large superstructures provided a lee against the wind and somewhat calmed the seas for rescuers who worked from small boats to recover the deceased.

Rescue efforts by the U.S. Coast Guard, U.S. Navy aircraft, surface vessels, and merchant vessels resulted in the recovery of all but seven *Marine Electric* crew members, who were presumed missing.

The overturned stern of the *Marine Electric* was visible until late morning. At 11:30 A.M. it sank in one hundred and twenty feet of water.

The investigation cited that the commandant did not determine the actual cause of the accident, only that "the most probable cause was determined to be the wasted top plating of the dry cargo hatch and wasted main deck plating which permitted boarding seas to flood the vessel's forward spaces."

"COUPLED WITH THE AIR FLORIDA ACCIDENT and the *Marine Electric*, Congress levied a mandate to the Coast Guard to develop a program which would provide a trained and capable individual to enter the water and essentially rescue people from the water," stated Coast Guard Master Chief Larry Farmer. "Prior to 1984 when the congressional mandate came down it was always a coin toss. We spent years dangling a rescue basket near a survivor or victim hoping they could get in. If they could not, then they would 'toss a coin' to decide who was going to go down and apply the hands-on rescue." This type of rescue would usually involve landing the helicopter for pickup or sending someone down the a steel hoist cable in the rescue basket.

In the Sikorsky HH-3F Pelican, a medium-range, amphibious helicopter, either the flight mechanic or the avionics man, also known as the radio operator, was an eligible candidate. It depended on the situation. "Back in those days, on the HH-52A helicopter the crew was only three individuals, two pilots and one crew member in the back. In some situations, the only other person who could go was the copilot," recalled Farmer. "Most of the time they would sit in the basket and go down and grab the individual that needed to be saved, pull the person across their lap. Then the flight mechanic would hoist the two people up."

Surprisingly, as far back as Farmer can remember no one in the Coast Guard ever got hurt daring to execute those types of rescues, but there were a lot of close calls. "Even with an amphibious HH-3F helicopter it was kind of a dicey proposition," according to Dana Goward. Six months prior to the SS *Marine Electric* accident, as part of his work as a lieutenant in the Coast Guard Headquarters Office of Operations, Search and Rescue Division, Goward developed a planning proposal for a Coast Guard helicopter rescue swimmer program. "You could stick the helicopter's tail rotor in the waves and die, you could be overwhelmed by a wave and die. You could land too close or too far from a survivor and they would die. So it wasn't something you did lightly—it was sort of a last ditch effort."

Goward's planning proposal needed to go through the formal congressional budget process, but the idea was not seen as a top priority within the Coast Guard.

"Probably ten to twelve times a year around the Coast Guard, a copilot or extra crewman would go down to help somebody who could not help themselves," Goward discovered. "Fortunately, no one got hurt. I think it was only a matter of time before something bad happened.

"I estimated that we lost between thirty-seven and forty-two lives a year because we weren't able to act quick enough. Hypothermia was a big issue for survivors."

NEARLY TEN YEARS BEFORE THE TWO TRAGEDIES, a few pilots and aircrews believed there should be a better way and took action. They aimed to help people who could not help themselves, particularly hypothermic survivors. In the 1970s, their beliefs were realized. They developed a team of self-taught aircrewmen who could deploy out of Coast Guard helicopters.

The Coast Guard employed two types of amphibious aircraft during the 1960s to the 1980s. The Sikorsky single-engine HH-52A Sea Guard was first to come online in 1963. The second was the twin-engine Sikorsky HH-3F Pelican, purchased in 1968.

To mitigate a portion of the apparent risk, these ad hoc teams of volunteers trained on their own. Most notable of such initiatives were New York's Air Station Brooklyn and California's Air Station San Francisco.

San Francisco's Sea Air Rotor Wing Evacuation Team (SARWET) was "a unique, highly trained group of SAR aircrewmen established at Coast Guard Air Station San Francisco to effect difficult rescues when exceptional competence is required," according to the spring 1973 issue of: *Flight Lines: The US Coast Guard Flight Safety Newsletter*. The article "This is SARWET, CGAS San Francisco" credits the originality of the concept to AT2 William J. Thrall, who was later promoted to ensign in 1970. The commanding officer of Air Station San Francisco, Captain C. E. Larkin, encouraged the creation of a pilot team to test the feasibility of SARWET. The test team consisted of AT2 Thrall, ASM2 David G. Hobson, AT2 Craig O. Cross, and AE3 Karl H. Kochishan. They founded the original training, criteria, and syllabus.

According to the article, "SARWET candidates are selected for attitude, physical condition, swimming ability and strong motivation towards the SAR effort. Training consists of eight full days of physical conditioning which includes three mile distance running, underwater swimming, a 2000 meter swim in under 50 minutes, the ability to do 50 sit ups, 20 push ups and 10 pull ups."

In addition to physical conditioning, SARWET members were trained by the air station medical department in first aid. They were prepared to treat shock and burn victims, "fractures and dislocations, neck and back injuries, trauma, resuscitation and dealing with unconscious an uncooperative patients," the *Flight Lines* article continued.

To adjust to the environmental conditions offshore, they practiced swimming along the coast in the kind of surf they would likely have to experience during a rescue. They wore a wet suit, flippers, mask, special flotation gear, and carried a UHF radio and a medical bag.

"We received excellent support from the USAF swim team at Hamilton AFB in Marin County who were the rescue swimmers for the Apollo program," said Sean Rafter, one of the original members of SARWET and retired from the Coast Guard. "They gave us their manual, PT [physical fitness training] requirements, and swim gear that we had no budget to acquire. The support of the medical staff at the air station was excellent."

On November 15, 1972, the Pacific area commander (Twelfth Coast Guard District), Vice Admiral Mark A. Whalen, presented SAR-WET certificates to the new ten-man team at a ceremony at Air Station San Francisco. The members of the first functioning SARWET team were Lieutenant Junior Grade Sean Rafter, AD2 Jack Geck, ASM2 David Hobson, AT3 Clinton Ressler, HM3 Doug Cole, AD3 Charles Dewey, AM3 Ralph Oliver, AM3 Donald Lockwood, AT3 Greg Simmons, and AM3 Gary Hecq.

A few weeks later, AT3 Clinton A. Ressler would make the first SAR-WET save after a Beechcraft Bonanza crashed into the San Francisco Bay in heavy fog. The injured pilot was trapped in the sinking plane's wreckage. Ressler "dove from the HH-52A helicopter into the water where he maneuvered the survivor . . . to the Sea Rescue platform. The survivor was then delivered to a waiting ambulance at the Air Station. Extensive first aid treatment was administered enroute," according to *Flight Lines*. "The long-range goals recommended for SARWET are a service wide program of SARWET teams at all Air Stations where their special skill can be utilized, and the eventual establishment of a descriptive qualification code and pro-pay designation. It is not envisioned that SARWET would duplicate the Air Force pararescue program, but would concentrate on the Coast Guard's particular needs."

Rafter ran the program until he departed for a new assignment in March of 1973. SARWET did not flourish servicewide, nor was it well known. In fact, Lieutenant Ron Simons noticed its momentum was waning even at Air Station San Francisco. Simons, an experienced helicopter pilot, had completed tours working in two challenging environments, Air Station Traverse City in Michigan and Annette Island in southeast Alaska, which would later move and become Coast Guard Air Station Sitka in 1977.

When Simons was first assigned to Air Station San Francisco, he looked into the initiative. "I immediately wanted to find out what that was all about," he recalled.

He learned from his peers about the reasons for SARWET's development and response. For Simons, an officer with a safety background and personal focus, this plan of action made him nervous. He asked: *Who are these guys? What training do they have that we're going to take them out? Put them in the surf. What are the possibilities of someone being injured or not coming back?*

SARWET continued to fade while Simons was assigned to the air station. As the flight safety officer, Simons knew the need still existed. He talked with the commanding officer of Air Station San Francisco, Captain Bob Branham, and requested permission to give the SARWET program, which was filed away as a contingency plan, some impetus. "I asked if I could come up with a training program, one which would have helicopters available for training. I needed funding so that we could get wet suits, flares, radios, strobe lights, everything that we would need to deploy day or night from the helicopter into the water," said Simons. "He was very accommodating."

Fully supported by the command, Simons put out a call for anyone interested in the program to respond. With the support of the engineering officer, Commander Larry Montali, Simons knew volunteers would be available for training, and they had their shop chief's permission. Lieutenant Steve Pearman, one of twelve people to respond, assisted Simons with laying the groundwork and "putting the program together as we went." One critical element remained. Where would they find a swimming pool to train?

Simons, a bachelor who lived at the Treasure Island Naval Air Station, eyed the pool there as a potential training facility. "I talked to them, and they agreed to let us use their Olympic-sized pool for training every Friday," stated Simons.

With the essentials in place, the group started to train off the California coast in Half Moon Bay. "We tried to go out twice a month with the HH-52A helicopter, two of them if we went offshore. We'd drop out of the eighty-three-hundred-pound helicopter into the surf," Simons recalled.

Similar to the original SARWET concept, they focused their training on helping someone on a boat or caught in the surf or on the rocks. In cases where there were injuries, they trained to administer first aid and to use the Stokes Litter, a stretcher used for rescues, as a means of hoisting a survivor. "There were not any EMTs [emergency medical technicians] at the time in the Coast Guard. Part of our training was to go to sick bay to have them give us first-aid training," Simons added.

The first time they trained, the seas were ten to twelve feet off the coast. The swimmers were dropped four at a time into the surf before the helicopter flew out of sight. The men needed to become accustomed and comfortable being alone in the ocean. They carried a radio to call for the helicopters to return. After about an hour of bobbing up and down in the rolling surf, they were amazed to find they got seasick—something else they would need to adjust to.

"It was fun to do it so there wasn't anything unnerving, and we were cautious," said Simons. "I wasn't going to jeopardize anyone's safety."

What surprised Simons nearly thirty years later about their training ground was a fact he learned from a television special. Apparently, the most populous great white shark area was right off Half Moon Bay. "Here we were in black wet suits looking like a bunch of seals, I'm just thinking, holy mackerel, we're lucky we weren't devoured!"

Not wanting to take credit where it was not deserved, Simons acknowledged that the initiative had started before he arrived. "They saw the need and said they would meet it. It was late in 1973 when we started the program in this way," recalled Simons of his team's focus. "We had a number of times we were launched but never utilized. The day that I left, the SARWET team got a case. It was around March of 1974. Mike Belaumeny got the call. A beaten sailboat and panicked crew were in the Pacific surf near the Cliff House."

The SARWET volunteer deployed out of the helicopter into the surf. With the help of a forty-four-foot motor lifeboat standing by, Belaumeny was able to calm the survivors and get a towline from the Coast Guard lifeboat to the sailboat. It was towed safely into the harbor while a local television crew recorded the rescue from an ideal observation site on the adjacent cliff. It was one of the evening's top news stories.

Simons, unfortunately, missed the case. He had transferred to Washington, DC, that very day. For the next couple of years, he flew CG-01, the commandant's Gulfstream II jet, followed by a plum assignment as the aide to the commandant, Admiral John B. "Jack" Hayes. "He was the best commandant that ever lived," reminisced Simons.

The SARWET program was again but a memory by the end of 1974. In part, it was difficult to continue when dedicated members would transfer and there was a lack of interest among the incoming people to participate.

"Steve Pearman did his best to keep it going, but I think it died a natural death," Simons admitted. "For one thing, if you didn't love to swim, it wasn't for you. I was real fortunate we put together a team where every one of them loved doing it."

IN MAY OF 1974, THE COMMANDANT had directed commanding officers to reprioritize unit training in order to bring helicopter aircrewmen to the prehospital-care capability level of metropolitan ambulance attendants.

In fall of that year, the U.S. Public Health Service Hospital on Staten Island offered the new Department of Transportation standard emergency medical technician course to Coast Guard Air Station Brooklyn's helicopter crews. Lieutenant Junior Grade Hugh O'Doherty, the aircrew-training officer, solicited for volunteers to attend the course. The EMT-trained aircrewmen would fulfill the commandant's orders and also enhance Brooklyn's first response treatment of survivors and injured patients transported in their short-range HH-52As and medium-range HH-3Fs.

O'Doherty's commanding officer, Captain G. J. Budridge, directed him to pursue providing these EMTs with capability similar to their SAR-WET brethren in the Golden Gate city. Budridge's idea was a deployable rescue specialist who could enter the water to assist the survivor, then provide primary care en route to the hospital.

O'Doherty, an experienced HH-52A pilot and qualified EMT and scuba diver, had worked as a survival swimming instructor for lifeguards. He sketched out a program similar to that of the West Coast that would train EMT volunteers to be physically fit and become rescue swimmers.

They met for calisthenics and running during their lunch break, three days a week. At the start of the summer season they trained in the water once a week at Coast Guard Station Rockaway.

These "special aircrewmen," as they were called, were very enthusiastic EMTs. "They went to EMT classes, assisted in hospital emergency rooms, and worked out together, largely on their own time," recalled O'Doherty. "We bought resuscitators, the ASM's prototyped medevac bags, and soon we had an EMT in each duty section." They were assigned to fly on the HH-3F or the HH-52A. The air station's engineering department and sick bay covered equipment expenses.

Yet, participants never got their feet wet in the line of duty. Too soon they were faced with the reality of the Coast Guard budget. "No money for rescue swimmer equipment, no man hours or billets to cover the extra training time," said O'Doherty. "Like SARWET, the program could not sustain itself just on enthusiasm. Although our EMT program survived, the 'special aircrewman' program died on the vine. Some of the disillusioned volunteers 'voted with their feet' and left the Coast Guard to become civilian paramedics and firefighters."

When the Coast Guard's EMT school opened in Petaluma, California, in 1978, it provided all Coast Guard units standardized training for prehospital care. Again, the program was largely "out of hide—with no mandated extra billets and little funding," O'Doherty noted.

O'Doherty transferred from Air Station Brooklyn to fly C-130s out of Air Station Sacramento in 1978. He was assigned in 1981 to the 413 Transport and Rescue Squadron, Canadian Forces, on a helicopter rescue pilot exchange program. He was amazed by what he discovered. "Now, I got to fly with rescue specialists, SARTECHs! We could assist people in the water, on a mountain ledge, in a crashed aircraft, and in all cases, provide appropriate medical care," O'Doherty exclaimed. "It was the normal way to do a rescue." The Canadian SARTECHs were supported with appropriate rescue equipment, assigned people to do the job, and had the proper training to help them rescue in a variety of demanding environments. "Not only were these rescue specialists enthusiastic, they were professionally and operationally consistent."

One of O'Doherty's friends, Lieutenant Dana Goward, with whom he always enjoyed arguing on just about every subject, was assigned to Coast Guard Headquarters in Washington, DC. Goward was in a position to make a difference.

Goward worked in the Coast Guard Headquarters Office of Operations in the Search and Rescue Division with Lieutenant Commander Terry Cross (2004–2006 vice commandant of the Coast Guard) and Lieutenant Commander Jim Brockenik. Goward was given the latitude to develop an initial proposal for a helicopter rescue swimmer program within the U.S. Coast Guard.

Prior to Goward's staff job assignment, he had piloted helicopters on many rescues and earned a master's degree in management at the Naval Postgraduate School, focusing on human resources. He knew whom to talk to in the field to figure out what an ideal program would need.

While refining his proposal, Goward contacted O'Doherty to find out more about the Canadian SARTECHs.

"I immediately told him that it would never work in the Coast Guard, citing the SARWET, 'special aircrewman,' and EMT examples,"

O'Doherty recalled. "Dana countered by saying that he had a congressional mandate, money, and bodies. Only ASMs would be rescue swimmers/EMTs and that he was going to build up the rate [rating or job classification] so that there would be a swimmer in every duty section, Coast Guard-wide."

O'Doherty replied, "We'll see."

SIX MONTHS PRIOR TO THE SS *MARINE ELECTRIC* accident, the Coast Guard's rescue swimmer program had been under development. Lieutenant Goward spearheaded a planning proposal, and Commander Al Steinman, a flight surgeon responsible for survival equipment and a proponent of the EMT program, agreed to help. The two officers would split the workload to further develop the proposal. They would also address associated issues, which had stalled the plan's advancement, or added "friction."

"We were unable to get a lot of budgetary interest until the *Marine Electric*. Even then, the Coast Guard was slow to adopt the idea, as it was seen as hazarding our own folks," according to Goward. "However, the HH-52A was in the early stages of being replaced by a nonamphibious helicopter, the HH-65 Dolphin, and that helped sell the program internally."

Following the SS *Marine Electric* investigation and based on conclusions developed from the congressional Merchant Marine and Fisheries Committee hearings regarding the Coast Guard's existing techniques and equipment, Congress mandated the swimmer program as a part of the Coast Guard Authorization Act of 1984. This act required the commandant of the Coast Guard to establish a helicopter rescue swimmer program to train selected Coast Guard personnel in rescue swimming skills.

GOWARD'S PROPOSAL HAD A GREEN LIGHT, and the Coast Guard had funding and authority to establish its own helicopter rescue swimmer program.

A larger team was assembled to turn the dream into reality. Lieutenant Commander Ken Coffland, chief of aviation life support and charged with supervision of the EMT program for the Coast Guard, was assigned the additional duty of Helicopter Rescue Swimmer Program manager.

One of the first phone calls to solicit enlisted leadership was to a senior aviation survivalman, Master Chief Petty Officer ASMCM Larry Farmer. Farmer graduated from a Navy Class "A" school, a job training program for recruits in a specific field, as a parachute rigger in 1969 as a Third Class ASM in the Coast Guard. He served primarily at Coast Guard operational units for the next fifteen years. He was recognized for his leadership and his aviation operational and engineering expertise. He was also interested in the advancement of those in the aviation survival-man rate. Promoted to ASMCM in 1983, one of only two of that stature in his job classification, he was subsequently assigned as ASM Rating Subject Matter Specialist at the Coast Guard Institute in Oklahoma City where there wasn't a hangar deck or aircraft. This was something he was not particularly happy about.

When Coast Guard Headquarters asked if he would be interested in leading the ASM program, he was immediately on board with its plans and offered his expertise.

ONE OF THE EARLIEST CONSIDERATIONS for the team was where a rate of this specialty would work best in the current aviation workforce structure. Should a new rating be created? Or, would it work best as a collateral duty?

Of critical concern was the perception of creating a "rating of heroes," which could affect the morale of everybody else negatively. The swimmers might be looked down upon for seeming elitist because of the nature of their work.

Goward was also concerned that being a rescue swimmer should be a full-time job. It would be too demanding and hazardous to be something that was an add-on to a crewman's primary duty. Others campaigned that folks from every rate should have the opportunity to do this job. The job should be open to anyone, man or woman, who served in the Coast Guard. Goward later commented, "This was all uncharted territory for us as an organization and there were a lot of concerns and anxieties."

Goward now worked alone. Steinman had transferred to another job, and this was before Ken Coffland would be assigned to assist as the program's manager. Goward decided after careful analysis that the program was a natural fit within the aviation survivalman rate, a trade that involved the fabrication and maintenance of rescue and survival equipment and the training of the rest of the air station crews in the use of that equipment. Additionally, he chose to not make it a collateral duty. To be good at lifesaving, an ASM needed to specialize. It would be a full-time job.

Initially, Goward did not want to model the Coast Guard's program after the U.S. Navy's, an easy choice. "I wanted to model it after the British Royal Navy's SAR divers," Goward said. "I had a friend who was on the exchange with them at the time, Al Gaston, and it was obvious that they had a much more advanced and sophisticated program. It was their job and their primary focus. However, since a program like the U.S. Air Force PJs [Pararescuemen] was too expensive, the U.S. Navy program was the only source of training for what we wanted."

Goward conceded that the Coast Guard was too conservative at the time to start with a model with more sophisticated capabilities, although it was ironically similar to what it evolved into. "Just duplicating the Navy's program in the U.S. Coast Guard was as far as the outfit was willing to go in the beginning." There was one exception. "In terms of training, techniques, and procedures, we had one hugely important difference. The Navy swimmers did it as a collateral duty and did not have a career path," recalled Goward. "I knew that would be a horrible way to go in the U.S. Coast Guard, since we would be using these guys all the time in hazardous conditions, unlike the Navy. Our folks had to be physically fit and have it as their primary focus. So we campaigned pretty hard and pretty successfully to make it a rate, a career."

Another concern was that of the long-term strain and stress on one's body from the strenuous work. Swimmers would get older, suffer injuries, or develop back and joint problems. They may not always be able to stay as physically fit. So they built into the rate model a promotional pyramid that moved senior people up and into supervisory positions and out of the line for duty.

Goward agreed to follow the established U.S. Navy rescue swimmer program from the beginning, knowing it would mean a delay in adopting techniques, like the use of direct deployment. Direct deployment kept the rescue swimmer attached to the helicopter's hoist cable, and the British Royal Navy had developed an expertise in it.

"I think we had a sense that leadership was taking enough of a leap of faith with this that if we said we could do it better than the U.S. Navy initially it would be too much of a jump." There was a lot of internal anxiety and resistance to the push toward this organizational change within the Coast Guard.

"The important point is that we got the program started and it had sufficient critical mass that it became self-sustaining and self-improving," said Goward. "That's really what you want in a quality organization. Even if you don't get it right the first time, and you know you won't. The people are there, the programs are there, the folks involved with it see it as their life's work and they will just feed off each other and improve things."

This was an exciting mission, a career, for highly motivated people.

The commandant, Admiral James Gracey, issued a message that solicited volunteers for anyone interested in becoming a rescue swimmer. Those who responded would attend the U.S. Navy Aviation Rescue Swimmer School in Pensacola, Florida, before being ordered to Air Station Elizabeth City to establish the first operational unit with rescue swimmers and develop the pilot program for subsequent units to follow.

Meanwhile, ASM3 Kelly Gordon and ASM2 Steve Ober were among a half dozen or so ASMs who had gone through the Naval Aviation Water Survival Instructor Training Program. They would in turn train others how to use a new underwater rebreather for emergency egress from helicopters. Because of a design flaw, they did not start the servicewide training but were now known as notable ASMs. When the Coast Guard needed to find people to fill the first few classes at the Navy rescue swimmer school, they were on the list to call. Ober and Gordon were asked if they would be interested in being part of the first class to go to the Navy's rescue swimmer school. Of those polled, they were the only two to say yes.

GORDON HAD BEEN IN THE ASM PROGRAM for about four years. "I went to ASM school thinking I was going to work on life support equipment and pack parachutes." There was no notion of any type of helicopter rescue swimmer program on the horizon. Gordon had also flown as a flight mechanic on the HH-3F helicopter.

Gordon was born in 1962 and grew up in Redmond, Oregon. He didn't know what he was going to do after graduation from high school and had turned down an offer from his father to go to college. He was a marginal student, swam competitively, and said he went to school mostly for the social aspects. One day his father told him what his options were. "He gave me that look across the table one night at dinner, and said when you turn eighteen and graduate, your free ride is over, you can live in my home under my rules," Gordon recalled.

A couple of weeks later, a Coast Guard recruiter visited his high school. "I liked the water, helicopters, and flying. It seemed like a natural fit."

The inaugural group of five volunteers was selected to attend the grueling training at the U.S. Navy's helicopter rescue swimmer school.

"Boy, we were in for a rude awakening," Gordon said. "It was the hardest school I had ever been to both mentally and physically. Their philosophy was they wanted to break you, they didn't want you to pass because they really wanted tough, tough individuals that without fail could deploy independent from the helicopter into just about any type of situation and effect a rescue. They were very proud of their program and of their school and I think they weren't too happy about entertaining the notion of training some Coasties, so we really got put through the paces."

ASM2 Ober and ASM3 Gordon were a little more senior than the majority of the class, which was made up of mostly nonrates, men who had just finished boot camp and were not yet specialized. Gordon's motivation was in part the pressure of being one of the first two from the Coast Guard to ever attempt that school. "Failure was not an option," Gordon said. "In so many words, it was you will represent the Coast Guard and you will represent the Coast Guard well." Gordon finished the last half of his time at the school injured. He remembered swimming an eight-hundred-meter buddy tow with a taped sprained ankle. "I had to finish, I didn't have a choice," said Gordon.

"The scenarios we were put though, the instructors told us, were five times worse than what we'd ever experience in the real world," said Ober, "thus ensuring our survival in any type of situation. I was bound and determined not to be sent home. I wanted to be the first and the best, to set the example for the Coast Guard Helicopter Rescue Swimmer Program."

On October 5, 1984, the first Coast Guard rescue swimmers to graduate from the Navy's four-week school were ASM2 Steve Ober and ASM3 Kelly Gordon. ASM2 Ober was distinguished as the honor graduate of his class and the fourth honor graduate in the history of the U.S. Navy school.

By the end of November, ASM1 Rick Woolford, ASM2 Matt Fithian, and ASM3 Butch Flythe joined Ober and Gordon as graduates of the school in Pensacola. These five men, helicopter rescue swimmers, made Coast Guard aviation history, known ever since as the "First Five."

AN INTERSERVICE CONFERENCE WAS HELD AT Naval Air Station Pensacola in January of 1985 to formulate U.S. Coast Guard Rescue Swimmer Operating Procedures. Experts in their fields attended, including the U.S. Navy Search And Rescue swimmers (SAR) manager from the Pensacola Naval Air Station, two U.S. Air Force Pararescuemen from Eglin Air Force Base near Destin, Florida; and a Canadian Armed Forces SAR technician. U.S. Coast Guard presence was represented by the First Five; Lieutenant Commander Ken Coffland from Air Station Elizabeth City and Captain Dave Dingley, U.S. Air Force exchange rescue pilot and the unit's rescue swimmer implementation project officer and HH-3F standardization officer; Lieutenant Commander O'Doherty, who recently transferred from the Canadian exchange program to Elizabeth City; ASMCM Ray Stalvey, charged with the transformation of the ASM Shop to be the center for the new training, equipment, and crew readiness; ASMCM Larry Farmer; ASMCS David Hobson from Aviation Technical Training Center, Elizabeth City, one of the original San Francisco SARWET members; and pilots and aircrew STAN Team members from Air Training Center (ATC) in Mobile, Alabama.

The group exchanged ideas during its initial meetings and demonstrated individual service techniques and procedures. Following these informative meetings, the Coast Guard contingent relocated to the Aviation Training Center (ATC) in Mobile where its members developed, tested, and finalized initial operating procedures and choices of equipment. "We huddled separately in groups and sorted out what we liked and didn't like," recalled O'Doherty.

They decided that as part of the swimmer's duties, when not conducting rescues, the individual would continue to perform the jobs traditionally assigned to the aviation survivalman. He would maintain the survival equipment that pilots and other aircrew depended upon should they have to abandon the aircraft in an emergency.

One of the things Lieutenant Commander Ken Coffland, the rescue swimmer program manager at the time, was passionate about was the professional demeanor of the SAR Tech participant, Canadian Master Warrant Guy Parent. His image was that of a "quiet professional": one who didn't boast or seek recognition, just did what one had to do, without airs, with modesty. He was just part of the team.

By February of 1985, Captain Dingley coordinated Air Station Elizabeth City's pilot program training. He instructed the pilots, avionicsmen and flight mechanics in the new and sometimes uncomfortable method of rescue with swimmers. Until it became routine, it was often unnerving for them to deploy the swimmer outside the HH-3F helicopter.

By June of 1985, the commandant announced the permanent change of the ASM rating to include rescue swimmer and emergency medical technician duties and training criteria all ASMs were required to meet and maintain. As part of the transition, to make it fair for those already in the rate and who had no desire to become rescue swimmers, chief petty officers and above were exempt. All other individuals were given a lenient period (five years and four months) to become a swimmer, change to a different rate, or be discharged on July 1, 1990.

That same month, the commandant announced implementation plans that would be phased in over five years to include a rescue swimmer for each duty section. Members of the aviation survivalman rating would become rescue swimmers and emergency medical technicians. Additional billets for personnel would be added during the implementation phase to provide for "on-the-job and recurrent training requirements."

Master Chief Farmer started to write the *Coast Guard Helicopter Rescue Swimmer Manual* with the help of the First Five in an effort to standardize operational procedures and policies.

The First Five tested Navy equipment, methods, and techniques before they were approved for standardized use during Coast Guard search and rescue. The tests were based on the HH-3F helicopter as the search and rescue platform.

"I wouldn't really call the equipment state of the art, it was adequate for what we were doing," Gordon recalled. "Picture this testing starting in October and we were told, 'Be ready to go operational in February.' We were training, in the middle of the winter in these wet suits, which were not adequate for preventing hypothermia." Gordon and the other First Five were asked to endure long periods in the cold water to determine what was going to be adequate equipment. Before too long, with medical personnel taking their body core temperatures, the decision was made to replace the wet suits with dry suits.

They also tested deployment altitudes and methods. "Played with the notion of leaving us connected to the cable at all times, have us swimming around like a lure," Gordon said of the things considered. "Testing different life rafts, procedures for leaving a swimmer on scene. We used some of the Navy deployment methods and some of the Canadian's. One of which was dragging a swimmer with a cable by his feet at a ten-knot forward speed toward the survivor. The rescue strop would be donned on the survivor very quickly, and the swimmer could effect the rescue in ten to fifteen seconds," Gordon described other ways, which could take minutes. "It was a little too challenging, and the notion of dragging somebody through the water like a piece of meat didn't go over too well."

In the end, they chose equipment and methods that were simple, less prone to human error and mistakes. Even though the air station would be considered operational, the First Five were still learning, and continued to refine and develop the program.

"With Master Chief Farmer the common sense was always there. He had the final say on what we were going to do," Gordon said. "We didn't need the quick or flashy, just the stuff that would get the job done. And the program really needed somebody who was going to take charge."

That same month, Captain Dingley's training goals were achieved, and Air Station Elizabeth City officially became the first operational unit, the birthplace of the Coast Guard Helicopter Rescue Swimmer Program, whose members adopted their service motto: So Others May Live.

Shortly thereafter, in May, twenty-seven-year-old ASM1 Rick Woolford got the first call to duty. "We were all waiting to see who would get the first one, that's my claim to fame," said Woolford. "It took place during the day on the Alligator River in Elizabeth City. A squall had just come through, and a man in his bass boat had capsized. I did a free fall from the helicopter, the first time we had ever done it for real, and reached for him to put him in the rescue basket. He wouldn't let go of his boat. 'Sir, you've got to let it go so I can put you in this basket,'" Woolford said, trying to encourage him. "He was very reluctant but did let go."

Woolford had the first rescue, and Ober would be the first rescue swimmer to receive an award, the Coast Guard Commendation Medal, for saving the life of an injured crew member aboard a fishing vessel that same year.

BEFORE RETIRING IN 2003 AS A CAPTAIN, Dana Goward's final assignment on active duty (which in fact is his current civilian position) was as chief of Coast Guard boat forces. He helped standardize small-boat equipment and procedures.

Goward has been recognized by the Coast Guard as the founding father of a profession that has received notoriety for what he calls "the service's most visible heroes."

Goward was presented with an original set of Coast Guard rescue swimmer wings, mounted on a plaque, on May 24, 2002, for his vision, which is inscribed, in part, with: "Thousands live today because of your dream, 'That Others May Live,'" a slogan that dates back to an 1884 Life Saving Service annual report.

COMMANDER HUGH O'DOHERTY SUCCEEDED Ken Coffland as program manager while the program was still being implemented throughout the country. Before retiring in 1995 he was the operations officer at Air Station Cape Cod. On his last Coast Guard flight, his crew deployed its rescue swimmer to save a girl who had attended high school with O'Doherty's daughter.

He comanages a corporate jet business based in Hyannis, Massachusetts. O'Doherty still credits Goward with making it happen. "Dana didn't just sit and complain, like some of us. He did the legwork, and persuaded the right people to get the bodies and bucks for that program to start, implement, sustain, and evolve. He 'made the impact' that changed the way Coasties save lives . . . and, of course, he proved me wrong!"

Commander Ron Simons retired from the U.S. Coast Guard in 1983 and flew the bush in Alaska for a few years before he worked as an airline captain for Northwest Airlink. He lives in Minnesota and drives a school bus for children in kindergarten through middle grades to "get me out of bed in the morning."

Master Chief Larry Farmer retired in 1997 after thirty years of dedicated service. Some of his many military awards and decorations include two Coast Guard Meritorious Service Medals, the Coast Guard Air Medal, Coast Guard Medal for Heroism, Coast Guard Commendation Medal, and the Survival and Flight Equipment Association (SAFE) Award honoring his career achievements.

Farmer founded a consulting firm, LEF Right Systems, where he is a senior consultant and marketing and sales representative for manufacturers that develop and provide safety, rescue, or survival equipment systems for military and commercial applications. He lives in Maryland and is married to the former Christine David of Agawam, Massachusetts. He has three children from a previous marriage. Arthur Farmer residing in Tuscaloosa, AL, Jim Farmer AST2, USCG, of fifteen years, currently stationed in Mobile, AL, and Laura Farmer living in Mobile, AL.

What is he most proud of? "I used to contemplate that all the time until we watched the U.S. Coast Guard perform during Hurricane Katrina . . . Rescue swimmers lowered to waist-deep water and rooftops, hacking their way through to save individuals, that just sums it up in my mind of how well that program has developed over the last twenty years."

Kelly Gordon, promoted to lieutenant, works as chief of the Port State Control (Foreign Vessel Inspections) Branch in Portland, Oregon. Of his time as a Third Class ASM working with the First Five he said, "Being on the leading edge of something like that, you couldn't ask for anything better. We were really committed to the program, we had a lot of pride; it was our lives for a while. It was that significant and important a program." For a short period of time when there was continued resistance "from the hangar deck," Gordon admitted that they did have doubts. He wondered, "Are we always going to be that extra piece of rescue equipment that sits in the back of the aircraft that's never used?"

"There is no bigger rush than going out and rescuing, saving somebody's life. It is so fulfilling, I could live off that kind of adrenaline for weeks," Gordon explained, satisfied.

ASM2 Steve Ober was promoted to chief petty officer before he was selected for and attended Officer Candidate School. Following his commissioning as ensign, he served at Coast Guard Headquarters to work on survival systems and later transferred to work for the Captain of the Port of New York. Ober qualified to stand duty as a vessel traffic service officer, port operations and marine inspections officer. He became the Coast Guard's Gulf Strike Team operations officer and served another tour in headquarters as the marine environmental protection and security liaison for the Coast Guard's Deepwater Program, an initiative to modernize aviation and surface fleet. Ober was the lead for all chemical, biological, radiological, and nuclear initiatives for the Deepwater Program. He retired from the Coast Guard as a lieutenant commander in 2004 with twenty-six years of active duty service. "What I learned from being a rescue swimmer was risk equals success. Without the self-confidence I gained and my life experience from being a swimmer, I probably would never have gone as far as I did in the military or civilian world."

Ober is now a civilian contractor in the Coast Guard Headquarters Office for Security and Defense Operations. He works as the program manager for the Coast Guard's Weapons of Mass Destruction initiatives, overseeing equipment, training, and policy.

ASM1 Rick Woolford attended Officer Candidate School and became a career Coast Guard helicopter pilot. He was assigned to many different units including Air Station Clearwater and Air Station Sitka in Alaska. He was also a helicopter instructor pilot at Naval Air Station Whiting Field in Florida before retiring from the Coast Guard as a lieutenant commander with twenty-seven years of active duty. Woolford works in Florida as an air ambulance helicopter pilot. He has been married for twenty-five years to Angie. Together they had three boys. "She kept the home fires burning, kept the family running, and stayed with me through it all. She is just phenomenal," said Woolford.

ASM1 Matt Fithian served at Aviation Training Center Mobile in the ASM shop. He retired from the Coast Guard in the mid-'90s and started work as a truck driver.

ASM3 Joseph "Butch" Flythe, promoted to master chief petty officer, was very influential and a key figure in developing the training techniques that are used today. Chapter 2 describes how his efforts helped shape the success of the program's next twenty years of service.

2

IF YOU'RE NOT SCARED, YOU'RE NOT LIVING

There is no greater gratification than to be a part of the saving of another human being. It's indescribable. EMTs, firefighters have this—but it's not the same because the ASM is battling incredible elements."

—Master Chief Larry Farmer, USCG (retired)

WHAT COMPELS SOMEONE TO WANT TO descend into chaotic, even terrible conditions to risk his life to save a stranger? What does it take to be a successful Coast Guard helicopter rescue swimmer and *come back alive*?

The work is that of professional lifesavers, individuals who are part of a team. They depend on partnerships with pilots, flight mechanics, and engineers who enable them to descend from the helicopter into the plight. To achieve the level of skill required to be successful demands a mastery of mental and physical conditioning that only comes from specialized training. In the end, it can make a difference in whether both rescuer and survivor come back alive.

Training serves as the foundation, the core, of all rescue swimmers' success. It sustains them in a panic, the moment they make a choice to stay or to leave the helicopter to descend into the chaos below. A trained swimmer, with the assistance of the aircrew, can battle the odds and come back up a winner. Together they overcome challenges of monstrous proportions.

Over the past two decades, the Coast Guard rescue swimmer training program has broadened its scope and perfected its focus to prepare aircrews not only for the routine but also the unpredictable.

Its members have retooled the training standards, redesigned lifesaving gear, and fine-tuned the craft to such perfection that it has become an art of rescuing women, children, men, and even pets from unimaginable situations.

The profession has garnered respect within the Coast Guard from commandants down to the seaman who envisions becoming a rescue swimmer. Externally, military services around the world have sent their swimmers to train with USCG helicopter rescue swimmers. Presidents have stood next to them in recognition of their heroism.

It is said, quietly, to be the best of the best of lifesaving professions.

GETTING THERE WAS NEVER, EVER EASY.

ASMCM Larry Farmer was first in the hot seat to spearhead the program's start as the STAN Team senior enlisted manager from 1984 to 1991. Then he worked in headquarters as the Aviation Life Support Equipment and Helicopter Rescue Swimmer Program manager from 1991 to 1997.

"It was a major, major paradigm shift. That was my obligation at the time, travel around the Coast Guard and convince the various aircrews it was 'OK' to lower a Coastie in the water and leave that person if need be," recalled Farmer. "Always the big golden rule was 'Never put a Coastie in harm's way.' It was a difficult task, to say the least."

Among the many issues they dealt with was the elementary question of how to mold every rescue swimmer's professional focus and image. Could they simultaneously nurture among the "brothers" an esprit de corps without alienating pilots and the aircrewmen?

"It was difficult to keep the status of trying to transition the ASMs into having a new capability but not allow the air stations to put that person in a corner or put them on a pedestal," recalled Farmer. "We had something special and wanted it to stay that way, without making this person special."

Electing to keep the rate's profile low key or that of quiet professionals was one way. Another was resisting the call for helicopter rescue swimmers to distinguish themselves in uniform by wearing breast insignia or swimmer's wings, anything flashy. "In trying to maintain that quiet, low-profile individual, I was dead set against it," Farmer admitted. "We had enough difficulty at the time with the ASMs being considered to be prima donnas and getting to go swim when everybody else was working on airplanes, and the list goes on."

Farmer did not want the people who delivered the swimmers into and from the water to end up with an attitude. "The last thing you want is for someone in control of your life when you're hanging on the end of the hoist cable to be upset about your position in life or place in the Coast Guard," Farmer said. "This guy may have some physical capabilities that enable him to go into the water and swim around and rescue people. Other than that, he's a part of the crew because realistically a swimmer cannot do his job unless the pilot and the flight mech do their jobs."

"A lot of us, the young guys full of adrenaline who wanted to be the rescue heroes, closely identified with the Air Force Pararescue guys," recalled Gordon on his perspective as one of the First Five rescue swimmers. "They got to wear a different hat, they had the special uniforms and all the best gear . . . Yeah, we want to be like those guys!"

Gordon admits that the initiative had great potential to ruffle feathers and to not be a smooth fit.

"I see fully now, looking back at it, how important it was for the success of the program to keep it low-keyed."

Air Station Elizabeth City was identified as the first air station to begin the implementation of the Coast Guard Helicopter Rescue Swimmer Program in 1985. It would take six years to build the rescue swimmer numbers up to a force of three hundred members assigned to every air station duty section servicewide.

Elizabeth City was ideal for a couple of reasons. It had an established working relationship with Coast Guard Headquarters for the C-130 STAN Team, located on its grounds, and a swimming pool, which would need to be brought up to par. The long-range goal after the first unit was fully implemented was to move the rescue swimmer program STAN team to Mobile, Alabama, to be co-located with the helicopter STAN teams based at Aviation Training Center (ATC) Mobile.

Additionally, "Headquarters had accumulated a lot of data from the time they got the congressional mandate. Elizabeth City, as it turned out back in those days, had a very high occurrence of personnel in the water that needed to be rescued," Farmer said.

"The initial phase of the implementation was to get Elizabeth City up and running as not only the helicopter rescue swimmer pilot program for all of Coast Guard air stations but also the jointly located Rescue Swimmer Standardization Team," Farmer explained. The STAN Team would develop the concept of operations and train aircrews by traveling around the country to each air station.

Air Station San Francisco's HH-52A helicopter crews became the second air station to come online in November of 1985. The third and fourth were Air Station Astoria in Oregon, by January 1986, and Air Station Clearwater in Florida, August 1986. Air Station San Francisco's HH-3F helicopters and Air Station Sitka, Alaska, followed in November of 1986.

Other first implementations were chosen because of their proximity to cold water and their "highest degree of peril, persons in the water." Air stations in warmer climates like Puerto Rico, Hawaii, and Miami were last.

Even with the implementation completed at a few air stations in the mideighties, helicopter rescue swimmers were not entirely accepted or encouraged by the Coast Guard's own. In some cases, swimmers were not considered a resource on rescue missions, but were told to sit in the back of the helicopter's cabin.

One of the First Five, ASM1 Kelly Gordon had conducted a STAN Team visit at Air Station Sitka in Alaska when this reality caught his attention. During his brief with the officers at the command before he left, he heard why. "I basically got the story, 'Petty Officer Gordon, rescue swimmers are like firemen up here, and we don't have that many fires up here in Sitka. They're just a piece of equipment we will use if we need them, and we highly doubt we will need them.'"

A few months later, Air Station Sitka had a major search and rescue case, one that was so intense that the skin on the HH-3F helicopter was wrinkled because of the stress on the airframe. The only way the crew would make the rescue was to put the rescue swimmer, Petty Officer Jeff

Tunks, in the water. As recounted in chapter 3, Tunks miraculously saved a father and his six-year-old son from their sinking fishing vessel. His courageous efforts combined with the skill and determination of the entire aircrew changed the unfounded perception of many people throughout the entire Coast Guard—not just in Sitka—regarding the capability and value of rescue swimmers. "Commander Whiddon's [one of the HH-3F pilots for the rescue] attitude toward the whole program turned one hundred eighty degrees out. He was standing on every soapbox possible singing the praises of the swimmers," Gordon recalled.

"What saved us too was the direct commissioned aviators from the Navy and the Marine Corps who were used to using swimmers. Those were the guys that helped break down that barrier and change the paradigm saying, 'What are you all sweating this for, what's the big deal, the guy's a swimmer and a big help if you've ever had to use one,'" recalled Master Chief Butch Flythe, another one of the First Five rescue swimmers.

"In a very short time after employing rescue swimmers Coast Guardwide, we started to see situation messages which indicated, "Jeez, how did we ever do search and rescue before without this capability?" Farmer said.

"Then it went from one extreme to another. Everybody wanted to use a swimmer," Gordon stated. "We started to hear of swimmers getting burned out, how the first thing crews wanted to do was throw a swimmer out of the helicopter."

With many more believers within the Coast Guard there was additional momentum for future implementations. Commander Hugh O'Doherty succeeded Commander Ken Coffland in 1987 as the Helicopter Rescue Swimmer Program manager in Washington, DC.

O'Doherty and Farmer worked together to resolve other developing personnel issues. Aircrews had to be retrained when the Aérospatiale HH-65 Dolphin helicopter joined the fleet in 1984 and the Sikorsky HH-60 Jayhawk in 1990. The HH-52 Sea Guard and HH-3F Pelicans were both retired by 1993.

Additionally, "Eighty-eight guys had not gotten off the fence to become swimmers," O'Doherty said, referring to the 1985 requirement that all ASMs train to become rescue swimmers during the first five years of the program's implementation. "I had to respond to a lot of congressional inquiries." Those who were ASMs prior to the policy change were told they would have to qualify as a helicopter rescue swimmer within five years to remain an ASM. "I had to tell them they were going to end up out of the Coast Guard if they don't change their rate or qualify," recalled O'Doherty. This was a difficult choice for many ASMs especially if they had already worked halfway toward retirement as an aviation survivalman.

PERHAPS THE MOST IMPORTANT CHALLENGE for the program was training, the foundation of every swimmer's success. Ultimately, the Coast Guard would have to start its own school.

There was good reason to begin training with the U.S. Navy. "The Navy program best suited Coast Guard training procedures down to what the crew said in the middle of a hoist on the hot mike [internal communications system]," reflected Farmer. "Looking into the Navy, the training was free in the interim—a big incentive." Other programs, like the Air Force PJ's training, were pretty expensive.

A couple of months after the Coast Guard's First Five graduation from the grueling Navy Aviation Rescue Swimmer School in Pensacola, Farmer attended the school as a student himself. He was thirty-six years old, the oldest and most senior enlisted man to attend the Navy training at that time.

One of Farmer's Navy instructors was Petty Officer James McCann who was decorated by the Navy for his performance as the rescue swimmer during the SS *Marine Electric* tragedy. "He leaned harder on the Coast Guard candidates. Although he was pretty young at the time, he realized the significance of the CG attending the training and had a pretty good grasp of where we were headed," Farmer revealed. "He leaned on me pretty heavily because he knew I was the man, so to speak, and at the time I was the senior enlisted ASM. It was no breaks, no movies for me."

During an interview with TAM Communications for a one-hour program, produced by Tam and Susan O'Connor Fraser, called *Coast Guard Rescue Swimmers* broadcast on the Discovery Channel on November 22, 1998, he said:

> It is the most intense, finest, enlightened, terrifying, awe-inspiring training I've ever had. It shows you what your metal is. For two weeks of the training you deal with your inner self. You learn what

your physical and emotional capabilities are when you're exhausted. This is critical for Navy and CG ASMs because they're the only rescue swimmers that do not work in pairs. When you perform by yourself, you have to function *on your own.*

Upon completion of the Navy's swimmer school, he was selected to lead the newly established STAN Team in Elizabeth City with the assistance of ASM1 Richard Woolford and, later, ASM1 Kelly Gordon.

The STAN Team relied on input from the First Five, who tested equipment and procedures on the fly during their own qualification process. They "wrote the playbook" and from their experience created the foundation for the Coast Guard's rescue swimmer program.

Their concept of operations included a Coast Guard preparatory session essential for success while at the U.S. Navy's fast-paced and intense four-week school.

"In the beginning of the program we mirrored the Navy requirements," said Master Chief Butch Flythe, who also served as the enlisted program manager of the Helicopter Rescue Swimmer Program. He described what was needed to graduate from the grueling U.S. Navy course in the mid-1980s and early 1990s: forty-two push-ups, fifty sit-ups in one minute, eight pull-ups, run one and one-half miles in twelve minutes or less, and a five-hundred-yard swim in twelve minutes or less.

The Coast Guard modified these minimums in the 1990s. "When I was a school chief, we were still mirroring the Navy standards," Flythe said. "I would graduate students at a minimum level and six months later I would be getting phone calls about kids being grounded because they couldn't pass a PT test. I realized that the Navy standards were not working."

Flythe knew that the University of Alabama and U.S. Army had formed a partnership to conduct an extensive study to develop a physical fitness standard based in part on push-ups, sit-ups, and running. "I used those numbers because they were geared towards nineteen to twenty-four year olds which was 97 percent of our students. I then chose the old Navy standard for pull-ups because the Army had no data for those, and pull-ups are crucial to this job." He developed a Coast Guard model based on the combined standards and had it evaluated by an exercise physiologist from Elizabeth City State University Physiology Department. The physiologist recommended adding step ups to work hip extensor muscles. With approval from the rescue swimmer program manager, MCPO Keith Jensen, the established minimum field standard to graduate ASM "A" school was now on a par with the level of "excellence" for the twenty- to twenty-four-year-old level under the Army Master Fitness Program and University of Alabama standards. Flythe explained that a later, the minimum standard was updated to allow for "no room to fudge, one little slip and they are not standing duty anymore." The numbers are:

- Sixty push-ups, seventy sit-ups
- Eight pull-ups, eight chin-ups
- Two-mile run in fifteen minutes or less
- Five-hundred-yard swim in ten minutes or less
- Four underwater swims of twenty-five yards with thirty-second break before the
- Two-hundred-yard buddy tow

"They were trying to allow a guy who maybe can't run but can swim to stay in there as the population ages," Flythe said. "Tunks, for example, who's forty-eight, was working Katrina rescues!"

Now, swimmers are required to maintain the following fitness level for the rest of their careers:

- Fifty push-ups, sixty sit-ups, five pull-ups, five chin-ups, five-hundred-yard swim in twelve minutes or less
- Four twenty-five underwater swims followed by thirty-second break before
- A two-hundred-yard buddy tow
- Twenty-five-yard underwater swim repeated four times with sixty-second break
- Two-hundred-yard buddy tow

EARLY ON, THE NAVY HAD CONCERNS ABOUT TRAINING Coast Guard candidates. It felt the addition of Coast Guard students would add numbers to the course's already high attrition rate. From the very beginning, the First Five alleviated this issue by excelling in the course. ASM2 Steve Ober, one of the First Five, was the honor student in his class.

"What actually turned out was that the Coast Guard attendees started winning honor student in their various classes and started to excel because we had a fairly extensive preparation process before the Coastie went to the Navy school," Farmer said. "They had to meet minimum physical fitness requirements validated by their command before going."

It was not too long before the Coast Guard, progressive in nature, decided to send women to the Navy Aviation Rescue Swimmer School too.

"We called up the Navy one day and said, hey, we're sending women through this program, and it started a battle," Farmer said. "They wanted to change the obstacle course, have steps on it like the *GI Jane* movie, and we said no. We never had female standards. We had the basic, required standard, which enabled a swimmer to get into the water from a hovering helicopter and rescue three people within thirty minutes."

Captain George Krietemeyer, chief of training and education for the Coast Guard, was aware the Navy was territorial about who they trained. With the news of a woman in the training pipeline, he received a call from the Navy commander managing the Pensacola school. "Captain, we don't take women in the Navy rescue swimmer school," Krietemeyer recalled of their conversation. "I replied, 'She's not in the Navy is she?' I never heard another word about it and Kelly Mogk made it through just fine." Mogk, the subject of chapter 4, was the first woman to complete the Navy rescue swimmer school and the first woman to qualify in all the military services as a helicopter rescue swimmer.

The upper-body requirements tended to be the barrier for many female candidates. "Due to the differences in physiology, on the average a female has to work twice as hard to achieve that eight chin-ups, eight pull-ups than a male does," said Flythe. He has been pressured to lower the standards, but he protests such an action knowing that to do the work requires this level of preparedness and strength.

The Coast Guard qualified enough swimmers the first three years to stay on track with the commandant's five-year implementation schedule. It became evident that because of their training, they were comfortable at a much higher risk level than other people. "It's a very small percentage of the population that has or possesses the tools to be able to do that [dangerous rescues], but the ones that can do it usually excel. Although to casual observers it is a very dangerous and risky maneuver, they are quite comfortable with it because they possess the tools and the emotional and physical capability to perform that particular task," Farmer said. "I'm sure that Tristan [rescue swimmer Tristan Heaton profiled in chapter 5] was aware of the risk, but because of the capabilities and training he had, it was not as scary going into that cave as it would be to someone else."

IN MARCH OF 1988, the U.S. Navy Aviation Rescue Swimmer School closed after the tragic death of nineteen-year-old Airman Recruit Lee Mirecki on March 2. The effects of this crossed service lines.

The Navy school had a 40 percent attrition rate that was under study even before Mirecki's death, and major changes to the difficult training were proposed, according to a 1988 Associated Press (AP) wire story. "Mirecki died after instructors allegedly dragged him into a pool against his will and held his head under water after he failed a rescue drill," reported Bill Kaczor for AP.

When the school reopened later that year, its curriculum no longer included the "sharks and daisies" rescue drill that was in progress when the recruit died, according to the AP story. "In that drill, instructors randomly grabbed students in head-holds to simulate people panicking in the water. A student was supposed to pull his instructor underwater to break the hold and make the rescue." Instead students would now practice drills on each other.

"The drowning shut down our pipeline for qualifying swimmers," said O'Doherty, who had to quickly devise an alternative. "The ASM School in Elizabeth City created their own rescue swimmer school." During that time, ASM instructors, Butch Flythe among them, improvised. They built a platform in the pool to train from. They prepared the pool, outfitting it with other required tools, like the rope climb and life rafts and rescue swimmer gear. The instructors even quickly developed a training program using the existing Coast Guard rescue swimmer requirements while the students in the pipeline were at EMT school in California. "They were ready for the students when they came back," O'Doherty recalled. "A lot more lives would not have been saved the following year if we could not graduate rescue swimmers."

The Coast Guard trained with the Navy until 1997.

"DUE TO THE SEAMLESS IMPLEMENTATION of the rescue swimmer program from Elizabeth City and because we were bringing in new aircraft into the fleet such as the HH-60 and HH-65, we quickly realized the place we needed to be was colocated where our pilots were," explained Farmer of the STAN Team move to the Coast Guard Aviation Training Center in Mobile, Alabama, in August of 1988.

From there, the STAN Team provided on-site implementation training to pilots and their aircrews. It assumed responsibility for testing and evaluating rescue swimmer equipment, operational concepts, aircrew training, and certifications. ASM1 Jeffery Tunks and ASM1 Scott Dyer joined the STAN Team during this period. ASM1 Jim Sherman replaced ASM1 Kelly Gordon, who remained with the STAN Team until 1991 when he was promoted to chief petty officer and transferred to the Coast Guard Training Center in Petaluma, California, where he would continue to train rescue swimmers as chief of the Coast Guard's Emergency Medical Technician School.

Interestingly, certain air stations were identified that needed to "throttle back" deployments of rescue swimmers. "They were using the swimmers too frequently and unnecessarily and enduring more risk than they should have," said Farmer. "We had a lot of issues to deal with. For instance, the CG helicopter would arrive on scene, and there would be a smoking hole from a military jet. They would lower a swimmer to check things out and we had to deal with what kind of bio and chemical issues we were exposing a swimmer to."

Even in the Caribbean, which involved the Coast Guard's counterdrug interdiction efforts, there were cases when the swimmer was the only option a helicopter crew had to retrieve evidence. "The swimmer was lowered to retrieve bails or packages of every illicit drug you could think of out of the water," said Farmer. Their involvement created a new kind of medical issue for the service when these individuals tested positive for drugs because of their unprotected exposure. "They had never used drugs in their entire lives," Farmer stated.

By October 24, 1991, the Coast Guard's rescue swimmer program was completely implemented at all twenty-eight helicopter air stations. Rarely did a Coast Guard helicopter launch without a rescue swimmer on board.

Gordon and Petty Officer Scott Dyer kept a rescue swimmer deployment synopsis of missions where a rescue swimmer "assisted" or "saved" lives. From that log, which covered the time period between March 1985 and February 6, 1992, the following was recorded:

> Of 428 cases, the total number of lives assisted during that period was 368. The total number of lives saved was 176, a number determined by the essential use of the rescue swimmer to affect [sic] the rescue versus being able to rescue without the swimmer's direct assistance.

> If the helicopter crew could have successfully prosecuted the SAR case without the rescue swimmer then the rescue was classified as an "assist." If the helicopter would have probably deployed an untrained crewmember to complete the rescue, without a rescue swimmer on board, then the rescue is deemed a "save."

Despite its early success, unresolved issues continued to arise for the newest program managers who transferred into that seat at headquarters. O'Doherty was followed by Lieutenant Commander Richard Wright in 1990. ASMCM Farmer transferred a year later to serve as the headquarters ASM Program manager until 1997.

Initially the budget for the initiative was based on assisting incapacitated people in the water. Five years later, this parameter was outdated and too limited. It became apparent that the scope of situations rescue swimmers would have to handle was very diverse, dangerous, and required techniques they had not yet customized the training to achieve.

Master Chief Aviation Survivalman (ASMCM) Darell Gelakoska was well aware of the risks. He would advance the program's training to unmatched levels as the senior operational rescue swimmer, or "top fin," in charge of the STAN Team.

In 1991, Gelakoska was assigned to lead the Coast Guard STAN Team in Mobile. He was responsible for ensuring that all operational swimmers at twenty-six air stations passed annual certification. The certification program consisted of six types of rescues, pool work, and an EMT exam. This work would keep Gelakoska and the STAN Team on average deployed to the water twenty-five times a month for the next five years.

Gelakoska was the Coast Guard's first aviation survivalman, qualified as a parachute rigger and aviation ordinanceman. He worked as a drop master on eight different types of aircraft, dropping lifesaving equipment to mariners in distress. He was a hoist operator and got his feet wet as a survivalman on hundreds of search and rescue cases, saving numerous lives.

He was eligible to be "grandfathered" into the ASM rate without question. Instead, he enrolled in the program and at the age of forty-four graduated from the arduous Navy rescue swimmer school in 1990.

Gelakoska realized that pipeline training was needed to advance and adapt to the variety of cases rescue swimmers were deploying into. The Navy's training was specific to Navy missions. The Coast Guard's search and rescue cases involved civilians in harrowing and diverse environments, while the Navy's focus was primarily on downed fighter-jet pilot recovery.

"We had so many of these rescue swimmers out there that were fully trained as Navy rescue swimmers. In the Coast Guard we had boaters in distress, injured fishermen in the water without survival suits on or wrapped up in cable winches, so our first-aid training needed to be improved to an EMT level; Petty Officer Donald Patrick Chick [a Coast Guard rescue swimmer] fell down a cliff trying to make a rescue," recalled Gelakoska. "We had guys out their in fifty- to seventy-feet seas and were asked to jump in the water. They look down at the water and were scared to death and they didn't want to do it, and refused, which they had the right to do."

One case Gelakoska felt that particularly highlighted this weakness was the tragic attempted rescue of an injured fisherman from the *Sea King*, a fishing vessel that had taken on a disastrous amount of water crossing the Columbia River bar near Astoria, Oregon, in 1991.

A Coast Guard team of rescuers from a nearby small boat station, Air Station Astoria, and the Coast Guard cutter *Iris* worked for nearly ten hours to assist the sinking vessel.

It ended when the rescue swimmer nearly lost his life, another Coastie perished, and others drowned as the vessel rolled and sank. "As it rolled over, the swimmer was in the pilothouse holding onto the litter with this injured man in there trying to get him undone. They all scrambled as the whole boat filled with water," recalled Gelakoska. "The swimmer was so close to dying but made it up to the surface. Three people drowned."

In 1993, there were at least two other cases where aircrews and rescue swimmers had near-death experiences. As recounted in chapter 6, during the "Storm of the Century," some swimmers refused to deploy into the dangerous high seas while others, including aircrews, almost lost their lives. There were also cave rescues such as the one described in chapter 5, where swimmers and the aircrew almost lost their lives trying to rescue survivors and save their own.

It became evident that there was a serious gap between the level of training rescue swimmers received and the real-world environments they would have to contend with by the very nature of being in the Coast Guard.

The commandant, Admiral Robert E. Kramek, took notice and tasked the STAN Team to develop new deployment procedures with Lieutenant Commander Dick Wright, the Helicopter Rescue Swimmer Program manager at that time.

Gelakoska worked with ASM1 Jim Sherman and ASM1 Scott Dyer and Bob Lee, a civilian audiovisual specialist assigned to ATC Mobile, and met with Canadian and British forces to test, evaluate, and videotape their procedures and equipment for consideration to use them for Coast Guard missions. They developed the direct-deployment method whereby a swimmer would remain attached to the hoist cable while the helicopter hovered just feet from the steep cliffs, wet rocks, or over big surf for rescues and situations that merited it for the swimmer's safe return. Direct deployment was fully implemented fleetwide in the summer of 1993.

They videotaped their own tests of new procedures for all different kinds of scenarios a swimmer might contend with, including surf exceeding fifty feet and rescues in shark-infested water, underwater, in caves, and even at night. They took the videotapes to Coast Guard Headquarters as part of a pitch package for an advanced rescue swimmer school. They illustrated the need for a new school to teach seasoned rescuers skills that were above and beyond what they learned in "A" school or basic school—skills that would equip them for situations in real life based on experiences of other swimmers such as cave rescues, extreme surf and high seas, and capsized vessels.

This unique vision also included training everyone in the aircrew, pilots and flight mechanics side by side with rescue swimmers, applying the Total Quality Management principles the commandant's policy supported.

"What we tried to do was change some of our training scenarios on the pool deck to match message traffic we had seen. How can we recreate this or at least this type of scene management to a young buck as opposed to baptism by fire?" said Flythe.

"About midnineties, that's when the culture had changed enough to the point where everybody had accepted it," recalled Flythe of the helicopter rescue swimmers. "That's when there were plenty of new, young flight mechanics who had come up with the rescue swimmer program and started referring to it instead of "the swimmer" as "my swimmer."

With blueprints drawn up by USCG Pacific Area engineers and an obligated one hundred thousand dollars for building a school, there was still trouble agreeing where the school would be located. Gelakoska risked ending his career by calling out for support from others after he was thwarted by the 13th district commander who did not want the school in his region. With support from the three-star Pacific Area commander, Admiral Dick Herr, and the chief of Coast Guard operations, Rear Admiral Norm Saunders, the two-star District 13 admiral was overruled. In March of 1995, the Advanced Rescue Swimmer School was established in Astoria, Oregon.

The site of operations was selected for its intensive nature and because of "its many versatile training sites and rough sea state at the mouth of the Columbia River." Often referred to as the "Graveyard of the Pacific," it has a natural point of rugged coast in Washington state to the north, called Cape Disappointment and is bordered on the south by the state of Oregon.

The commanding officer of Coast Guard Group Astoria, Captain Dave Kunkel, initially allowed the STAN Team to use his facility's training room. As the need for space expanded, Kunkel's final offer, one that the STAN Team accepted, was the use of the Tongue Point Coast Guard Exchange. The building was renovated to the tune of $225,000 in improvements and is where the Advanced Rescue Swimmer School has operated for the past ten years.

Rescue swimmers pulled together to determine what they needed to do to run the school. After realizing they would not be getting small-boat support from the local command to use during their training, the STAN Team worked with Lieutenant Commander Karl Baldessari, who was the new Rescue Swimmer Program manager in headquarters, to procure jet skis. After several hours of learning heavy surf rescue with an experienced jet-ski team from Southern California, the ASMs built platforms off the back of the craft and were ready to train in the Pacific Northwest.

"We handpicked the first class by gathering all the senior and junior guys with the most experience. We asked them to critique our proposed training. Add to it or subtract from it, we talked about what was good and what was bad," Gelakoska said.

"Even though it has that name, Advanced Rescue Swimmer School, we think about it as the advanced aircrew school. They really approach it from a crew position although a lot of the information is geared towards swimmers," said Flythe. "They'll all go out together and help each other out."

The Mobile-based rescue swimmer STAN Team holds eight one-week sessions per year during March and October when the sea's conditions are increased. Each class is one week in length and includes six ASMs, now referred to as ASTs (aviation survival technician), who train with the aircrews on board HH-60 Jayhawk helicopters and HH-65 Dolphin helicopters. By the end of the session, the Rescue Swimmer STAN Team trainers from Mobile qualified two dozen ASTs and four helicopter crews.

"In advanced school they expose you to environmental elements you're not used to dealing with," said Flythe. "For instance, rough surf swim teaches you how to dive into and operate in rough surf, how to free-fall into the swell and time it with the crest as opposed to the trough, cave hydraulics so you wait and time it so that you wait for the fill cycle to stop and you ride the currents out on the dump, cliff walking and ocean survival where they drop you with the one-man swimmer raft, let you experience being left on scene."

Morning classroom sessions also include lectures on Crew Resource Management (CRM), previously known as Cockpit Resource Management, whereby, in the past, the pilot was the one in command and made decisions without necessarily including the input of the other crew members. CRM focuses on all members of the crew contributing their knowledge and experience to the success of the mission.

Another segment of the course includes Critical Incident Stress Management (CISM). Sometimes a "seasoning" type of rescue can also be unnerving and can be something a person or aircrew will frequently think about and not talk about. The effects are long-lasting on the entire aircrew, not just the individual rescue swimmer. CISM helps an aircrew deal with the post-traumatic stress of the ordeal. "It addresses the psychological issues and gets a guy back in the game," said Senior Chief Jimmy Brandt, the current chief of the rescue swimmer STAN Team. "We talk about it, debrief, to try and normalize it. If you are on your own, you can think you're the only one affected."

Run by the safety program managers at Coast Guard Headquarters, CISM (see the Epilogue) broke tradition when it came online. "There were issues where people were having bad cases, and the old guard mentality was, 'Hey, it happened. Suck it up, go do your job,'" reflected Master Chief Scott Dyer, current Rescue Swimmer Program manager in headquarters. "People got to the point that they would have so many bad cases that they were scared to go out on a case for fear that it would go bad."

"It's not just used for rescue swimmers. It is used by the entire Coast Guard responding to the dangerous jobs that we do," said Master Chief Dyer. "What the program does is allows you to talk to trained peers, process what happened during the case, and it allows them to relieve some of the stress from the case." The effort keeps people on the job and allows them to continue to work. CISM helps work through issues that could cause someone to get burned out.

In the afternoon, the class is taken across the Columbia River to Cape Disappointment.

Here the rescue swimmers and aircrews practice together a variety of techniques including high sea recoveries and deliveries, vertical surface deployments and recoveries, wet rock boarding, cave rescues, litter procedures, surf and beach swims, large frame pickups, and raft survival.

Although pilots and flight mechanics participate in the school, rescue swimmers are on the list to attend every three years.

IN 1995 THE COAST GUARD RESTRUCTURED the enlisted aviation workforce. In October 1998 the Aviation Technical Training Center (ATTC) in Elizabeth City began training and graduating petty officers in three newly created aviation ratings: aviation survival technician (AST), formerly ASM or helicopter rescue swimmers; aviation maintenance technician (AMT); and avionics technician (AVT).

The Helicopter Rescue Swimmer AST "A" School was completely independent of any other military service training.

Annually eighty-four students enroll in the AST "A" school's Airman Program. The majority are white males from the ages of nineteen to thirty-two. The Airman Program is the first phase of an AST's journey to becoming a fully qualified helicopter rescue swimmer.

The first phase of the journey is a four-month training curriculum based at the candidate's assigned air station. While they learn about the three aviation rates, they are also evaluated. One requirement is they must not have a fear of water. The candidate, designated as an airman, must complete the course syllabus, pass a demanding physical training test, and receive the unit commanding officer's recommendation to proceed to the AST "A" school.

"When they are at the air station, we are able to start assessing the candidates to see how hard they apply themselves," said Master Chief George Waters, one of the first instructors and the AST school branch chief. "A rescue swimmer is, at the core, a person who willingly enters the aquatic environment for the purpose of saving other people and will not stop until he completes the mission."

Candidates have to meet minimum physical requirements before even being recommended to go to "A" school. They are screened as airmen at their air station to test their abilities to punch out forty-two push-ups and fifty sit-ups in two minutes, five pull-ups, five chin-ups, complete a twenty-five-yard swim four times underwater with ninety-second rest intervals, and run one and one-half miles in twelve minutes or less before swimming five hundred yards using the crawl stroke in twelve minutes or less.

If the airman receives the commanding officer's endorsement, the next phase begins at ATTC in Elizabeth City, North Carolina, where trainees are enrolled in an eighteen-week AST course followed by three weeks of EMT training at Training Center Petaluma, California.

"The mission is so important that the person has to break past administrative 'fit for full duty' kind of stuff boundaries," said Waters. "We would really like to find a way to come up with some type of mental assessment. If they make it through our curriculum, we believe they can continue on." Water's added that an essential trait for this job is to want the action, that fix, and that nothing can distract them from it. He continued, "If they haven't been scared to death in the last twenty-four hours, then they are not alive."

"The first eight weeks of the journey here applies hard to the PT program," according to Waters. "The hardest thing about the curriculum is living with the day-to-day fear that something is going to occur tomorrow that is going to cause you to quit. The actual events of the next day are not as stressful as the anticipation. Living with that for eighteen weeks, you can really tell a lot about a person."

After the initial eight-week course, the students focus in phase two on learning how to sew and repair gear, parachute packing for fixed-wing aircraft equipment drops, inflatable lab work on a variety of life rafts, and some indoctrination classes on aircraft oxygen systems.

Of the number of students reporting in for school and dropping out, "If four people show up, two make it."

Waters recognized the merits of those who complete the school, "They will become strong, capable, aquatically adapted, and extremely confident in themselves. They know about the John Halls, the Bob Watsons, and Jason Bunch's [the Coast Guard's more decorated rescue swimmers]. Our staff of instructors is selected because of their own remarkable cases; they are good role models."

The staff of eleven AST instructors, comprising two chief petty officers and nine first class ASTs and below, review the curriculum and rework parts of it to make it reflect what they experienced in the field. "We're constantly validating our curriculum when new instructors come in and look at it. They tweak the edges but the core remains the same," Waters revealed. "A lot of water work, lifesaving drills, panicky situations, multiple survivor situations, and very aggressive, unpredictable survivor scenarios with communication issues."

Although parts of the Coast Guard school are designed to be scary, Waters felt that it was different from what the Navy school was like prior to the death of the recruit. "In the old days—the Tunks, Flythe time frame—it was a dangerous place pre-Mirecki. After, it was merely difficult, you were never in fear for your life," stated Waters, who emphasized that he was not of the same category as Senior Chief Jeff Tunks, Master Chief Butch Flythe, and Master Chief Scott Dyer and that he went through the school after the incident.

The Coast Guard school's stress comes from the intensity of the physical training. "What we're trying to do here is train three different aviation rates. The AST physical intensity is the much more stressful one. Contrary to a lot of public thinking, this builds strength and creates camaraderie," Waters admitted. "It gives them pride."

"The people that come out of this thing are able to do this job. They get worked. We scare them to death," Waters confessed. "Some of the training at our school is designed with no-win situations, which the staff does not always like, neither do the students. What we do see is that this person does not quit, and that's what we want. Knowing that when they get through this, it instills confidence in them, and they want that stamp of approval from the staff."

Upon graduation a student has become an apprentice, assigned to an air station for final performance qualification and testing. It can take up to one year to completely certify the apprentice as a qualified duty stander.

TODAY's ASTs PERFORM ROUTINE AIRCRAFT INSPECTIONS as well as servicing and maintaining survival equipment, dewatering pumps, and storing aviation ordnance and pyrotechnic devices and aircraft oxygen systems. They function as helicopter rescue swimmers and EMTs. They can also be assigned aircrew positions as dropmaster, loadmaster, or sensor systems operator for the two fixed-wing aircraft in the Coast Guard's fleet: the HC-130 Hercules and HU-25A Falcon.

"We were the last resort in the eighties, and now we're the Swiss Army knife and the American Express card where you don't leave home without us." Flythe said.

Of all the recognition that helicopter rescue swimmers do receive in the form of awards, the occasional top television news story, or being honored at the Coast Guard Foundation Salute to the Coast Guard dinners, many do not display their letters, plaques, and mementos of their heroic work. Often when asked to provide a copy of the award citation, they admit that they'd have to dig it out from under the bed or find the box upstairs in the attic where they think it might be stored.

"What they want, they won't say this, is to hear stories about themselves from the other guys that do the job," Waters confided. "When their brothers say, 'Hey dude, did you hear what this guy did?' And, if you haven't faced the beast and won, your opinion doesn't count. That's what we do here, we give our students the thumbs-up by those who have faced the beast."

For Waters, in the business for twenty-nine years, "It is the most personally rewarding thing that you can do. The monetary value? I never asked what I was going to be paid when I joined the Coast Guard . . . It is an extremely hard job, very hard on the body. It's worth the gamble for a lot of these guys. Why risk your life? None of us gets out of here alive; we're all going to die one day or another . . . None of these guys want to die, but they want the songs of glory to be in their head!"

"I don't care who walks through that door, if they can get through this thing, then they can hear that song of glory from their peers too!" exclaimed Waters. "We all would like to see more diverse representation in this business, but we don't think recruiting is the way to go. We want people who want this desperately."

BETWEEN 625 AND 650 HELICOPTER RESCUE SWIMMERS have served in the U.S. Coast Guard over the past two decades. Of those, six have been women. Three hundred and thirty-three men and three women make up the current force of ASTs on active duty. "That's really not enough to get everything done," said Master Chief Scott Dyer, current Rescue Swimmer Program manager in headquarters. "There are new initiatives for the rate like the aerial gunner program, airborne use of force, under the Department of Homeland Security."

"The aviation life support equipment community has constant upgrades and advances in technology. We've got protective suits for WMD [weapons of mass destruction] incidents so our aircrews can be protected when they go into a chemical or biological environment," Dyer said. "With our airborne use of force initiative we are having to field new survival vests that integrate with the mission to include body armor and those kinds of gear."

New harnesses and suits that have fire protection are being developed so that rescue swimmers are more protected on boats.

"The future looks bright for the Coast Guard," Dyer stated. "Under the Department of Transportation we were a search and rescue agency that did law enforcement. Under the Department of Homeland Security, we are a law enforcement agency that does search and rescue."

"We need more rescue swimmers on the job," Dyer said. "We're hoping everything settles out in five years to increase our rate by one hundred and fifty folks."

"THERE IS NO GREATER GRATIFICATION than to be a part of the saving of another human being. It's indescribable. EMTs, firefighters have this—but it's not the same because the ASM is battling incredible elements," Farmer said.

"We have not lost a swimmer while actually conducting a rescue or while performing swimmer duties in the twenty years of the rescue swimmer program," stated Farmer. "Mike Odom was as close as we come." Mike Odom's lifeline, the HH-60 Jayhawk helicopter's hoist cable, broke after he had successfully rescued five stranded sailors aboard their vessel *Mirage* on January 23, 1995. The punishing seas had caused Odom to swim hard and, exhausted, he watched as his best friend, Mario Vittone, tossed out an inflated life raft for him. The helicopter's fuel supply was past "bingo," and they risked not being able to reach land. They had no other way to rescue Odom, who nearly died spending the night in the life raft and braving the tumultuous Atlantic Ocean seas, three hundred fifty miles east of Georgia.

Within five months after Farmer's retirement, rescue swimmers finally got breast insignia. He received a lot of e-mails informing him about it.

"I KNEW IT HAD COME FULL CIRCLE when I got a call from the Navy [in 1998] asking me if I'd train their guys," stated Flythe. "We allowed Navy swimmers, Air Force PJs to all go through our advanced school.

"To me the nail that would be put in the coffin, to say this program is finally taken care of, would be if they built us a decent aquatic training facility," said Flythe. "Every year it comes up, and every year it's taken off the list to be funded. It's a darn shame. All the people that come and look at our pool can't believe we train in this. They expect a lot more and they should.

"I'd say these kids coming out nowadays are twice the swimmer," Flythe said. "They are locked, cocked, and ready to roll. They are learning direct deployments, double pickups, all this stuff that in the beginning we didn't have. They have better equipment, the old harness really wreaked havoc around our backs, we redesigned this stuff and you know what, the Navy usually follows our lead now for rescue swimmers. They went to the TRI-SAR harness after we did."

Maybe it was a longtime dream to be in the U.S. Coast Guard. Perhaps a family member or friend influenced their decision to join the service. For some it was hearing the stories of others, their rescues, and their daring deeds. Most swimmers find it hard to describe the feeling of the moment when they made a difference. Some would wait for years to do so while others would have the "big one" the day after they qualified. All of them believe this was what they were meant to do.

The following chapters are some of their stories.

MASTER CHIEF GELAKOSKA RETIRED from the Coast Guard in 1996, with thirty years of distinguished service. He and his wife, Marianne, who is a member of the Coast Guard Judge Advocate General (JAG) program, live in the Pacific Northwest.

Gelakoska, born in 1947 in Grand Haven, Michigan ("Coast Guard City, USA"), entered the Coast Guard following the footsteps of his older brother.

In the early 1970s Gelakoska qualified as an EMT, nearly fifteen years before it would be required for all rescue swimmers. Intuitively, he used this skill to apply first-aid techniques to the injured in crucial moments between rescue and delivery to a hospital while aboard rescue helicopters.

He received the Robert A. Perchard Memorial Trophy for most outstanding enlisted aircrewman, twice, an honor bestowed upon him by air station personnel when he was stationed at Traverse City and Astoria.

MASTER CHIEF BUTCH FLYTHE WAS BORN in Ahoskie, North Carolina, in 1961. He began his military service in 1979 as an Army National Guard combat medic. He had dropped out of college and later finished his degree on active duty. A friend of his who enlisted in the Coast Guard encouraged him to consider the service. He liked the aviation survivalman rate description and enlisted in 1983.

Now, as the life support and equipment manager for Coast Guard Aviation, all rescue swimmer and aviation survival equipment is maintained, researched, and developed under his supervision.

"I wouldn't trade it for the world. When I dropped out of school and man I'm just drifting, I never would have thought that I'd have the privilege and the honor to participate in such a profound program that would have such an effect on this country at large. Well, after Katrina now, there are seven thousand people on the face of this earth that possibly would not be here if this program had not been in place. It makes me humble and grateful, gosh, what a ride."

Flythe worked as a subject matter specialist on the set of the Disney feature film *Guardian*, with Kevin Costner and Ashton Kutcher, about rescue swimmers, which is scheduled to premiere in fall 2006.

MASTER CHIEF SCOTT DYER, Rescue Swimmer Program manager in headquarters today, was born in 1957 in Des Moines, Iowa. Of the twenty-three years he has served in the Coast Guard, twenty-one were as a helicopter rescue swimmer.

After high school he went to college and earned degrees in business management and history. In 1983, Dyer enlisted in the Coast Guard with the intention of being either a boatswainmate, corpsman, or aviation survivalman. He was picked up for ASM "A" school. While attending ASM classes, he learned from Senior Chief Dave Hobson about the development of the rescue swimmer program. Of the initiative, Dyer said, "Whoa, I don't know if I can do that." He changed his mind a little later and believed, "This would be cool." He was given orders to go to Astoria with his family to be a part of the second air station implementation. Before completing ASM "A" school, then Seaman Scott Dyer received a telephone call from Commander Ken Coffland, the headquarters' Rescue Swimmer Program manager. "I was packing parachutes when he called and asked me to go directly to the U.S. Navy rescue swimmer school in Pensacola," Dyer said. "I promised to go but requested time to move my family and pregnant wife, Debbie, to Astoria first. By May of 1985, Dyer graduated as an ASM3. In August he was standing duty at Air Station Astoria as a qualified Coast Guard rescue swimmer.

Dyer's personal drive comes in part from a personal motto of his: never give up. It is a belief he shares with others he mentors and encourages.

3

BELIEVERS

JEFFERY D. TUNKS

It's not easy to be brave all the time; your first instinct is to survive.

NIGHT FELL JUST NORTHWEST OF SITKA, Alaska, leaving Jim Blades and his six-year-old son, Clint, to fight for their lives aboard their twenty-six-foot wooden trawler, *Bluebird*. An unexpected weather system, which entered Sitka Sound from the Gulf of Alaska, was cause for their battle. The incoming storm on December 10, 1987, was unforecasted, and its ferocity was hard to describe.

Second Class Aviation Survivalman Jeff Tunks, a rescue swimmer assigned to Coast Guard Air Station Sitka, unknowingly readied for what would become for him and the Coast Guard Helicopter Rescue Swimmer Program an evening of historic renown. He ran into the hangar and quickly put on his dry suit topped by an inflatable vest, which contained a knife, flares, and strobe lights. He tightened his mask and snorkel. He grabbed his swimming fins and antiexposure coveralls, extra survival bags, and made his way out toward the flight line to join the "controlled chaos" surrounding the HH-3F Pelican helicopter, tail number CG 1486. Men scurried about the flight line preparing the craft for the search and rescue.

For a brief moment, Tunks looked up at the moonless sky. It was blanketed by thick cloud cover, and his face was pelted with bullets of ice. The downpour also blistered the tarmac. He questioned his first rescue mission, "Is this for real? Why me?"

Tunks was assigned to the Alaskan air station immediately after graduating from the Naval rescue swimmer school in Pensacola one year earlier. Rescue swimmers had not had a major case at the unit during that time or in the entire Coast Guard for that matter. This would be his first one; a feeling of apprehension flooded his mind.

He was confident in the team of pilots and aircrew that would join him on this mission. What he feared most was his own failure. "It's not easy to be brave all the time; your first instinct is to survive," said Tunks.

At thirty-one years old, Tunks was in extremely good shape. He was five feet ten inches tall and one hundred seventy pounds of handsome man, respected and affectionately known as a "Grandpa" to the other swimmers, who were mostly in their early twenties. Tunks carried a full head of sandy blond hair and a ready smile to match his friendly, jovial manner.

He willingly joined the rescue swimmer community during its infancy as a way of remaining in the Coast Guard. As an ASM his choices were change his job, be released from the Coast Guard, or become a swimmer. Before making the lateral change into the program, Tunks had worked as a flight mechanic, repairing gear and emergency equipment for aircrews.

To qualify as a swimmer he had to first graduate from the four-week rescue swimmer course at Naval Air Station Pensacola. Tunks knew that men attending the course were coming back unqualified. It was a brutal program of instruction. Regarding the course he said, "They can't kill me. How bad could it be?"

For Tunks, completing the course was a matter of fighting for his survival. He had a wife and one-year-old son to provide for back home. This was not just a job but also his profession, and he needed to succeed.

Luckily for Tunks, he had always been a runner. From this sport he had developed a strong lung capacity and endurance. "I was not a swimmer any more than when I was water skiing, and I had to get the rope to get back up." Every day of the course he dreaded going to the pool where men were routinely pushed beyond their limits and even feared for their lives. He lived by what others who passed it told him, "If you don't quit, you'll make it." Of the thirty-five men in his class, twelve finished.

As natural as the change was for the Coast Guard's echelon, the development of and the acceptance in the field of the rescue swimmer program was slow. Sometimes it was viewed as unnecessary. Many aviators did not want the swimmers around, much less in their aircraft.

By 1987, when Tunks was assigned to Sitka, standard procedures at that time deployed swimmers only as a last resort and only into known training scenarios, which often were not like real-life conditions. The program was still being developed and the skill of the swimmers still being tested.

"I did feel discriminated against—it was a difficult time with a lot of unknowns," reflected Tunks, who was a distinguished and respected role model for the profession. "The program was being resisted with as much force as was being used to push it through."

This issue was not on Tunks's mind as he leaped into the cabin of the helicopter to join the rest of the experienced aviators. "It was my first time in the fire, and I was hoping to get back alive."

A WEATHER SYSTEM HAD DEVELOPED hurricane-force winds and forty-foot seas from its journey eastward across the vast stretches of the cold north Pacific Ocean before entering the Gulf of Alaska. By the time it approached Sitka Sound, located on the eastern shoreline of the gulf, it raised havoc with anything in its way. It descended down the side of Cape Edgecumbe, a dormant volcano that soared to thirty-two hundred feet above the town of Sitka.

The cape and a myriad of small islands provided modest protection for Sitka, located on Baranof Island. Saint Lazaria Island, a bird sanctuary nestled just below the cape, was surrounded by prime fishing grounds for fishermen and the wildlife that venture there.

In an extraordinary ambush, the storm approached the Blades, who, unaware, had settled down for the night aboard the anchored *Bluebird*.

Around three o'clock that afternoon, the father and son had completed a profitable king salmon fishing trip aboard the blue-and-white painted boat. Still twelve miles from home, the winter sun set early bringing a consuming darkness between the *Bluebird*, a nearby reef, Vit-skari Rocks, and the warmth and comfort of the fisherman's home. Jim decided to anchor near Saint Lazaria Island on the leeward side of the prevailing winds. He sensed the waters could get a little choppy during the night.

He radioed his wife, Jill, who was home caring for Kurt, their three-year-old son. "We had talked and he mentioned he was gonna stay back behind the island . . . He said the weather was marginal which meant it was gonna blow a little bit and he was going to probably be awake half the night watching the anchor," said Jill. "We said good night and I turned off the radio." Jill then climbed up the ladder to the loft bed where Kurt was drawing pictures before going to sleep.

The Blades usually moored their boat to the one-room float house. Fishing was a primary source of income for them. Jim and Clint were under way a lot together, which enabled Clint to become a capable boat crew member. He could steer a course, help with the trawler's hydraulic gear, and call Dad over when there was a fish too big to haul up himself.

Unknowingly, they were in the storm's track. Jim had missed an emergency weather update of an incoming, fast-moving gale crossing the Gulf of Alaska.

EARLIER THAT EVENING, a few miles to the east, Jeff Tunks had worked inside an aircraft hangar at Coast Guard Air Station Sitka. He was on call as the duty swimmer. Having completed a routine training flight that evening with the on-call pilots and aircrew, he followed procedures and prepped the helicopter for any future mission they might be called upon to perform.

Tired and hungry from a busy day of practice hoists and aerial exer-cises, Tunks walked over to the galley just after six o'clock. After eating a significantly overcooked hamburger, he returned to the hangar. As he walked down the hallway, he heard the rat-a-tat of the wind and rain pelting the windows and realized the weather was fast deteriorating.

BY THEN, THE GALE'S WINDS HAD STARTED to accelerate down the leeward side of Cape Edgecumbe toward *Bluebird*, which was on top of an al-ready big swell. It "came out of the west pretty hard . . . That's where I got in trouble," said a soft-spoken Jim who had been icing their catch in the fish hold. "The wind set me in right towards the beach with very little warning. Just one cat's-paw and the next thing you know it's blowing forty then seventy and snowing."

Seeking shelter from the "storm of unforecast ferocity," Jim started *Bluebird*'s engine and put it in gear. He attempted to stop the anchor from dragging. Then he set *Bluebird* on a course, hopeful it would lead them to deeper water. Limited by the darkness and heavy, snow-laden gusting winds and mushrooming seas, Jim was lost. Without radar, the best he could do was direct the beam from his spotlight into the snow-packed, watery darkness encircling them. He hoped it would illuminate a safe passage.

Clint, who was on a bunk in the fo'c'sle, remembered feeling a large wave lift the entire boat then forcefully drop it. "I heard this huge crunch, and Dad got me out of the bow right away and put me in the cabin," said Clint. "I remember, real vividly, Dad going up to the bow and shining the light down in the water and then running back into the cabin to try and back off the rock. Another wave picked us up and the back end slammed into another rock. He basically picked another direction, and went for it. This happened to be the right way."

"We couldn't see anything but snow," said Clint. "Gusts of wind came from the wrong direction. Within minutes waves and winds started rising from the northerly direction . . . It got so rough, so fast."

Suddenly, a car horn hooked up as the bilge alarm blared, announcing to Jim that they were taking on water below decks. "That was pretty annoying so I ripped the wires off of that!" Jim said. With that silenced, he ran to the bridge and made a desperate radio call for help on Channel 16, the emergency VHF marine distress frequency.

Fearfully Jim reported to the Coast Guard that Vitskari Rocks had holed *Bluebird*. He erred in giving his location. The boat was actually a few miles away from where he had reported. He was disoriented by the darkness and heavy snow. The storm was worsening.

BACK AT THE SMALL, RED CEDAR FLOAT HOUSE, a sudden gust of wind had violently spun it around and drew the shore cables tight with a jolt. The strength of the winds loudly smacked water against Jill's front door. Alarmed by the unwelcome movement of her home, Jill recalled her reaction. First, she wondered if her husband and son were OK. "I tried to get Jim on the radio. He wasn't on Channel 70, so I turned it to Channel 16 because I thought, *Boy, if he's in trouble, he'd be talking on that.*" On the distress channel, she overheard Jim talking to Coast Guard Air Station Sitka. Then she guessed that he must really be in dire straits. While she listened, the Coast Guard asked Jim if there was any way to contact his wife. Jill immediately interrupted them, "I'm here, listening in." Jim cautioned, "You better get off the radio, honey, it's a distress frequency."

Air Station Sitka received Blades's Mayday at 7:36 P.M., four hours after sunset. The watch stander immediately sounded the search and rescue (SAR) alarm. Following its jolting blare was an emergency announcement over loudspeakers broadcasting throughout the air station and hangar, "Now, vessel in distress at Viscary *[sic]* Rocks, taking on water, rescue swimmer provide."

The pipe was unusual. The call was for a rescue swimmer to go on the mission too. The swimmer program was still in its infancy. The use of a swimmer was rare, at the pilot's discretion, and even if they were airborne, rarely were they called into action.

Tunks knew this was a prime fishing ground and guessed it was a fishing boat in distress. He quickly made his way out to the helicopter where men were preparing to put the amphibious helicopter on the flight line.

Lieutenant Commander John B. Whiddon, the duty aircraft commander, rushed to the operations center to get the updated information on the situation. Whiddon, a thirteen-year veteran and distinguished Coast Guard pilot, was known for his 1980 Gulf of Alaska case, where he helped hoist many people from the fire-engulfed cruise ship *Prinsendam*. For his aviator's skill and courage, he was awarded the coveted Distinguished Flying Cross, the military's highest peacetime honor for heroism, the same medal awarded to Charles Lindbergh for his transatlantic crossing. Whiddon spoke with a heavy English accent, having emigrated as a young man from England to the United States.

Reviewing the information the SAR desk had received, Whiddon decided to launch immediately. Current weather conditions at the field were snow showers and twenty-knot winds with gusts to forty knots. "There were no indications of any pending bad weather," recalled Whiddon.

Lieutenant G. B. Breithaupt, the copilot, was very experienced and known to have a good sense of humor. Less than a month ago, though, he had to turn his helicopter back from a sinking fishing vessel case because of dangerous weather conditions. The only thing located after the storm passed was a hatch from the vessel. This loss affected not only the townspeople of Sitka but also the Coast Guard community living there.

AD1 Carl E. Saylor, a seasoned flight mechanic, was in charge of operating the hoist and troubleshooting any mechanical problems during the flight. He was a tall, lanky fellow standing over six feet. He flew on the *Prinsendam* cruise ship fire mission and was also awarded the Distinguished Flying Cross for his gallant efforts hoisting survivors from lifeboats to the Coast Guard helicopter.

AT3 Mark A. Milne, the avionics technician, was responsible for plotting their course and maintaining communication with the air station. He was five feet nine inches tall. A rather quiet guy, he loved to work out and lift weights.

Whiddon buckled into the pilot's right seat of the ten-ton aircraft with his copilot and crew. "As we were just turning the helo up, a really strong gust of wind knocked it sideways, thirty degrees to the right. The first time that had happened in my career. That was our first indication that there were going to be problems, and it just proceeded to get worse from there," said Whiddon.

Seventeen minutes after the Mayday call the helicopter was airborne. "As we lifted off, it was like we were flying into nothing it was so dark," recalled Tunks. "It was all stick and rudder." With no road or lights to follow, the helicopter's spotlight illuminated the waters below as the only road map.

The intensity of the storm had magnified. "The helicopter was immediately hit with heavy snow and tossed by severe turbulence," wrote Whiddon in his case summary. They descended from seven hundred feet to five hundred feet to shed snow that had been collecting on the sponsons and windshield. "The windows were obscured by snow build-up, and ice started to accumulate on the airframe necessitating a lower than desired search altitude to avoid further icing," declared Whiddon.

Adding to the dangerous flight conditions, mountains were on either side of the helicopter's flight path into Sitka Sound. The sound "is still relatively wide, but we had no forward visibility, only the water below us, two hundred fifty to three hundred feet below," said Whiddon.

"The Coast Guard couldn't find us," said Clint of what seemed like a long time waiting for rescue.

Finding *Bluebird* was indeed a complicated matter for the Coast Guardsmen. They communicated with each other by using the helicopter's internal communication system (ICS) wired into headsets in their helmets. As they flew toward a repeatedly reported inaccurate position, the pilots were forced to fly at low altitudes; the radar returns illuminated on the scope were so intense that they could not distinguish land from water, and they were limited in the use of loran, a long-range navigation system in which pulsed signals are sent out by two pairs of radio stations to provide position information for aircrafts or ships, as a navigational aid.

Ramping up the fear factor another notch, Whiddon and Breithaupt had to carefully guide the nose of the aircraft down to prevent it from getting pushed up too high by the powerful winds trying to force it into a dangerous, out of control, aerial acrobatics.

Lieutenant Breithaupt contacted *Bluebird*'s captain on Channel 16 and asked him to provide a long countdown in order to directional find (DF) the boat. Using this tracking equipment, the radio signal received would register a direction relative to the helicopter's position.

Jim provided the countdown, backward from ten to one, a technique used to keep him from speaking too fast into the microphone: "Ten, nine, eight, seven, six, five, four, three, two, one . . ."

The pilots instructed Jim to prepare to be hoisted off.

EARLIER, JIM HAD DONNED HIS SURVIVAL SUIT. He placed Clint in a sleeping-bag-style suit on the floor of the cabin where he fell asleep, comforted by the warmth. He was too young to be fearful of the dangers just outside the cabin door.

Jim realized the dangerous situation they were in, though, and planned to clip Clint onto the front of his own survival suit in order to hold them together, hands-free, when it became time to evacuate. Unfortunately though, Jim was unable to zip his suit up entirely to keep him warm. The repair shop had removed the toggle from the zipper. Without this device, Jim was helpless. Jim didn't let his son know how much he feared for their lives. He remained outwardly calm, aware that his son watched him closely. They were ready to be rescued and anxiously awaited the arrival of the helicopter.

JILL BLADES, WHO HAD LISTENED on the distress frequency to her husband's conversations with the Coast Guard, switched her radio to a routine channel. She called her friends and neighbors Bob and Laura Hubbard. Jill explained that Jim and Clint were in trouble. She begged them to start the Sitka Trinity Baptist Church prayer chain. Pray for her family and the rescuers she pleaded before tuning back to the emergency marine channel. Scared and nervous she listened, not quite aware, yet, of how bad things were for her husband and son as well as the Coast Guard rescuers.

LIEUTENANT COMMANDER WHIDDON, with Milne providing navigational and communications assistance, decided to fly toward the Cape Edgecumbe Light. From this point, they could fly along the shoreline toward Saint Lazaria Island where they knew the helicopter would be in the neighborhood of the twenty-six-foot vessel's reported position.

Briethaupt, Saylor, and Tunks painstakingly looked out the aircraft's windows into the snowstorm hoping to see a glow from *Bluebird*'s masthead light. "I tried to use night vision goggles, but with the flood hovers and searchlight on, reflecting off the snow, the goggles did not work," Saylor wrote in his case summary.

In an effort to help the rescuers locate him, Jim turned off all his boat's lights and pointed his powerful battery-powered spotlight into the darkness. He directed it forward then backward hoping to point it in the approaching helicopter's position.

As the helicopter neared St. Lazaria Island, Saylor spotted the intermittent light at the aircrew's two o'clock position. The pilots were able to use the radar, which had cleared, to fly toward the light, a blip on the radar. Navigating within a mile of the light, Whiddon made a slow, right, three-hundred-sixty-degree turn, to descend to three hundred feet. He would make a straight, precision approach to a hover. "During the turn, the wind blew the helicopter six miles to the south causing the crew to lose sight of the light. They had been blown completely off course!

Realizing what had happened, the pilots adjusted their course to head back to Lazaria in time for Saylor to regain sight of the light.

The storm unleashed a fresh gust of wind, forcing frigid waters up onto the decks of the *Bluebird*, which had already taken on an ample amount. Seeing the demise of his boat, Jim feared they had little time left afloat and called out to the rescuers over the radio, "I'm going to be in the water pretty quick. Where are you guys at?"

JILL, WHO HAD MAINTAINED A VIGIL next to the radio, was terrified. "At one point I overheard Jim say that the decks were awash with water, they were sinking. That really freaked me out. My little baby was out there," Jill said in anguish.

JIM COUNTED DOWN FROM TEN again over the radio.

"Ten, nine, eight, seven, six, five . . ."

According to Saylor, the signal was not strong enough to get an accurate direction of where it was coming from.

To improve their visibility, Whiddon and Breithaupt descended to three hundred feet and again commenced a precision approach less than a mile from the sinking boat in an effort to descend and fly into a hover.

When they were hovering above the *Bluebird*, the situation became dire. The winds were rushing down the side of Cape Edgecumbe faster than an Amtrak train to join seas exceeding forty feet in height.

"The pilots noticed that at 60 knots, the indicated airspeed, the helicopter wasn't making any headway but was actually being blown away from the boat," noted Whiddon in his summary.

"The pilots used their flight instruments to adjust but the altitude was still varying from fifty to one hundred feet . . . and I could see, looking at the water, we were flying backwards," wrote Saylor.

Whiddon carefully inched the helicopter forward into another hover above the *Bluebird*. "The aircraft was crabbing about thirty degrees—we got up to the boat in about a forty foot hover," stated Saylor. "The survivor told us he was taking on water and did not have much time left." It was then they learned that Jim was accompanied by his six-year-old son.

Saylor and Milne provided positioning information to Whiddon over the ICS while looking out the aircraft's cabin door. They planned to lower the rescue basket to the *Bluebird*'s stern hoping that Jim and Clint could climb into it.

After three to four attempts, the rescuers realized that the limited deck space on the small boat was not enough to enable the father and son to be safely hoisted. All they needed was a clear three-foot-by-four-foot area to place the basket. The wildly pitching hull, the boat's rigging, and the gear on deck created dangerous interference.

"We were standing mid-boat, waiting for the basket," said Clint. "We'd have to go whichever direction the basket went."

Some of the helicopter's aerial maneuvers above the *Bluebird* became close calls. *Bluebird*'s mast almost impaled the body of aircraft. It was unpredictable, swatting back and forth near the hovering frame positioned less than the height of a child's step stool above the masthead.

Saylor hand signaled for the skipper to come up on his radio located in the wheelhouse. Breithaupt spoke with Jim and convinced him to get into the water with his son. It was the only way to save them, he advised.

"Dad picked me up and strapped me in facing forward," said Clint. With Clint secured to his chest, Jim moved to the stern of the boat and gave instructions to his son. Clint had, up to this point, remained calm.

"Dad shouted, 'We're going to go over the side.' I got scared. I tried to hold on to the side of the boat I was so scared!" recalled Clint. They surrendered their fate to the snow-filled, turbulent waters with the rescuers hovering above when they jumped off *Bluebird*'s stern.

Despite numerous attempts by the Coast Guard team to get the basket close to the survivors, the Blades were not able to distance themselves from the sinking boat, making the pickup impossible.

During one of these attempts, the winds forced the helicopter backward into a descent. All the instrument gauges went red. "I felt the helicopter rise and start to shudder," said Tunks. "You could hear the pilots yell "Full power! Full power! Full power!"

Whiddon had felt the helicopter violently pitch twenty-five degrees nose up. "The winds just picked us up, and we were going backward and descending completely out of control at sixty miles per hour," recounted Whiddon. "Greg, the copilot, and I, looked at each other and just knew we were going to crash. I thought, well this is it, we knew we were going into the water."

Whiddon and Breithaupt pulled maximum power (122 percent torque) using the collective and cyclic in full up positions, but the helicopter continued to back down and descend.

Whiddon felt the aura of someone's presence standing behind him. He assumed it was Saylor conducting a safety check of the helicopter, required every thirty minutes. Knowing they were about to ditch, "I turned back to yell at him to sit down, get strapped in," Whiddon recalled. Looking for him Whiddon discovered that Saylor was in his seat. "Right then the descent stopped, our backward motion stopped. We were fifteen to twenty degrees nose up, fifteen feet above the water and the helicopter's tail was just a few feet from hitting it!"

When the pilots pulled power again to regain control of the craft, the helicopter engines were over torque. Miraculously they were still airborne. Whiddon credited this miracle to the intangible feeling that remained with him. Something else was in the mix; he could not explain it.

Tunks, who had witnessed the wave tops and sea foam up close from just outside the cabin door, was thinking, *Let's not do that again*, as they repositioned for another attempt to send the rescue basket down to the survivors.

Whiddon was one of the best pilots Tunks had ever flown with. Yet, Tunks was aware that this case was a little too much for the pilot.

Whiddon reported, "The pilots nearly lost aircraft control three additional times during the rescue attempts as these extreme gusts tossed the helicopter about like a paper airplane."

A mere ten minutes had passed since the helicopter had arrived on scene when the *Bluebird* rolled over and sank stern first. Fortunately, this loss provided more room to try and hoist the father and son without the basket getting caught in the boat's rigging.

Jim and his son were under increasing duress. "They became too incapacitated to help themselves," noted Whiddon. "They just got too cold."

By now, Jim's hands were disabled. He couldn't hold his son to his chest. The clips were the only reason Clint was still there. He began to wonder if they would survive.

In an unprecedented moment, considering the weather and conditions they were in, Whiddon turned to Jeff Tunks for help. "The only way we will be able to rescue these guys is if you go in the water. Are you willing to do it?"

"Yes sir. OK, let's do it," Tunks responded without hesitation. *This is insane*, thought Tunks. He knew he just had to do what he could do even if he was uncertain of the outcome. He hoped it would be a good one. "It's not easy to be brave all the time; your first instinct is to survive."

Up until this moment, no one in the Coast Guard had ventured into conditions as fierce as these for any rescue or even a training exercise, Whiddon said.

Following procedures to lower Tunks down to the turbulent seas, the helicopter was repositioned in a sixty-foot hover above the Blades. In the rear cabin, Milne and Saylor prepared Tunks to be lowered by a horse-collar-style sling.

Tunks descended into the relative darkness and observed close at hand the environs. The magnitude of the rushing seas and winds, punishing him, were illuminated by the helicopter's dual hover lights mounted on its undercarriage and its nose-mounted searchlight.

He reached the water's surface and prepared to release himself from the cable.

"Unfortunately the moment his feet hit the water we got dragged backwards again!" recounted Whiddon. Tunks was able to free himself from the sling after being dragged back the length of a football field attached to the helicopter.

Whiddon and Breithaupt recovered the aircraft from the treacherous moment again by using all the power they could demand from the engines. Breithaupt continually called out what the pilot called in his report the "drastic changes in altitude (25 to 100 feet) and attitude (from 20 degrees nose up to 10 degrees nose down and 20 degree rolls of either wing down)" to help a fatigued Whiddon counter them with his skilled hands. He also helped Whiddon by assisting on the controls.

Milne was able to keep the Blades in sight and assisted Saylor in conning the aircraft into position for another attempt to hoist once the pilots recovered.

Tunks was in no position to help Jim and Clint. He had recognized that "it was better to be out of the sling than attached." Three pool lengths separated him from the father and son. The radio he would use to communicate with the helicopter was not operating properly in these conditions.

"Of course he was on the other side of forty-foot waves, in the dark. He had absolutely no idea where they were, he didn't know how to reach them, and he couldn't yell for them because it was too loud out there to be heard," remembered Whiddon.

In an effort to help, "Dad would wave his arms to catch the spotlight's beam on his survival suit's reflective tape," said Clint. "So I raised my arms too. I could see the chopper, looked like a big dome or theater above us . . . the lights blaring right above us . . . really an amazing thing."

With the nose light off to the right illuminating Tunks, Whiddon looked for and spotted the Blades. Unwittingly he had grabbed the light's directional controller and swung it straight ahead to spot them. "Somehow Jeff knew to follow that beam of light. He just followed that beam of light and it took him right to the Blades," Whiddon said.

Tunks swam up to Jim and his son, guided by their reflective tape.

Father and son did not realize Tunks was in the water until he was right next to them.

"Dad asked, 'Are you going to get us out of here?'" said Clint.

Tunks, despite the fact that this was his first rescue replied, "We do this shit all the time!"

Jim laughed through chattering teeth.

Tunks himself was the father of a three-year-old son. "He looked at me and shouted, 'We've got to get you out of here!'" said Clint.

Tunks noticed Jim was suffering from the cold. He was floating lower in the water than his survival suit was designed to do. Clint, who was chilled too, was calm. He trusted his dad had everything under control.

Tunks focused instinctively on what he had to do. He worked with fierce determination, matched by his pumping adrenaline, to save them. Tunks reached across Jim's shoulders and swam with the Blades into a hoisting position. He gave Saylor a wave with his chemical light, signaling they were ready for the basket.

Saylor lowered the rescue basket again and again only to miserably watch it be consumed by a wave one moment and then shoot out the backside of the wave as it rolled past.

Tunks, unable to maneuver the Blades toward the basket, recalled, "You could hear the strain on the helo's engines as the plane was buffeted around by the winds."

After another ten minutes of precision effort, five attempts by the pilots, Milne, and Saylor to deliver the basket, Whiddon started to give up.

"What do you think about giving them the life raft?" he queried over ICS. He predicted Tunks and the Blades could ride out the gale inside the raft.

Breithaupt, Milne, and Saylor were silent. "All right, we'll give it one more try," Whiddon remarked.

With the helicopter repositioned, Saylor inserted the basket in the water close to Tunks while simultaneously giving positioning instructions to Whiddon.

Tunks grabbed the basket. In one swift motion, he rolled the Blades inside seconds before the seas swept it away.

Ready. Tunks gave Milne the thumbs-up sign to start the hoist. "I noticed Milne was not taking the load," said Tunks. "He wanted me to go up with them. There was no room and too much weight on the hoist." It was also not the way they had trained. Tunks pushed the basket away.

Saylor started to hoist.

Immediately, the storm raged against the helicopter. "The violent movement of the helicopter drug them [the Blades] fifty feet through the seas and set them swinging wildly as they cleared the waves," according to Whiddon's case summary.

"The basket shot out of the water, swinging like a pendulum," observed Tunks. He watched the Blades rise up into the cabin. Milne and Saylor tried to stabilize the steel basket, which was swinging like a wrecking ball.

During this entire rescue attempt, Breithaupt had called out the drastic changes in altitude and power demands. Attitude ranged "from twenty degrees nose up to ten degrees nose down and twenty degree rolls of either wing down." The power demands on the engines were "exceeding the transmission limitations caused by the severely gusting winds." At least three times, Breithaupt assisted on the controls to help Whiddon stop the helicopter from crashing into the water. Whiddon reported, "the torque indicator climbed to 123%—the point where the transmission linking the engine to the helicopter blades would be damaged." The pilots "used the entire range of all flight controls just to maintain a hover."

Now, safely deposited in the helicopter's cabin Jim and his son got out of the rescue basket with assistance from Saylor and Milne. Clint noticed the life raft. He confessed, "I was glad to be in the chopper."

Tunks rode out the waves below.

Moving into position to retrieve Tunks, the team tried with great difficulty to position the basket close to him. On the second attempt, Tunks pulled himself inside.

Yet, Tunks's recovery was even more difficult than the Blades'. Suddenly, the helicopter was lifted by the winds and shuddered as it was propelled back at speeds in excess of fifty miles per hour, against the demands of the pilots who countered with full power on the controls. Saylor released more cable but the helicopter was moving too fast.

Tunks gripped tightly onto the sides of the steel basket as it surged. "I was hit with a freight-train—a really hard wave." Its wall of water knocked the air out of his lungs. He was stunned. Now fifty feet out in front of the helicopter he witnessed it veer out of control and descend toward the water.

Inside the craft, "Whiddon had the nose of the helicopter down ten degrees and was pulling maximum torque, he could not stop the helicopter's rearward movement as ASM2 Tunks impacted the waves ahead of the helicopter."

"We had to pull all the power we could to keep from crashing," said Whiddon. As forces careened them backward, Tunks was hit by a thirty-foot wave. The helicopter's hoist cable dragged him at high speed through the wave, slamming his back into the rear of the basket. Without delay or time to think about his pain, a third wave attacked him with equal punishment, tearing away his face mask and snorkel.

The pilots and aircrew had noticed the explosions of white water as the waves collided against Tunks. Whiddon heard yelling from the back of the cabin, "We've killed him, we've killed him." Whiddon said, "That was the one and only time I ever heard anyone say that to me. The only time anyone ever had to say that."

As the gust subsided, Whiddon regained control of the helicopter. Milne and Saylor did all they could to quickly hoist Tunks to safety.

As the basket was pulled free of the water, Tunks swung dangerously from side to side almost hitting the helicopter. "Only by Herculean efforts were they able to bring the basket into the helicopter," wrote Whiddon.

Once inside the safety of the cabin, Tunks fell out of the rescue basket onto the deck and vomited, twice. "I could still taste that overcooked burger I ate before the mission," Tunks said. "Everything came out of me, seawater, nerves, everything."

The pilots conducted an instrument takeoff, unable to see their surroundings and navigated the battered helicopter back to Air Station Sitka. They were on deck within ten minutes. "The helicopter was out of service for seven days due to the overtorqued transmission, the overstressed hoist and wrinkles on the skin of the tail pylon [extended tail of the helicopter back to the tail rotor]," Whiddon reported in his case summary.

Talking about the ordeal, Tunks admitted that he dug in so hard on the basket he bruised his fingertips. His back was also bruised and red hives broke out all over his body, which a doctor later identified as adrenaline induced. "It was an unbelievable, euphoric feeling of achievement. I loved seeing everybody smiling when we got back," Tunks said.

Whiddon, who has since retired from the Coast Guard and lives in Kodiak, Alaska, wrote that the *Bluebird* rescue was the most difficult and demanding case he had been involved with in over twelve years of Coast Guard aviation. Of the men he flew with that night, he said, "The performance of the entire crew was, without exception, truly super and most certainly deserving of recognition at the highest level for the courage, skill and professionalism displayed." Regarding Jeff Tunks's actions that night, "It was a superb example of what the rescue swimmer could be and turned out to be. Tunks is just remarkable!"

Each of the Coast Guardsmen was awarded the Distinguished Flying Cross. Tunks was the first Coast Guard helicopter rescue swimmer to be awarded this medal. The five-man crew received the 1987 National Naval Helicopter Association Award, the Association of Naval Aviation Outstanding Achievement Award, and Tunks was selected as cowinner of the Coast Guard Foundation Admiral Chester R. Bender Award for Heroism. The governor of Alaska, Steve Cowper, presented the state's highest honor, the Medal of Heroism, to the five Coast Guardsmen. This medal had only been presented thirteen other times since its establishment by law in 1965. The governor wrote to Jeff Tunks in January of 1988,

It sounded like a pretty harrowing experience in those weather conditions, but I'm proud to see that you stuck with it and saved Jim Blades and his son. I also noted that you used the occasion to test your equipment to the max. Genuine heroes are hard to find these days but I think you and other members of the crew qualify. On behalf of all Alaskans, I'm honored to have you in Alaska and thank you for a job well done.

Whiddon believes that he was helped that night. "The presence kinda never went away. I became a born-again Christian a couple of years ago—I'm convinced I knew what it was. I didn't know it at the time but the Blades were very religious Christians, they had activated their prayer chain."

Lieutenant Breithaupt retired from the Coast Guard and flew for a commercial airline.

Petty Officer Carl Saylor has retired from the Coast Guard.

Petty Officer Mark Milne left the Coast Guard after completing his tour in Sitka.

For Senior Chief Petty Officer Jeff Tunks, who is still in the Coast Guard working at Air Station Mobile in Alabama, "I think I was the fortunate one—I used to feel lucky, now I feel blessed."

From that day on, when Whiddon put his stamp of approval on the rescue swimmer program, it just took off. "This mission showed we were here to stay. It grounded the program and showed that we could make a difference."

Jim and Jill Blades still live in Sitka, though they no longer live in the float house. In a 1987 letter to the aircrew Jill Blades wrote, "You have made this a very special Christmas for our family in the thankfulness of the opportunity to keep our family whole. Can one ever casually thank another for risking his life for you? I'm afraid I cannot. But that remembrance will ever be with me."

Clint Blades is married and lives in Sitka. He remembers Carl Saylor taking him out of the helicopter when they landed. "I kept going up and up and up! I should have died that day," said Clint. "I believe everything I do in my life has meaning. I remember it pretty vividly—I get a lump in my throat."

Many nonbelievers became believers—within the Coast Guard, among the helicopter rescue swimmers, and in their own personal lives.

4

FIRST

Kelly Mogk

> What gave me my determination was everybody telling me I was
> going to fail . . . but mostly I wanted to be a rescue swimmer . . .
> the frontline person in a rescue.

ASM3 Kelly Mogk, the first woman to qualify as a rescue swimmer in
any of the U.S. armed services, had agreed to jump into the Pacific
Ocean, thirty-five miles offshore. She made final preparations; donned
her mask, snorkel, and fins; and wearing her dry suit, waited for the right
moment to deploy from the Coast Guard helicopter the morning of January 3, 1989.

From her elevated position, Mogk could see the injured F-4 pilot.
Second Lieutenant Mike Markstaller, Oregon National Guard, was trying to keep his head above the surface. He was not aware of the helicopter circling above him or of the rescue swimmer observing him every
moment. He was entangled in his parachute. In repetition, twenty-foot
swells washed over his body.

The helicopter hovered fifteen feet above the surface. Mogk was
pretty "stoked" to deploy into the water as she sat in the cabin door.

With one swift movement and full of confidence and determination, she free-fell as she was trained to do.

"She was a really strong swimmer and got over there quickly," noted Lieutenant Commander William W. Peterson, the pilot of the HH-65 Dolphin helicopter. "We were sort of helpless and watched her work like crazy."

Before Mogk jumped, Peterson had briefed her on the situation. Because the survivor didn't look to be in great shape, Mogk was informed that to save time they might depart the scene once she got the survivor into the cabin. An incoming helicopter would hoist her and bring her home.

Mogk repeatedly dove below to investigate the bowl of spaghettilike entanglements surrounding Markstaller. She noticed his shoulder, was it dislocated or broken? Straps and lines were around his broken leg, abdomen, and chest holding him prisoner. Hypothermia dangerously lowered his body core temperature.

"I noticed he was taking a pounding from the waves crashing over the top of him," she stated. "He probably sucked in a lot of seawater, he didn't have a helmet on. I didn't feel the cold temperature of the water. My adrenaline had kicked in." Mogk did have a rip in the side of her suit but didn't feel the water seeping in and ignored her own body getting cold. "Nothing else matters, I didn't care about myself, I wasn't consciously aware of potential danger to myself. All you care about is getting that person out of the water. You're just so focused."

MOGK'S DETERMINATION AND INNER STRENGTH helped guide her through many difficult steps just to qualify as a rescue swimmer and be the one on scene that particular day. A self-declared tomboy, Mogk was born in Minnesota and grew up in Seattle. Interested in the military at an early age, Mogk listened when her father asked, "Hey, what about the Coast Guard?" Talking with recruiters, she discovered that the Coast Guard, unlike the other military services, did not restrict women from certain jobs and duties. The missions intrigued her, and she discovered any of the jobs and missions she wanted to do she could.

Still a teenager, Mogk enlisted in the Coast Guard in 1984. An attractive, athletic woman with hazel eyes and wavy, light brown hair she was all of five feet seven, one hundred twenty pounds. Her first career choices were not in aviation at all. Initially she sought opportunities as a yeoman, gunner's mate, and even quartermaster.

"What changed my life was a Christmas assignment to work at Air Station Cape May for two weeks," said Mogk of the opportunity to get airborne on helicopter flights and work with the aviation survivalman. Mogk enjoyed every moment and especially liked the fact that the ASMs had their own shop to run. As a result, she updated her career request to join the rate.

Meanwhile, the Coast Guard changed the requirements for the ASMs. They were now required to qualify as rescue swimmers to stay in the rate. "My name went from 118 on the list up to 19," recalled Mogk. This new stipulation effectively ended what would have been a two-year wait for her to start the training.

When she heard about this additional job standard, Mogk naively thought, *Rescue swimmer, oh, OK. I started swimming when I was three and could go underneath the water, the whole length of the pool, when I was four years old. So water doesn't intimidate me. I'm a great swimmer. I can do that. Is that it?*

"Everybody went into it not realizing how big a deal it was," said Mogk.

The nineteen-year-old was not deterred. As a child growing up she was accustomed to flipping boats over with other kids, roughhousing, and being forced underwater—something she knew would be a part of the ASM training in addition to other tests under more strenuous conditions.

The eighteen-week Rescue Swimmer Program took place in two geographic areas. The basic school, located in Elizabeth City, provided the trainees with the fundamentals: classroom, pool lessons, equipment familiarization, and fitness drills. It also served as a test bed, weeding out those not capable of meeting the rigid standards. Qualified trainees then attended three weeks of specialized training at the Navy's Aviation Rescue Swimmer School in Pensacola. If they made it through this school, they would return to Elizabeth City for graduation. That was if they made it.

The Navy school taught Marine Corps, Navy, and Coast Guard students. It had the reputation of being so difficult that many participants felt some of the harsh training conditions put their lives at risk. In 1988, it shut down temporarily to review procedures after the death of Airman Recruit Lee Mirecki.

Two years before this tragedy, Mogk had attended the training. "I really worked out and got myself into great shape," said a determined Mogk. The instructors at the Navy school had already seen a woman go through before her and resign. Mogk believed passing was within her reach despite their efforts to eliminate her and her classmates. Being the first woman to complete the training, accommodations were created out of what existed. Her locker was a converted closet. While her male classmates were in their locker room, she'd wait outside, on many occasions doing push-ups.

"They were doing everything in their power to make me quit," said Mogk. "Once they realized I would not give up and was doing well, it became less and less a big deal to them. It was tough, a tough school for everybody. A lot of people failed." The other students in her class melded into a support group with Mogk—"my brothers," she affectionately referred to them.

"What gave me my determination was when the instructors were telling me, 'You're going to fail; I'll give you two weeks.' So there was a little bit of 'I'm going to prove them wrong,'" said Mogk. "Mostly, I want to be a rescue swimmer. I want to be in aviation. This is a part of it, and yes, I want to be the frontline person in the rescue. So, yes, I was all pumped up!"

Mogk was the first woman to complete the difficult Navy Aviation Rescue Swimmer School in Pensacola, Florida. She returned for graduation from the Coast Guard program in Elizabeth City and became the first woman to qualify as a rescue swimmer in the Coast Guard and in all the military services. Since then only five other women have achieved the qualification of rescue swimmer in the Coast Guard.

About being the only woman, "I just happened to be the first," said Mogk. "It's a new program, and someone had to do it."

MOGK WAS PHYSICALLY AND MENTALLY FIT, having graduated from the grueling training. She was ready to go to work. "I was pretty excited about it, brainwashed, ready to save the world."

Two and one-half years later, with several rescues to her credit, Kelly Mogk would again have to prove her worth.

It was a typical rainy, foggy, low-visibility morning in the Pacific Northwest when the distress call came into Coast Guard Air Station Astoria, situated near the Columbia River.

"Now, put the ready helicopter on the line. F-4 ditched thirty-five miles off the coast," announced the operations center watch stander over loudspeakers. Mogk, a third class petty officer and one of a handful of Coast Guard rescue swimmers assigned to the air station, was repairing survival gear in the ASM shop. Not on call, she witnessed the duty swimmer respond to the emergency call. He got his gear and scrambled out the door to the waiting helicopter.

Meanwhile, inside the air station's Operations Center, Lieutenant Commander William W. Peterson was engaged in discussions about the Coast Guard's response plan. He realized that because there were two pilots in the F-4, it would be best to send a second helicopter. Given permission, he began to build the flight team to support him as the aircraft commander of the backup helicopter.

The telephone rang in the swimmers' shop. Mogk quickly answered it. The caller asked Mogk if she would join the second helicopter crew on the mission. She eagerly agreed, grabbed her gear, and ran out.

Peterson, in the right seat, taxied the helicopter behind the primary Dolphin helicopter. The copilot and navigator, Lieutenant Junior Grade William Harper, entered position information into the flight computer from the left seat. The flight mechanic, Aviation Electronicsman Second Class James Reese, in the cabin with Mogk, was the hoist operator. Each had dressed in insulated, red-orange flight suits, affectionately known as "Mustangs." The suits were designed to provide flotation and protection against hypothermia if the aircraft were to ditch in the frigid water.

While they waited for takeoff, Harper entered the F-4's last known position data into the helicopter's flight computer.

Peterson briefed the crew on mission details using the internal communications system mounted inside their helmets.

North America Air Defense Command (NORAD) had contacted the air station by using SARTEL, a search and rescue telephone. NORAD reported to the Coast Guard that two F-4 Phantom jets were participating in aerial combat maneuvers thirty-five nautical miles west of Tillamook Bay, Oregon. The pilot and his weapons systems officer were in an uncontrollable flight and had to bail out during basic fighter maneuvers because something catastrophically broke.

"They bailed out at a very high speed. Their playmate out there had followed them until the clouds covered the chutes," said Peterson.

NORAD monitored the western sector of operations known as "BIGFOOT" and had tracked the F-4's radar position down to the crash site and relayed the data to the Coast Guard. To provide search and communications assistance, the second F-4 would remain on scene as long as possible.

Per standard procedures, the Coast Guard launched a Falcon fix-wing jet to provide overhead communications support for the rescuers. With any clearing of the cloud cover, its crew might even locate the pilots in advance of the rescuers' arrival.

MARKSTALLER'S PARACHUTE WAS FULLY BALLOONED in the depths beneath him. The weight of it wrenched his body downward toward the bottom of the Pacific Ocean. He had suffered multiple bone-crushing injuries ejecting from the cockpit. Even at an altitude of twenty thousand feet and a velocity of five hundred miles per hour, "Ejection was better than the only alternative—not ejecting," Markstaller said. "It was a lot of windblasts and some tumbling followed by having the parachute open. I started descending through the under cast."

When he collided with the surface it felt like concrete—he could have landed on a city sidewalk. It was all he could do to hang on to the life raft attached to a ten-foot cord extending from his chute. Presumably, he would have jumped into it. "But if your arms are broken, you can't," said Markstaller, who also had a broken leg. "I was only able to partially inflate one of the life vests. You're supposed to pull vigorously, but with broken arms I pulled a little." Adding to his distress, he couldn't talk on the radio to the second F-4 circling above the clouds or to his weapons systems officer, First Lieutenant Mark Baker, who had ejected from the rear seat a fraction of a second before him. *Where was Baker? What had become of him?*

Determined to live, Markstaller countered the forces tugging his dying body toward the deep. He hooked his only employable arm over the side of his life raft, which leisurely inflated. Weakened further by the cold waters, he was unable to pull himself aboard. Nearly unconscious, he held on instinctively for air and hoped for rescue.

AFTER A FEW MINUTES ON THE RUNWAY, Peterson was informed that the duty helicopter, which had just taken off, was forced to return to the hangar with engine problems and torque splits. At this point in time, the Coast Guard was experiencing extreme problems with the engines and cracks in the power turbine wheels for the HH-65 engines. The causalities were said to be part of working out the "glitches" of transitioning from the HH-3F Pelican airframe into this new one.

Peterson and his team were airborne in less than nine minutes, not only as the primary search and rescue helicopter for the mission but the only capable one. All of the other helicopters at the Astoria air station were in "Charlie," or repair, status. The Coast Guard immediately ordered the launch of a second helicopter from the nearest unit to the south, Air Facility Newport, Oregon.

Immediately crossing over the beach line, Peterson guided the helicopter into a descent to a hundred feet, just below the ceiling of clouds. As it flew toward the coordinates of the downed F-4, the helicopter's use of loran failed.

In 1989, global positioning systems were not a technology in play. "I put in some set and drift," recalled Peterson. This was a technique he had learned from standard surface navigation to account for winds and currents moving an object in the water.

Looking down at the ocean, he noticed, "We did have a good swell system . . . close to eighteen feet. In the Pacific, because of the fetch [distance waves travel from shore to shore], there was a large swell system. We were in and out of fog. The fog reduced our visibility to just a couple hundred feet."

After about thirty minutes of flying, the crew arrived at the F-4's reported crash site. Peterson, Mogk, Harper, and Reese searched intently for the two men. They hoped to spot a marker or visible sign to identify their location like a dye marker, raft, flare, or a signal from one of the pilots. As they searched, Peterson saw something off to his left.

"Cross-cockpit! Oh, I've got something over here," he yelled while making a sharp twenty-to-thirty-degree course change to intercept it.

"Shoot!" exclaimed Peterson at the sight of whales spouting. He then turned the helicopter back to the right. "Just as I turned back, I caught the glimpse of what was a pilot's raft. They are in combat gear, it's dark, and there was nothing really visible. It was just 'Oh my God there he is.'"

As they inspected the situation, Peterson and his crew questioned why he wasn't getting into his raft. He had one arm draped over the side of the raft, and it seemed that what held him above the surface was his partially inflated life vest or water wings.

Following procedure, Reese dropped a data marker buoy out the cabin door to mark the position. The buoy would also serve as a beacon that could be located electronically. It would track the effects of wind and current on the pilot's position in the water and provide an approximate location. As they flew back around to reposition for recovery, they located the second raft. It was empty, adrift, and about two hundred yards away.

MOGK DOVE BELOW THE SURFACE, assessing the situation. "He was so tangled up. His leg was disjointed, I knew it was broken." Mogk sensed his tension increased when she dove beneath the water to untangle him. When she surfaced again he relaxed his shoulder a bit. "He must have thought I was leaving him," she recalled.

If there was anything good about Markstaller's situation, he was slightly coherent. He followed her with his eyes. They were not alert eyes. Only eyes aware of her presence.

Following procedure, Mogk swam around behind him where she could get a good grip on his harness without endangering herself. "You don't want to be in front of them because they see you and think 'Hey, buoy, let's grab on to you,'" recalled Mogk. "I noticed his purplish lips moving between swells, like he was trying to tell me something."

"Hey, I'm here. I'm going to take this parachute off you," she informed him. "Bear with me."

He couldn't respond.

"There was a lot of coughing and gurgling."

She squeezed his hand and, miraculously, he squeezed back.

Of critical importance, Mogk knew she needed to release the harness connecting him to the parachute. The National Guard–styled mechanism was different from what she worked with during training. She removed one of her gloves to get a better grip. With concentration and effort she managed to release it.

Yet, when the suspension lines came loose he was still tangled up in the chute. All the while she worked diligently behind the pilot. "I kept thinking, *God how did he get so tangled up in this?*" She remembered from training that if she cut one line she'd have two lines to deal with. Cutting was a last resort.

"It seemed like an absolute eternity. But it really wasn't that long," recalled Peterson of the wait for the second helicopter's arrival. He immediately directed them to search the other raft and surrounding areas for the second pilot.

Mogk worked line by line. Slowly and methodically she untangled him. "I remembered the last line, when I got it off, the parachute slowly just floated down and faded away. It was pretty wild to see."

That part's done, thought Mogk. If there were any predators around, such as sharks, Mogk didn't even notice. She had more to do.

The situation did not get any easier. He would not let go of the life raft.

"I was yelling at him to let go. His grip was like they say a 'death grip,' he was not letting go for anything," Mogk decided.

"You've got to let go! Let go of the raft!" she commanded.

"He finally let go, about the time I was going to reach for my knife to pop the raft," noticed Mogk. "Then he kind of relaxed into my grip."

Mogk held him in a cross-chest carry, a position that enabled her to control his position in the water. She held him by reaching with her left arm over his left shoulder and across his chest. Her left hand gripped his harness on the right side. With her body supporting him underneath his back, she could swim with him or hold position as needed in preparation for the hoist.

They were ready for the helicopter and got into position for the hoist. As she waited for the rescue sling, Mogk saw the raft tumble across the ocean, pushed by the steady winds, and disappear.

Peterson, Reese, and Harper simultaneously observed what appeared to be Markstaller's last moments of life. "He looked like he was dying of hypothermia, right then," exclaimed Peterson. "We called the other helicopter and asked them to come back and stand by to pick up our swimmer. As soon as we got the pilot in the cabin we could take him to the hospital."

"This guy was huge, over six feet," recalled Mogk. "And over two hundred pounds." Because of his injuries and his size he would not be easily placed into the rescue basket. They had decided not to use the basket and instead hoist him by using a rescue sling or "horse collar" looped under his armpits and attached to the hoist cable.

Ending a twenty-five-minute rescue procedure, Mogk snapped the rescue sling in place after positioning it around him.

She gave a thumbs-up sign to Reese signaling that Markstaller was ready for pickup.

Up he went.

As they pulled Markstaller into the cabin, Petty Officer Reese observed that he looked like he was in really bad shape. He informed the pilots that the man's leg and shoulder seemed to be broken and he was severely hypothermic. As Markstaller was carefully released down to the cabin floor, he let out a weak, pain-filled scream.

Markstaller was close to death from his body temperature dropping very low, and he needed warmth to help him recover.

"Reese, can you get into that rewarming bag with him?" asked Peterson, aware that Reese was a rather large man too.

"No sir, I can't fit," said Reese. The hypothermia-rewarming bag, shaped like a very well-insulated sleeping bag, was too narrow for the two men. Turning to his copilot, Peterson instructed, "Bill, I know you can. I'd like you to get in."

Harper unbuckled from his seat and worked his way back into the cabin. In order to provide immediate body warmth to the stricken pilot, Harper stripped down to his underwear before getting into the bag with Markstaller.

"We hand signaled to Kelly that the other bird was going to pick her up," said Peterson as he prepared to fly home.

Peterson cranked up the aircraft's heater too. Reese "buttoned up" the helicopter and they proceeded to make best speed toward the town of Astoria.

Peterson reminded Harper to keep the pilot engaged and awake. "I've had people relax and die—he was slipping into unconsciousness—I yelled at Harper to get in his face, tell him to stay awake, he's not saved yet, he's got to stay awake!" As instructed, Harper continually yelled at Markstaller all the way to the hospital.

Mogk bobbed in the ocean. She watched with a sense of loss and loneliness as the helicopter flew away. "That was the correct decision; they couldn't take the time, even the three minutes to come in and pick me up," recognized Mogk. "I started to relax, knowing my job was done. I hoped too, that the pilot was going to be OK."

Waiting for pickup, Mogk had time to think. "Because of the height of the waves, I couldn't see the other helicopter, it seemed like it took an hour for them to arrive." It was the first time she started to feel the chill of the ocean, which had quietly leaked into one of her dry suit seals. During the rescue she had removed one of her gloves to better grip the lines. That hand had completely lost all feeling. "It's cold, that water's freezing!" Exhausted, Mogk looked down into the water. "It was extremely deep. I wondered for a moment what kind of critters are out here?" she asked. *OK, don't look down anymore.*

The Newport-based Dolphin helicopter hovered above Mogk, positioned for her hoist. Mogk grabbed the bare hook lowered to her and attached it to her harness. The harness she wore that day has since been redesigned. It was a half harness worn around her rib cage and offered zero back support and little comfort.

She gave the flight mechanic a thumbs-up sign, ready for pickup. Because the rescue swimmer program was still being rolled out, not all units had swimmers attached. This aircrew was in that predicament and not familiar with hoisting swimmers.

"I was kinda getting dragged . . . Just as I was starting to come out of the water, the crest of the wave went by, and I dropped into the trough between waves. It was jarring!" said Mogk. "The full brunt of the fall was carried by my rib cage, I remember yelling, 'Ohhhh God.' It was like a jolt, like somebody jumping off a building and then midway a line catching you right at your rib cage." The full impact wrenched the hell out of her back, Mogk said.

"I got into the helicopter and kinda laid down, relieved that was over," said Mogk before moving to the rear of the cabin. The pilots asked Mogk if she would go in the water again. They had briefed her that there was no sign of the other pilot during their previous aerial search over the second raft and vicinity. Assessing her condition and informed that other aircraft were on their way, Mogk responded, "I really shouldn't go back." Mogk was experiencing symptoms of hypothermia.

"If the second pilot had been clinging to the life raft or visible in any way, I would have gone in again," said a determined Mogk.

UPON RETURN TO AIR STATION ASTORIA to refuel, Peterson and Reese met with the Air Force air rescue group. "Their Para rescue folks are more highly trained than our rescue swimmers," said Peterson. He debriefed the Air Force team on what he knew and had seen at the crash site. "They wanted to go back out to find the other officer. Turns out their direction-finding gear wasn't working. They could not hone in on our data marker buoy's signal." Peterson called for another copilot, flight mechanic, and rescue swimmer to return with him to the search area.

"The weather was improving as we got out there, and I DF'd right to the spot and found the raft. After vectoring in the HH-3F, they released a couple of PJs to search," said Peterson. "They dove down, ten to twelve feet underwater and found Baker underneath the raft with his chute fully deployed. That's why we never saw him."

Using CPR, the staff aboard the HH-3 helicopter restarted Baker's heart. Flying in formation, Peterson escorted the aircraft back to Astoria where the pilot could be rewarmed and provided emergency care at the hospital. Baker was transferred to Emanuel Hospital in Portland, Oregon, where later that evening he was pronounced dead.

The press was critical of the handling of this rescue. The Coast Guard was questioned in media reports, reports that were not always accurate. Some of the articles even went so far as to inquire why a woman was sent to the rescue.

Even an Oregon congressman criticized the case; in particular, the helicopter engine problems and the lack of rescue swimmers positioned at the other Oregon air facilities.

Peterson elected to go to the Portland Air National Guard with the rest of the aircrew to provide the facts. Telling their story, they addressed a standing-room-only audience of the families, command, and their guests. By the end of the two-hour brief, and having had all their questions answered, the audience rose and gave the Coast Guard crew a standing ovation.

Peterson, Harper, and Reese were awarded Coast Guard Commendation Medals for outstanding achievement. Mogk received the Coast Guard Air Medal.

"I gotta tell you she is one extraordinary young woman," Peterson exclaimed. "I'd have her on my team everyday, anytime, anywhere . . . The Coast Guard is pretty well blessed to have somebody like her who's taken this on as a calling and that's basically what it is because we don't pay our men and women enough to do what we do out there. It was total teamwork; they performed outstanding, just like clockwork. These folks performed flawlessly."

"I feel that any rescue swimmer could have done what I did," said Mogk. "I was trained to do that. For me it would have been much worse if it were at night. Yeah, it was tough, very difficult, but I don't think it was worth any award.

"It was a pretty powerful event to be a part of saving somebody's life like that, but that is why we do it, not for a medal," stated Mogk. "For the rest of your life you have that bond, a special bond between you and the people you were involved with saving lives."

In April of that year, Major General Rees of the Oregon National Guard presented Mogk, Reese, Harper, and Peterson each with the Meritorious Service Medal in Salem, Oregon. Markstaller, in a wheelchair, was reunited with them.

Later when he had recovered further, Markstaller visited Air Station Astoria and presented each of his rescuers with a signed painting of an F-4 as a symbol of his thanks. "That is one of my most valued treasures," reflected Mogk. As they discussed the events of that day, she learned that Markstaller thought two men were rescuing him, one of whom wore wire-rimmed glasses. "To see him again was just very profound," recalled Mogk. "His body temperature was eighty-four degrees, he shouldn't have survived, eighty-four degrees!" Mogk shyly added, "It was so different to see his face with color and he looked alive. He was a really good-looking guy."

Understandably, she became the Coast Guard's role model. The Coast Guard flew Mogk around the country to be presented with awards from the Coast Guard Foundation. Mogk met with President George Bush, who congratulated her. The secretary of transportation, Sam Skinner, presented the Air Medal to Mogk in a formal ceremony. Additionally, Coast Guard recruiting posters featured Mogk.

Many entertainment shows wanted airtime with Mogk including *The Bob Hope Show*. The History Channel reenacted the case. Mogk turned down opportunities for publicity with *People* magazine, *Live with Regis and Kathy Lee*, and even a feature film proposal from Goldie Hawn's production team. Mogk felt she had just done her job.

"The attention I was getting, I didn't think was justified," stated Mogk. "If you keep putting me on a pedestal how am I going to be treated as an equal?" For Mogk, this is why she joined the Coast Guard, to complete the rigorous training and become a rescue swimmer. "This is why I put up with the crap, to have a great case. So let me enjoy the moment."

Sadly, Mogk endured criticism from other swimmers and Coast Guard personnel who didn't know her. They believed her recognition was because she was a woman. "I'd go to another air station and people wouldn't talk to me at first," said Mogk. "They'd be like, 'Oh, there she is.'"

A bronze plaque hangs in the entrance of the prestigious Explorer's Club in New York City that lists a few adventurous firsts: "first to the North Pole, 1909; first to the South Pole, 1911; first to the summit of Mount Everest, 1953; first to the deepest part of the ocean, 1960." Kelly Mogk, aviation survivalman third class, might be considered a member for her exploits: first woman to qualify as a rescue swimmer in the armed services, 1986; followed by first Coast Guard woman to save a downed pilot from certain death in the Pacific Ocean. Mogk is humble and modest about her achievements. In fact, she shunned the national publicity her heroism garnered in the aftermath of her storied rescue. That and the criticism she received almost made her resign from the Coast Guard.

Today Kelly Mogk is an officer and Coast Guard helicopter pilot. Lieutenant Commander Kelly Larson is stationed in the Pacific Northwest.

"I'm very grateful for her competence and expertise. Also for her willingness to put her life on the line for me and for anybody that needs it," said Mike Markstaller. "Due to a lot of those injuries it was sort of common thought that I wouldn't fly airplanes again let alone walk." After three years of surgery, bone grafts, and rehabilitation, Markstaller was able to continue his career in the Oregon Air National Guard. He flew C-26 aircraft and subsequently C-130 rescue airplanes in the Air Force Reserve. Today, he is a first officer with a commercial airline on the West Coast.

Captain Bill Peterson retired to Washington. He last served as head of the Coast Guard's aviation program in Washington, DC. Petty Officer Reese and Lieutenant Harper have both retired from the Coast Guard.

5

TO ALMOST DIE

Tristan Heaton

If I don't make it out of here, could you please tell my kids I love them.

Immense Pacific Ocean seas rolled ashore, given unusual power by the effects of El Niño on April 4, 1993. The saltwater swept into the mouth of a cave at the foot of Cape Lookout on the Oregon coast with a roar so loud the U.S. Coast Guard rescue helicopter hovering above could not be heard.

For Aviation Survivalman Second Class Tristan Heaton, the rescue swimmer looking wide-eyed down toward the cave from the protection of the helicopter's cabin, it was the kind of day he lived for. Nothing got his adrenaline going in such an incredible rush as when he was preparing to save lives. He was addicted to the natural injection. Looking down at the ocean he thought, *If I make it back from this one, I'm going to go back and do it again.* Heaton said he had waited all his life to "almost die" to help someone and, in his mind, cleanse his past.

MICHAEL FAHLMAN, SEVENTEEN, and John Fahlman, thirty-three, were trapped inside the cave. The only way out for the brothers was back through the cave's mouth, into the wild sea.

The waves sped into the cavern, which reached back more than two hundred feet. This was not a small cave by any means. About the size of the Statue of Liberty, its mouth was 125 feet high by 225 feet wide. The sheer force of the water picked up heavy logs and threw them like toothpicks into the depths. The air in the cave whistled like a teapot at full boil as it was sucked out and up through the cracks of the cave's damp walls to make way for the Pacific saltwater forcing its way in. The intensity of the surf was just getting started, the winds gusted to twenty-five and thirty knots while twelve-foot seas broke at the coastline.

This was slack tide. When the tide shifted to flood, the currents and wave heights would almost double.

HEATON HAD BEEN IN THE COAST GUARD Air Station Astoria aviation shop when the distress call came in. He had a few rescues under his belt, but nothing comparable to this one. He was excited to have the chance to pull two people from a cave; yet, a cave rescue was not something he had done before. In fact, it would be a first for the Coast Guard.

Motivated to help at an early age, having suffered from repeated abuse, Heaton had always tried to come to the aid of others and prove he was a good person. He joined the Coast Guard to make a difference, to save lives.

FROM PORTLAND, OREGON, the brothers had been walking on a deer trail located on the state's pristine coast near Tillamook Bay. It led them to the cliffs of Cape Lookout situated above the north side of the cave.

Having visited the interior of the cave before, John planned to show his younger brother how to navigate its dangerous crevices. John knew of a shoelike rock ledge that formed a rugged volcanic walkway into the south side of the mammoth cave.

Misjudging the magnitude of the surf and unaware of the timing of the incoming swells, John and Michael scaled down the four-hundred-foot cliff face toward the cave entrance. They made their way onto the ledge. Just then, a rogue wave caught John and engulfed him. The wave tossed him toward the cave's mouth. Michael tried to run after him and pull him back. But the ocean delivered a powerful one-two punch. A wave struck Michael broadside, forcing him into white water and currents on a direct course into the cave.

A couple on the trail, watched in horror from hundreds of feet above. They realized that the men were in trouble. One of them ran to call for help.

By then, Michael and John Fahlman were struggling for their lives. They tried to get out of the water's grasp while strong currents forced them toward the back of the cave just like the logs before them.

John's head hit a rock.

For Michael, the next couple of minutes were a blank. He was forced under the forty-seven-degree water again and again. When he could, he looked for his brother. He couldn't see him, but he could hear him. John was calling to him from the southwest interior of the cave. Michael looked over and saw John trying to scale the cave walls with his bare hands.

Michael called out for him.

John answered with desperate cries that he wanted Michael to tell their mother that he loved her and for Michael to hang on. In an instant, the waves plucked John off the wall.

He was never seen again.

Grasping for anything to hold on to, Michael was miraculously pushed back and up by the rising water to a narrow ledge. He dug his fingers into the cold, rugged rock and pulled his two-hundred-twenty-pound frame onto it.

Sixty grueling minutes had passed.

HALF A FOOTBALL FIELD AWAY, hovering above the cave entrance, the Coast Guard HH-65A Dolphin helicopter, tail number CG 6504, and its crew spotted the couple on the trail.

The flight mechanic, AD2 Craig Wyatt, lowered Heaton on the steel hoist cable down to the couple, thinking they were the ones in distress, but the couple anxiously pointed to the cave.

Looking at the cavern from the outside, Heaton's first thoughts were fearful. He realized that nothing in his life had prepared him for this. "It was so raw," he recalled. "Nothing, not my training, not my other rescues and experiences like helping car crash victims, could have prepared me for what I had to do that day."

Instead of letting his fear get the best of him, he found confidence knowing that the on-scene helicopter crew was supporting him. Heaton also sought motivation from what he learned during his training at the elite Navy Aviation Rescue Swimmer School and aviation survivalman schools. At these schools, where 40 percent of the rescue swimmers wash out, Heaton graduated believing that he would survive. He could do what was asked of him at all costs. Feeling invincible, he knew this was the day he was born for.

Heaton listened to the witnesses' accounts. Then, using his PRC 90 handheld radio, Heaton relayed to the flight crew that the two people they were looking for were in fact inside the cave.

"Our biggest concern was that the tide would keep rising and we were running out of time," said the pilot, Lieutenant Ed Gibbons. "We didn't have good communications with Tristan either. With the PRC 90 handheld radio, communications were scratchy at best."

Before going in, Heaton briefed the Coast Guard pilots and crew that he would probably give his life jacket to one of the men so that it would help the survivor swim out. As he made his final preparations to enter the cave by way of the same shoelike ledge the brothers had stood on before, Heaton radioed, "If I don't make it out of here, could you please tell my kids I love them."

Based on previous rescues, the aircrew realized this was a dangerous mission. Gibbons hesitated when Heaton proposed entering the cave. "I felt like there was something missing, something we should be thinking of to do, before Heaton got off his radio and went in," said Gibbons. "I 'rogered' his plan and he was gone.

"About thirty seconds later, Lieutenant Blake Burris, the copilot came up with the idea that we should have Heaton take a trail line in with him, which was not a routine thing to do," recalled Gibbons. "But Tristan had put his radio away. My regret is that when he said, 'I've got to go, got to go now,' I should have been more careful and told him to wait. Wait so that we could have talked this out a little more . . . If we had a better quality radio, we could have heard each other, and this whole thing would not have turned into a nightmare for him."

BEFORE LEAVING THE OPERATIONS CENTER at the air station, Heaton had checked the weather reports and calculated the tides and currents for the search area. He knew he had thirty minutes until the slack tide shifted to a flood. He would need to get the victims out of the cave before the flood tide started, or they would face waves and currents doubling in size and force.

HEATON'S DRY SUIT WOULD PROTECT his five-foot-seven-inch frame from hypothermia, which could set in within minutes if the icy Pacific water seeped in. Armed with only his mask, fins, snorkel, radio-equipped life vest, and his courage and desire to help for inspiration, Heaton moved toward the entrance. Watching the waves and timing their movements, he chose his moment to enter the cave.

Walking along the rocks Heaton spotted one of the men, Michael Fahlman, curled up on a small rocky ledge toward the rear of the cave.

Heaton observed that the interior of the cave reached back about two hundred feet, then turned to the left where there was an underwater entrance to a second cavelike tunnel. All the logs and water seemed to be rushing toward that entrance, then moments later were spit right back out. Heaton told himself that it was not a zone he wanted to be near or he'd be finished.

He lowered himself into the white water between twelve-foot waves. He flinched not only because it was frigid, but also because it was unexpectedly filled with so much air from the wave action of the water. The water felt as if four large washing machines were on the rinse cycle with a plentiful supply of saltwater and power from the Pacific.

Pushed by the surging water, Heaton swam along the rocky wall toward Fahlman. At first, as he inspected him for injuries, he thought Fahlman must be African-American because his skin was very dark, almost blue. Heaton realized that Fahlman's coloring was that of an extremely hypothermic person. By then, the brother had been in the cave for almost two hours.

When they made eye contact, Heaton noticed tears in Fahlman's eyes. Yelling over the noise, he said to him, "Hi, I'm Petty Officer Tristan Heaton. I'm going to get you out of here." Fahlman weakly described how his brother, hanging onto the cave wall, was lost while "trying to pull a Spiderman to get to safety." He also made it clear that he did not want to get back in the water.

Heaton said to Fahlman while clipping on the inflated life vest, "This is what we get to do. You're going to kick with all your might, and I'm going to kick to get us out of here." Fahlman wondered if they could make it and kept asking, "What if . . . ?"

"There is only one what if, and that's if I'm not able to do my job and get you out of here, then you will get yourself out of here and leave me be." Seeing the fear in Fahlman's eyes, he said encouragingly, "I need you to believe in me. You are not responsible to get me out if I fail because if I have any way to do so, I'll push you away and you will save yourself."

They had no choice but to get moving. Heaton radioed the helicopter, but Gibbons, Burris, and Wyatt could not hear his transmissions. They feared the worst. For their part, they were brainstorming to figure out a way to get the helicopter closer to Heaton. They were committed to remain on scene as long as they had fuel.

"Here we go!" Heaton commanded. Fahlman, who seemed to have some confidence now, jumped into the water after him. Just as rapidly, like a cat, he climbed on top of Heaton's head and shoulders. His fear of dying set in, and he was not letting go of his rescuer. Heaton gave him a couple swift punches, as he was trained to do, which subdued him, and told him to relax. Then Heaton put him in a swimmer's rescue carry and they started kicking together.

The currents and wave action surrounded them, pulling them toward the rear, second cave. Yelling at Fahlman to start kicking harder, Heaton tried to keep them out of the dangerous back tunnel and on the north side of the cave where it seemed, ironically, a little calmer.

They had to swim against the currents and incoming waves. These combined forces pushed them under. The waves acted like a wall between them and the surface. They gasped for air when they were allowed and tried to hold their breath when they were not. Every twenty yards they made forward, they were propelled back thirty. The eddy currents, swirling around and down, pinned them and swept them back into that same place. "There was this invisible line of force which Tristan couldn't get through," recalled Gibbons.

Twice they were forced and held underwater beneath a four-foot submerged ledge of rock. After what seemed like minutes, they would be released and gasped desperately for air. The third time they were pushed under the ledge, Heaton felt Fahlman give up. His entire body shook. Heaton heard his underwater scream. Then his body went limp. Heaton tried to give what little air he had in his mask to Fahlman. He blew into

Fahlman's shirt so that he might inhale it. But now, faced with no air of his own and desperate to breathe, Heaton decided, "Might as well inhale the saltwater. What harm could that do . . . ?"

Suddenly, they popped to the surface. Fahlman was unconscious. Both were alive.

Thinking of Moses, Heaton desperately prayed for help to part the waters and get them out. "Something has to give!" he pleaded. They were stuck in the hydraulic wave action of the cave. The cavern would fill with four to five sets of rolling waves before it would dump out the water and then a new series of waves would roll in. This hydraulic action and the ocean's tidal flow formed a barrier when the two collided, blocking their escape.

Forced under again, Heaton started to hyperventilate. He began drinking seawater as he swam for life, dragging Fahlman, as close to the north side of the cave as he could. They surfaced.

By now, Heaton thought he was going to die. But unbeknownst to him, he had made it through the barrier. Heaton looked toward the cave's entrance and gave the emergency signal even while he continued to hyperventilate.

Meanwhile, the helicopter crew made a daring and unprecedented decision. Knowing that Heaton must be stuck, out of their sight and reach, they decided to do the only thing they could do. Fly into the cave. "We realized that either the swimmer had to leave the victim or we had to enter the cave . . . or they both would die," said Burris.

Heaton, looked desperately toward the entrance. He saw the helicopter slowly moving into the narrow mouth and the vivid "U.S.C.G." painted on the bottom of the aircraft. It invigorated him with the strength of hope.

Flight mechanic Craig Wyatt sent down a couple of trail lines. But Heaton knew that if he took one of those lines, the rush of water toward the second cave would propel him right into it. Noticing he was not grabbing the lines, Gibbons, guided by Burris and Wyatt, flew the helicopter farther into the cave. They needed to get close enough to send the rescue basket down on the hook, a three-sixteenths-inch-thick stainless steel hoist cable.

Gibbons meticulously maneuvered the helicopter inside. Wyatt watched the rotors and judged how far they were from the cave walls on the right. Burris watched the left.

"Gibbons had the entire body of the helicopter inside the cave with the exception of the left side of the rotor head," recalled Wyatt. Now, close to thirty feet inside the cave, the flight mechanic quickly dropped the rescue basket. "I used the waves entering the cave to carry the basket to him as I let out slack in the hoist cable," said Wyatt.

Heaton grabbed it.

Looking at Fahlman, Heaton noticed that his eyes were blinking, signaling that he was checking out. Heaton gave him a slap, which from his training he knew would revive him. Heaton struggled to yell, "You've got to help me. Get in!" With great effort, Fahlman climbed in. There was only room for one. Heaton's choice was either to wait or hang on somehow. He was still hyperventilating. Waiting was not an option in his mind. Heaton hooked his hands with bent wrists inside the crab-traplike exterior of the basket and held on. He was not letting go.

Gibbons started to maneuver the helicopter out of the cave with navigational coaching from his team. Slow going at first, Heaton and Michael were dragged through the water. But what seemed slow to the helicopter crew ended up being like a sprint across the water for the two survivors. As they bounced and bumped, Heaton's back was hit by a twelve-foot wave, making the basket twirl into a full three-hundred-sixty-degree circle. The wave had knocked him so hard he stopped breathing. He felt blessed when he caught his breath; he was no longer hyperventilating.

Once outside the cave and its treacherous surf, Wyatt set up to hoist the basket. Heaton grabbed a lifeline dangling from the helicopter thinking, "This line better not fall off."

Fahlman was lifted into the cabin. The basket was returned. Heaton was hoisted into the cabin. The first things he saw were his flight team's tearful eyes. Heaton vividly recalls the words he heard from Wyatt, yelled out over the loud noise of the rotors, "We can't believe you are alive!"

"We had a seven-minute flight to the hospital. During that time, both of them fell asleep. I had to wake them up when we landed," said Wyatt.

At the Tillamook Bay Hospital, Fahlman was treated for hypothermia and shock. Heaton had a temperature of 106 degrees Fahrenheit from heat exhaustion and ingestion of saltwater.

Aviation Survivalman Second Class Tristan Heaton was awarded the Coast Guard's highest award for heroism, the Coast Guard Medal, on April 4, 1993, for "extraordinary heroism."

HEATON'S SUBSEQUENT CALLS TO DUTY were personally traumatic. He attempted to save a man in cardiac arrest who later died, and he also helped search teams recover deceased victims of a plane crash.

By March of the following year, Heaton transferred from Air Station Astoria and became a rescue swimmer instructor with the STAN Team in Mobile. Heaton said of this transition, "I was relieved that search and rescue was not a part of my life on a regular basis."

During this assignment, as part of the Rescue Swimmer Training Branch, Heaton was a member of an inaugural team tasked to develop an Advanced Rescue Swimmer School, which provided greater safety and better training for future rescues throughout the entire Coast Guard. Consisting of five enlisted petty officers who were also experienced rescue swimmers, the team was the first to make significant changes to rescue procedures, equipment, and the "mentality" of the Coast Guard–wide program by adding a dose of real-life experiences and situations.

At the time, the course used new procedures like direct deployment and exercised swimmers in real scenarios for cliff and cave rescues while also using an improved rescue harness. Heaton and the team were awarded the Coast Guard Meritorious Team Commendation in 1995 for their improvements and course development, which continues today.

Heaton decided to leave the Coast Guard in 1996 after he watched a training video of images of himself fearfully reliving his cave rescue trauma during a cave training exercise.

Disturbed by what he saw, Heaton realized he needed to get help.

That same year, Heaton married Carol McCann and moved to San Diego where he underwent three years of post-traumatic stress disorder treatment at the San Diego Veteran's Hospital. During this period, Heaton participated in a cutting-edge therapy called rapid eye treatment. This therapy helped Heaton relive and overcome a lot of suppressed memories enabling him to take control of his emotions and subsequently live a happier life.

Heaton graduated from the University of San Diego in the fall of 2005 with a degree in psychology. He is continuing his education with a master's degree in rehabilitation counseling. He currently lives in San Diego with his wife, Carol. Heaton's two children, Shelli and Chet, are "doing very well in their lives," said Heaton.

Awarded an Air Medal for this rescue, Commander Ed Gibbons is the executive officer at Air Station Cape Cod. He is an aircraft commander in the HH-60 Jayhawk helicopter, the Coast Guard's medium-range rescue helicopter.

Lieutenant Commander Blake Burris retired from the Coast Guard in 2002. He works in California City, California as a lead pilot for the EMS Air 19 helicopter rescue program, transporting people involved in car, motorcycle, and other crashes in the desert who need immediate medical treatment facility advanced care.

Lieutenant Commander Craig Wyatt was awarded the Coast Guard Commendation Medal for his part in the rescue. He now works in New Orleans for the Coast Guard District 8 Marine Safety Division.

6

STORM OF THE CENTURY

DANIEL W. EDWARDS

One never knows what he is going to do when he sits in the doorway of the helicopter.

IT WAS A FREAKISH THING. It was only mid-March, yet a hurricanelike storm spun into the Gulf of Mexico. Its course was a direct hit on Florida's west coast before it moved up the eastern seaboard of the United States. The repercussions of this superstorm were swift, vast, and disastrous. By the time it was over, it would strike twenty-six states and have an impact on the lives of nearly 100 million people, according to a University of Illinois case study.

"I'd never seen anything like it before," said rescue swimmer ASM2 Dan Edwards of the storm's unusual power and path. Edwards, assigned to Coast Guard Air Station Clearwater in Florida, defined the system, "like a nor'easter only they don't blow across the Gulf of Mexico. The air temperatures were mid- to high thirties and the water in the forties. Normally it would be closer to fifty to fifty-five degrees Fahrenheit." With this surprise package came wind speeds that gusted upward of ninety miles per hour, record low pressures, and snowfall amounts that "were more than enough for this storm to gain the status of "Storm of the Century," as documented by the University of Illinois. "The storm was monumental, killing over 250 people and canceling 25% of the United States' flights for two days."

"ONE NEVER KNOWS WHAT HE IS GOING TO DO when he sits in the doorway of the helicopter," said Edwards of the situation he faced. He had been on a week's vacation in Tampa, Florida, when he received the late-afternoon phone call from the air station. It was Saturday, March 13, 1993. Recalled to help with what became the second day of catastrophic events in the Gulf of Mexico and for towns along Florida's west coast, he drove as quickly as possible to Air Station Clearwater.

Edwards would immediately fill in for the rescue swimmer who had already flown too many hours and was "bagged" from multiple rescue responses. Edwards's return was hampered by bridge closures and washed-out roads. He had to follow back roads and detours. In Tampa Bay, the storm created seas of such increased height it was too dangerous for motorists to traverse the low-level bridges.

GROWING UP, EDWARDS HAD ALWAYS BEEN around the water, boats, and the Coast Guard. Before he enlisted, he knew he wanted to fly. Of the aviation rates, being a rescue swimmer seemed like a natural fit. He was willing to wait two years before going to the rescue swimmer school to be tested mentally and physically to see if he was capable to serve his country in this demanding profession. By the time he went to school, his heart and mind were resolute. He succeeded and was not washed out. He credited his family's support as part of why he achieved his quest.

Four years after he qualified, this quiet, self-described family man had perfected his skill as a swimmer. He was athletic, strong, and a force to be reckoned with at five feet eleven inches tall and one hundred ninety pounds. A fairly new guy at the air station, the brown-haired, brown-eyed swimmer did not know anyone he was assigned to fly with that night when they headed directly into the superstorm.

THEY LAUNCHED CLOSE TO SUNSET, after Dan Edwards jumped aboard the Coast Guard HH-3F Pelican helicopter, tail number CG 1486. The pilot, Lieutenant Tom Maine and copilot, Ensign Tim Tobiasz, flew the helicopter over the Gulf of Mexico toward their assigned area of operations. In the cabin, avionics man AT2 Ken Newbrough maintained the radios and kept up their communications guard with home base. He sat near the flight mechanic, AM2 Russ Jones.

"This was an all-hands situation," said Maine of the flurry to call Coast Guard men and women in the region into action. "Everybody was coming in to the air station to fly, and the orders given were like 'You're next, go!'" No one had time to develop flight schedules because of the fast pace of events. The operation required aircrews to quickly get on scene to help people in distress along the flooding shoreline and offshore in the churning waters of the Gulf of Mexico.

"It was like the wild, wild West. Confusion everywhere," said Maine. "Clearwater is a pretty pleasant place to fly generally, kind of fair weather flyers down there. The thing that struck me was that we had an old crusty lieutenant commander, Bill Kesnick, who had completed his second tour in Alaska. He was talking to us on the radio saying, 'This is just as bad as anything you'll see up in Alaska.'" Alaska, in the minds of many, was really the last frontier especially compared to the Sunshine State.

Maine had flown as an HH-3F aircraft commander for less than a year, accumulating a grand total of one thousand flight hours in that command position. Before transitioning to aviation, he had been enlisted and worked as a Coast Guard corpsman.

"I was green," said Maine. "Dan did not have a very capable guy in front of him that he trusted with his life. We were a very junior crew up front." The copilot, twenty-three-year-old Tobiasz had graduated from the Coast Guard's Officer Candidate School in 1992. He had served as a pilot in the U.S. Army for four years flying the UH-60 Black Hawk helicopter. "I had about twelve hundred hours of flight time and was brand new to the H-3," said Tobiasz. "Our experience levels were probably about the same, both fairly junior."

For Maine, this was his first really challenging case. In his words, "my first scary one."

THE TREMENDOUS SEAS AND STRONG WINDS were cause for multiple distress calls through the evening. Coast Guard helicopter crews were tasked with locating activated Emergency Position Indicator Radio Beacons (EPIRBs). These beacons, stored on boats in an upside-down position, would automatically broadcast a distress signal on 121.5 (VHF) or 243.0 (UHF) MHz via an antenna. The automatic signal was sent when the vessel overturned and the device rolled one hundred eighty degrees with the vessel, which was the beacon's upright or "on" position.

The Coast Guard correlated these distress indicators with all available information including active search and rescue satellite tracking. When the satellite passed, the Coast Guard's Rescue Coordination Center (RCC) in Miami calculated a composite solution or general latitude and longitude. RCC Miami relayed the information to Coast Guard Group Saint Petersburg and Air Station Clearwater. These units and others in the region would then launch resources by air and sea to locate the source of the distress.

BY TEN O'CLOCK THAT EVENING, Edwards and the aircrew located four distress signals by using the helicopter's electronics to hone in on the devices. The direction-finding equipment could track the "aurl" or audio strength of the radio frequency and its associated bearing to determine in which direction the pilots should fly to locate the beacon. As they flew toward the signal and got closer, the "aurl" would strengthen.

In some cases, signals they tracked down were correlated by land based SAR prosecution teams as left over from previous evacuations. Others signals were located, but no people were found in the vicinity.

"There were so many search and rescue cases. Our direction was that if we didn't see anybody, divert on to the next one," said Edwards.

The next one changed his life.

MAINE AND TOBIASZ, AS IT TURNED OUT, searched with the only available HH-3F in the region. Of the twelve helicopters assigned to the air station, eight or nine of them were either flying elsewhere or down for maintenance. "We flew the planes until they broke," recalled Edwards.

Suddenly, they were redirected. The aircrew received instructions to locate and rescue ten crewmen abandoning a sinking merchant vessel. The *Fantastico*, a two-hundred-foot Honduran ship, was in a reported position sixty nautical miles west of Fort Myers, Florida. It was an hour and a half flying time away. They entered the coordinates into the navigational equipment and made best speed toward its last known position.

From Friday into Saturday night the storm's force had magnified. Winds had continued to build and bellow from the west-northwest, driving the seas faster, larger, to heights exceeding thirty feet. Visibility was also restricted because of heavy rain showers.

"That's what caused the *Fantastico* to break up and what promoted severe flooding in the Clearwater region," said Edwards. "Many boats and people had trouble."

THE HELICOPTER WAS EN ROUTE when a Coast Guard HU-25A Falcon jet flew over the *Fantastico*'s distress beacon. It provided an advance report of the exact location of the emergency locator transmitter (ELT) hits. The fixed-wing aircrew also reported seeing two white strobe lights nearby.

"We never saw the *Fantastico*," said Maine of their approach, "we were coming down from the north, fighting the severe winds and turbulence. I remember vividly, looking through night vision goggles. I saw to the south strobe lights on the water and our direction-finding needle pointed toward the distress beacon. I thought, *Oh my God, there really are people in the water here*."

Maine circled the helicopter low over the area before establishing a hover. Edwards identified ten strobe lights attached to life jackets tossed up and down by the gigantic waves. He noticed that almost every second the strobes flashed white against the black seas and night sky.

"When the pilot asked that I get in the doorway and assess the situation, I pretty much knew I was going out," confessed Edwards. "I thought every person had a strobe light on them. All you could see was a bunch of blinking strobes."

Edwards felt that these helpless people were counting on him to get out there and rescue them. "I didn't even really think about it," said Edwards of his decision to go into the hurricane-force winds and seas. "I just gave the pilot the thumbs-up signal, which meant 'swimmer ready,' and started the rescue."

"Every swimmer has a choice about whether or not he's up for the task. A swimmer could say no, this is not something that I want to do," said Maine. "We talked about the situation. We knew this was something we had not done before and I wanted to make sure Dan was up for it."

Dan Edwards was unhesitant.

"Put me in, coach," Maine recollected Edwards saying.

Maine confessed that, because he was himself a relatively inexperi-enced pilot, he was concerned. "It scared the hell out of me when he left the aircraft. I thought, *I'm not sure I can get him back*. These were times, before direct deployment, when the swimmer would not stay attached to the hoist cable. Now, he's just another person in the water, albeit a good PIW [person in water], but in heavy seas."

Wearing a back-straining swimmer's sling adopted from the U.S. Navy, Edwards was hoisted down. About ten feet below the hovering helicopter, a thirty-foot wave rolled underneath and slapped his dangling body. "I jumped out of the harness and fell into the water. I started swimming. These waves were so close together it was like swimming up-wards," said Edwards who didn't have time to think about anything else. "Swimming up the crest of the wave, the wave would break over your head, I'd pop out and fall down the back side of the wave. Then, it was time to start swimming again."

The waves continued to charge by, one after the other. Occasionally, Edwards would be met with a smaller wave that enabled him to break out on top of it just enough to see a strobe light in the distance. The giant waves pushed the strobe lights in his direction.

Several things added to the severity of the situation. The pilots were not authorized to fly using their night vision goggles during hoists, only on the approach. Keeping an eye on their swimmer was extremely diffi-cult. The helicopter was not equipped with a powerful searchlight or nose light called the "night sun." The trainable, movable floodlights un-derneath the helicopter were burned out. With no time to replace them or install the night sun, crews just refueled the helicopters and sent them back out to sea. "We were just doing everything we could under the cir-cumstances," said Edwards.

With the reduction in visibility, they relied heavily on the fixed hover lights as a primary light source. This diffused light only illuminated the area directly below the aircraft. The searchlight would normally be used to track the location of the rescue swimmer and his work with the sur-vivors. Edwards would pop in and out of the illuminated area and fre-quently out of the pilots' view.

For the pilots and aircrew, maintaining the helicopter's position above the water and over Edwards was hazardous because of the sever-ity of the circumstances. Edwards's hand signals, when they could see them, were all his teammates had to identify what assistance he needed while battling the rough waters below to find survivors.

The first member of the *Fantastico* crew Edwards reached was in pretty good shape. It became a monumental task for the flight mechanic and pilots to coordinate placing the basket close and low enough for Edwards to reach it. When it was placed near him, a split second later the water moved so fast it was jerked out of Edward's reach. For twenty minutes, the team struggled to get the survivor inside. "I didn't think it would be so hard," said Edwards later.

With one man in the helicopter, Edwards was hoisted by the rescue sling and repositioned near the next blinking strobe light. He reentered the seas and began the exhausting swim toward the light. As he approached, he guessed the man was deceased but checked him anyway. He was facedown in the water and not responsive to Edward's attempt to revive him by lifting his head and shaking him.

The pilots hovered the aircraft above Edwards. He was picked up and deposited close to a third blinking light. Edwards reached out for the man and held him. He tried to talk to him. With no response, he shook him and slapped him on the face as he was trained to elicit any sign of life. Nothing, the man was dead.

Edwards was positioned near another twinkling light. He found another deceased crew member. "They must have been sleeping just before they abandoned ship," recalled Edwards. "They were dressed only in T-shirts and shorts. It was absolutely too cold to be out there in that."

Edwards was lifted by rescue basket to another light. This time the survivor was inside a swamped lifeboat. Edwards discovered that the man, who appeared to be in his late forties, did not speak English. Encircling his waist were no fewer than ten empty milk jugs for flotation. As Edwards encouraged the Honduran to leave the flooded little boat, he became combative. He did not want to be removed and fought to stay. "I kept motioning for him to come out of the boat. He refused," said Edwards, and they had a few words. "He didn't want to go, and I didn't want to stay. I was not going to go by myself."

Edwards was left with no choice. As he was taught to do, he took control of the situation. "I grabbed him by his life preserver, pushed him up and off the boat, and twisted him into the water. I put my feet on the side of the submerged boat to give me more leverage."

After about thirty minutes of "Herculean effort," Edwards was successful in maneuvering him into the rescue basket. "Once he was up in the helicopter, that's when I learned he had a steel spike or metal piece which went through his hip and out the other side," said Edwards. "At the time of his rescue, all I knew was that he was alive. I didn't see the spike."

"It was truly amazing that Dan was able to get this guy with his injury over to the basket and into it," commented Maine. "Truly amazing. We didn't know what he was going through down there. It was all I could do to keep the aircraft in a reasonably stable hover above the waves. I was working pretty hard just to do that."

Edwards admits he was scared and had asked himself, *What are you doing here?* "When your mind is in a kind of limbo, the repetitive training just kicks in. It works," recalled Edwards. For more than an hour Edwards searched and found people in the water, his state of mind conditioned by his training to not panic, but to do his job. Yet, he was doing it with a vigor enhanced by his pumping adrenaline.

Edwards was hoisted into the cabin. Standard rescue swimmer training was based on thirty minutes of effort. He had been in the water for over an hour. "I told them, give me five minutes to get my composure and I'll get back at it again." Edwards removed his helmet to attend to the two survivors. In doing so he was disconnected from the ICS used by the crew to communicate with each other over the loud noise of the helicopter and storm.

The flight mechanic relayed to the pilots that Edwards was puking up seawater while trying to attend to the survivor with a spike in his leg. "If he's asking for a break, I'm not going to put him back in the water," stated Maine, who had silently thanked God several times that he did get Dan back inside the aircraft.

The Coast Guard case summary described the ordeal: "Having spent nearly one hour in the water under the worst weather conditions imaginable, ASM2 Edwards was completely drained physically after rescuing the second survivor."

During that period of much needed rest, they searched for additional survivors. With the assistance of an HU-25A Falcon jet circling overhead, they located something. The pilots hovered the helicopter above two survivors and expedited the lowering of the rescue basket to them. It was a pretty difficult proposition. "We fought the basket for quite a while trying to get to them. The winds are blowing the helicopter around, the seas are blowing the survivors and the basket around, and we're trying to make it come together at the same time," said Maine. "The temperatures were pretty cold that night, and the survivors were getting hypothermic."

Jones, the flight mechanic, worked to control the hoist cable. He leaned out the door to better observe the basket below and control its violent movements. A wave crested and rolled underneath. As the basket rose with the wave top, its sudden elevation simultaneously created a loop in the hoist cable. This loop became a dangerous component of untamed cable. It snaked behind the flight mechanic's ear and became caught underneath his flight helmet.

In a breath, the wave dropped, released the basket. It toppled down into the seas. The hoist cable tightened. All slack was gone. Now taut, it jerked Jones headfirst right out the door.

His safety belt, hooked into the deck of the cabin, stopped his forward flight. Somehow a few feet outside the door Jones managed to keep his boots on the edge of the doorframe.

"I heard a scream," said Edwards, who had been working with the survivors and was not aware of the emergency situation. He had been disconnected from the ICS and was unable to hear the emergency shouted over the communication system. "When I looked up and turned around all I could see was his boots. He was hanging there by his tippy toes!"

Newbrough, the avionics man, reached over and grabbed the tether attached to the flight mechanic's safety belt.

"We heard him yelling, 'Shear! Shear! Shear!'" said Edwards. "When I reached up to do it, the light had turned green, which meant it was. The copilot had sheared it."

Newbrough swiftly pulled the flight mechanic inside as the cable released from around his helmet and neck. He was bleeding. "It looked like he had broken his nose, split his lip, and had lacerations around his neck," recalled Edwards. "It very well could have killed him."

The helicopter's hoist capability was completely finished. The basket was gone. The only way to rescue anyone would be if they landed the amphibious aircraft. The pilots discussed this in earnest with the inbound relief helicopter pilots. The approaching helicopter, tail number CG 1431, also an amphibious HH-3F, would arrive on scene in minutes.

Collectively the pilots decided not to attempt a landing in such terrible sea conditions. It was also important to transfer the rescued survivors to the nearest hospital for emergency care.

Edwards talked with his pilots over the ICS system. "They wanted to know if I wanted to help prestage, or set up, survivors in the water for the next helicopter's rescue," Edwards remembered. Because the hoist was broken, it would mean Edwards would have to free-fall at night into seas exceeding thirty feet. This was against rescue swimmer procedures. Even so, Edwards considered it. He was informed that there was another helicopter on its way with a rescue swimmer aboard. Edwards asked if anyone in his crew was trained as an emergency medical technician, a necessity for the proper treatment of two survivors who were hypothermic and one severely injured. No one spoke up. So, Edwards elected to remain to treat them.

Released from the case once the relief helicopter was on scene, Maine and Tobiasz flew to Naples, Florida, with their survivors.

"NEEDLESS TO SAY, WHEN THE OTHER HELICOPTER arrived on scene, the rescue swimmer elected not to deploy," recalled Edwards who learned of this after they departed for the Florida hospital. "I support the decision of the other rescue swimmer," explained Edwards. "Coast Guard policy supports a rescue swimmer not deploying if there is debris in the water, predators, or a dangerous sea state. We had two of the three and if he was not comfortable deploying then that's his call."

"The aircraft that relieved us worked for well over an hour trying to get the basket near two guys on an overturned life raft or piece of debris," recalled Maine. "They were getting too hypothermic to force themselves to reach out and grab the basket which was almost on top of them."

Still, Edwards felt terrible. For weeks he second-guessed his decision to remain and care for his survivors instead of going back down. Even though the men he saved were in critical need of his skill as a trained EMT, Edwards believed he did not do enough.

"Of the four living people we saw, we were able to get two out," said Edwards. "We never saw ten."

The STAN Team, which critiqued the rescue, supported his decision and helped provide Edwards the closure he needed. Edwards learned that the rescue swimmer who arrived in the second aircraft had held a life raft and data marker buoy (DMB), a device that is normally dropped to search for a survivor. He planned to take it with him into the seas that night. "Normally, we're in the water before the DMB. He was psyched out and did not want to go in," concluded Edwards.

The conditions during the Storm of the Century were above and beyond what any rescue swimmer had trained to work in before. The Advanced Rescue Swimmer School, which was commissioned years later, would train swimmers, pilots, and crews for rescues in big surf and seas, as well as in caves, on cliffs, and in other risky environments.

ASM2 Dan Edwards was awarded the Distinguished Flying Cross for his extraordinary heroism the night of March 13, 1993. "It changed my life," said Edwards. "It helped me shape who I am now. The experience definitely strengthened my belief. I feel that I have nothing to fear, so I go and do what I've been trained to do. It takes a lot of stress off you knowing that." Edwards has since been promoted to AST1 and works at Coast Guard Aircraft Repair and Supply Center in Elizabeth City as the office manager for technical services. "We take care of all the life support equipment, tests and evaluations of new gear, and procurement," stated Edwards. "Basically out in the field if they have questions about how to fix something, they'd call us, and we'd find the right answers for them."

Lieutenant Tom Maine was awarded the Coast Guard Air Medal. Promoted to commander, he is the operations officer at Air Station Cape Cod. After Hurricane Katrina devastated the Gulf Coast, he provided much needed relief to New Orleans–based aircrews for nine days. He flew missions and rescued people from the floodwaters and rooftops. Ironically, he filled in as the acting operations officer at Air Station New Orleans for Lieutenant Commander Tim Tobiasz who needed to rotate out for rest.

Lieutenant Tim Tobiasz received the Coast Guard Commendation Medal. He is currently assigned as the operations officer for Air Station New Orleans. His tremendous work helping to rescue thousands after Hurricane Katrina is included in chapter 14.

AM2 Russ Jones was awarded the Air Medal for his efforts during the rescue. He has since retired from the Coast Guard.

Admiral William P. Leahy, Coast Guard District 7 commander, summarized Air Station Clearwater's efforts in a report: "Throughout this

ninety-six hour emergency, HH-3Fs and HC-130s flew 55 sorties total-
ing 165 flight hours, prosecuted 32 SAR cases, saved 62 lives and assisted
27 others in extremely hazardous, hurricane-like weather conditions."

Air Station Clearwater was awarded a CG Unit Commendation.
Dozens of aircrew personnel received individual awards for their meritorious actions.

On the subject of the nature of rescue swimmers, Maine added, "We
think of these kids as being machines, just another piece of rescue equipment that jump out of the helicopter and do their superhero stuff. They
are human beings, and they know their limitations better than anybody.
For Dan, on this night with a couple of young knuckleheads up in the
plane in front of him with his life in their hands to say, 'Yeah, let's go,'
is pretty significant.

"These guys are macho to a fault, they are kind of our Special Forces
folks. It's a big deal for one of them to turn down a rescue. So for this
next helicopter to come out, with more experienced pilots by the way,
for that rescue swimmer to say 'No,' that is pretty impressive. To relay it
back to what Dan did, it is pretty impressive.

"As a young guy who was seeing my first real challenging conditions
for the first time, I don't think the magnitude of what Dan did hit me.
I don't think I appreciated it until later on. I've told the story many
times of what he did, went in the water with a couple of young knuckleheads and a flight mechanic he didn't know, trusted us with his life.
There is no question in my mind, as the guy at the controls, that he was
a fraction away from losing his life himself. There would not have been
any other options. He put himself right in the face of death to rescue
those two people. To me that is the most heroic thing I've seen in my
twenty years in the Coast Guard."

7

THE FALLS

Eric Mueller

> When we would show up on scene for a rescue, you'd never know
> exactly what you were going to get. There was always that
> excitement, that anticipation that every day was going to be a little
> different.

For Coast Guard Second Class Aviation Survival Technician Eric
Mueller, his first tour as a rescue swimmer was unusual. In just four years
at Air Station Detroit, he earned multiple, prestigious medals for a variety of harrowing rescues. About that period in his life, the twenty-eight-
year-old rescue swimmer recalled, "I was on fire. It just happened to be
I was in the right place at the right time."

Being in the right place was fortunate for Mueller, who had discovered the Coast Guard by chance. Pursuing a degree in recreational management at Sierra Nevada College in Lake Tahoe, he spent more time
snowboarding than studying. After switching colleges a couple of times
and averaging a 3.5 GPA, he decided that he did not want to continue
his college education. Sitting in class and trying to take notes made him
crazy because he believed he was missing something. He talked with his

father, a retired U.S. Army colonel, about his future. Serving in the Marine Corps seemed to be a fine idea and a good fit.

Mueller drove two hours to the joint service recruiting building in Cleveland, Ohio, to meet with the Marine recruiter. As he left the meeting to think things over during lunch, something caught his eye. It was a poster of a Coast Guard rescue swimmer jumping out of a helicopter. Halfway down the hall and almost signed up with the Marines, he turned into the Coast Guard recruiter's office. He told his story. When he finished, Mueller was surprised that the recruiter refused him. He told Mueller to finish college because he had great potential to become an officer. "He wouldn't sign me and told me the rescue swimmer program might be finished by the time I completed boot camp anyway," recalled Mueller. During this period, the Coast Guard was restructuring the aviation work force.

Mueller returned home to think over his options. The next day he returned to tell the Marine Corps recruiter he wanted to serve in the Coast Guard instead. It took another meeting with the resistant Coast Guard recruiter before Mueller would enlist. One year later, in 1994, he began his active duty service still convinced he wanted to be a helicopter rescue swimmer.

After finishing boot camp, he was selected to serve in the Presidential Honor Guard for two years in Washington, DC. From this plum assignment as a seaman, he transferred to Air Station Barbers Point in Hawaii in 1996. There, he was encouraged to consider another aviation specialty. It would be a lengthy wait to be accepted into the rescue swimmer school.

"I told them that this is all I want to do and if I can't do this, then I'm not going to stay in the Coast Guard," Mueller said. He chose to wait for his chance to go to rescue swimmer school.

Committed to his dream, he volunteered after hours assisting aircrews with their training requirements, or "minimums," by being the hoist "duck" (volunteer) riding in the rescue basket. Mueller would also come into work early to complete his assignments so he could justify going on the flights. "Being a seaman was a lot different from being in the Presidential Honor Guard. [As a seaman] I was cleaning toilets, picking up, doing lawn care, carpentry, and stuff like that," mused Mueller. He spent as much time as possible working for the rescue swimmers. "I probably did a lot of their work learning about their job."

Three years after signing up with the recruiter Mueller completed AST school and was officially qualified as a swimmer with his name nationally registered as a certified EMT. Mueller was ready. He had no idea that his vision of a perfect career would be cut short because of a crippling injury. Meanwhile, he would have the time of his life.

THE GOOD TIMES STARTED IN DETROIT. As a third class aviation survival technician assigned to Air Station Detroit, Mueller became known for his first rescue. During the night of December 29, 1998, he recovered eighteen hypothermic fishermen and their "rescuers."

The men were trapped on a fast-sinking ice floe in Lake St. Clair, Michigan. Firemen were first to arrive on scene aboard a hovercraft. They had tried to save the fishermen when a sudden increase in the lake's wave height combined with strong gusts of wind and snow showers capsized it. Everyone was tossed into the icy lake.

"When we were trying to find people in the ice, we hit a whiteout, where you can't see anything but snow," recalled Mueller. "The pilot started loosing altitude and the copilot picked up on it, grabbed the controls, and brought us back up to altitude."

The Coast Guard aircrew located the people and quickly deployed Mueller. "They were sticking up from the water, sinking, and coming up again for air," recalled Mueller as he was hoisted down to recover the men. "One of the fireman had shuttled people off the ice when it started to break up," Mueller recalled. "The waves were so big that the hovercraft overturned. The civilian they had rescued fell into the water again. I saw the firemen hold his hands, pull him off the bottom of the upside-down hovercraft. He looked like a crucifix he was so rigid."

After two hoists of survivors using direct deployment, the helicopter experienced mechanical difficulties, which mandated an immediate return to the air station. Mueller transferred from that helicopter to the waiting one, which immediately took him back to the scene.

The Coast Guard had also launched a forty-one-foot utility boat. It had to be pulled out of dry dock and deiced before the coxswain could navigate up the icy Detroit River.

The Coast Guard's work boat was directed in closer to be used as a platform to bring the men into shore. "The small boat coxswain called the helicopter and said 'I'm worried the ice is going to poke a hole in my hull. You've got to come get them,'" Mueller said.

Working together the small boat and second helicopter aircrew sent down Mueller who hoisted the four remaining firemen from the boat's deck out of the arctic-like conditions.

In all, one rescue swimmer and two Coast Guard HH-65 helicopters and aircrews executing thirteen hoists saved the stranded people.

There was one moment Mueller will never forget about that night. When he was coming up from a hoist with a survivor in his arms, he was pulled into the cabin by the flight mechanic who said, "Let me fix this, your strop is not around you right." Mueller had held the man with his legs and held on supporting himself during hoist, all the while not connected to the D-ring that should have taken the load. If he had let go too soon, Mueller would have fallen.

Mueller was awarded the Coast Guard Air Medal. By nature humble and modest, he credited his fellow men for enabling him to save the lives of many. They were the flight mechanic, Lieutenant Commander Joe Kelly and Lieutenant Rich Suskey, pilots for the first helicopter. The second aircrew comprised Commander Darrell Nelson and Commander Greg Hack and flight mechanic AMT2 Kevin Bunn.

Five months later, Mueller would be dramatically tested again. During the afternoon of May 12, 1999, while refueling a HH-65 helicopter at Port Clinton Airport in Ohio, the Detroit aircrew was called into action. Several Mayday calls were overheard on Channel 16. Before responding, they immediately dropped off a reserve commissioned officer in the aircraft for area familiarization. This left Lieutenant Rich Suskey to single-handedly fly Mueller and the flight mechanic, AVT1 Tom Carter, to the call.

When they arrived, a boat was sinking from a large hole in the hull. A father, mother, son, and their friend struggled to stay afloat in Lake Erie.

A Coast Guard forty-one-foot utility boat, CG 41487, arrived on scene, and the crew pulled the mother from the wreckage.

Mueller deployed. He swam through the debris and large, five-foot choppy lake waves toward the others.

The first man Mueller reached was in a state of panic from hypothermia and then shock. He became combative and ripped off Mueller's swimmer's mask. Mueller spoke to him to calm him, reason with him before he could have him hoisted by rescue basket into the helicopter's cabin.

Mueller turned to look for another person in the debris zone. "A wave dropped and there he was," said Mueller of the adult man. "He jumped on top of me screaming for his dad." Mueller managed to take control of the situation by repositioning the man for hoisting. Seeing that he was obviously distressed, Mueller tried to reassure the person by rationalizing with him. Mueller explained how he would hoist him into the helicopter and out of the dangerous environment before he could look for his father. Mueller asked, "Where is your dad?" He said, "I think he is under the boat."

Suskey held the helicopter in a low hover once the son was aboard. With Carter watching from above, Mueller looked under and around the boat. There was no sign of the father.

Carter and Suskey pointed Mueller toward a shadow just below the murky surface. The father, who apparently had tried unsuccessfully to put his life vest on, was submerged a few feet below. "I dove as deep as I could, with a dry suit on," said Mueller. "He was a big guy and unconscious."

Suskey, from the right seat continued to single-handedly pilot the helicopter and maintain a steady hover at just fifteen feet above the surface. Mueller prepared to hoist the man.

Carter saw exactly where the helicopter needed to be and aimed to pinpoint the rescue basket location there for the recovery. He gave the pilot instructions to move the helicopter and dangling basket into the position.

Out of the corner of his eye, Suskey saw the Put-in-Bay Express Ferry approach. It was trying to help with the rescue but was dangerously close to the helicopter. Suskey, afraid they might collide, instructed Mueller to come off the hook.

Mueller grabbed the basket. It was repositioned within his reach after the danger had passed. His adrenaline was pumping now. It supplied him with needed strength to move the heavy man inside. With the man in the helicopter, the flight mechanic sent the bare hook back down for Mueller to attach to his TRI-SAR harness for his hoist.

With Mueller safely aboard, Suskey began his forward flight. He flew to Port Clinton Airport where emergency medical crews awaited their arrival.

During the flight, Mueller and Carter began CPR to try and revive the father. "I remember the son was in the back of the helicopter watching me. The father threw up in my mouth, so much so that it went around the one-way CPR pocket mask, into my eyes and all over the helicopter cabin and Carter, everywhere," recalled Mueller. No matter how much effort Mueller put into reviving the man, he died.

While the aircrew dropped off the father, his son, and the friend, the aircrew received urgent news over the radio. The mother was hypothermic and going into shock aboard the Coast Guard utility boat.

Suskey banked the helicopter around toward the boat. Carter quickly lowered Mueller, a trained EMT, to the small boat. Mueller assessed her situation. He found the patient to be in critical condition and decided it would be an unnecessary risk to hoist her. It was safer and just as expeditious to transfer her in the boat to the medical treatment facility.

Mueller was awarded the Coast Guard Commandant's Letter of Commendation for his meritorious service.

ONLY EIGHT MONTHS LATER, ON FEBRUARY 18, 2000, Mueller was called for another daring ice case. Three people were stranded on ice floes in the vicinity of Marblehead, Ohio. He expertly recovered the survivors. For his superior performance of duty, Mueller was awarded the Coast Guard Achievement Medal.

"AS RESCUES GO, ALL OF US WANTED A CASE off Niagara Falls. It would be really cool," said the now thirty-one-year old Mueller, promoted to AST2. For Mueller, the chance came quite surprisingly on October 24, 2001. This would be the last rescue for which he would receive a personal medal for his valor. It was also shortly before he would suffer a disabling injury.

Following the September 11 terrorist attacks the previous month, Coast Guard aircrews were given weeklong assignments to the Niagara Falls Air Reserve Station. From there, their mission was to fly Homeland Security patrols over the Great Lakes, Saint Lawrence seaway, and other high-risk targets or waterways looking for unusual activity.

Mueller was seated in the back of an HH-65 helicopter with Lieutenant Commander Richard Hinchion, Lieutenant Eric Hollinger, and Avionics Technician Second Class Sean Lott.

Having just completed their morning surveillance flight of targets of interest along the lakes, they refueled the HH-65 helicopter, tail number CG 6558. Anticipating another surveillance flight assignment after lunch, the pilots had elected to take on a maximum fuel load, four hundred pounds above normal. This was the first day of their duty week, and they were looking forward to their lunch break.

As Mueller reached for the door of the Chinese restaurant, Hinchion's cell phone rang. Everyone watched as Hinchion listened intently to the call and mouthed to his team, "O-P-S." He motioned with urgency for everyone to turn back to the van; he had just spoken with operations, and they had been assigned a rescue. Hinchion increased his pace to a jog, and the others followed. Jumping into the van, the pilot reported to his team that a man was clinging to a rock at the top of the American Falls.

Lott, who had slipped into the driver's seat, spun the van around like it was a sports car and skidded out of the parking lot. Back on the base, "We were flying through barricades because we knew we had to move fast to save this guy," said Lott. Reportedly, the man had jumped into the white water and was carried downstream with the twenty-five-knot current. He clawed at anything with his bare hands and legs to stop his progression toward the falls. In a desperate attempt to stop, he grabbed on to a partially submerged rock.

Local fire departments and police had already tossed lines and a life raft to try and save the man. The lines were swept downstream before ever reaching him and the life raft toppled over the edge of the falls. "We really thought the park rangers were going to save the guy first," recalled Mueller of his thoughts as he prepared for the rescue. "We were out of our civilian clothes and into our dry suits with the rotor blades of 6558 turning in about five minutes."

Hollinger took the right pilot's seat and was at the flight controls. Next to him in the copilot's position sat Hinchion. He would oversee the mission as aircraft commander. As they taxied the helicopter, each expressed mutual concern about the aircraft's load weight being at its upper limit. Should they take precious time to jettison fuel, time that could be used to save a man exposed now to the frigid waters for over thirty-five minutes?

"They questioned if they would have enough power to pull up into a hover because we had so much fuel," said Mueller. Attempting to hover and rescue the man over the 176-foot falls even without extra fuel was extremely dangerous. According to www.niagarafallsalive.com, the volume of water flow could reach 150,000 U.S. gallons per second. Knowing that every moment was critical, the pilots decided to test the helicopter's power in a fifty-foot hover before they left the airport. Surprisingly, the available power was good. The pilots counted on the falls to provide some airlift too. Relieved that it was not crucial to jettison fuel, they pressed on.

Without a speed restriction, they traveled at airspeeds exceeding one hundred and twenty knots. In just three minutes, they were over the Niagara River executing a slow flyby of the American Falls to search for the man. He was visible from the air only because his presence made a much bigger white spot in the dark green and blue rapids, giving away his location. He appeared as an interruption, a break in the water's rush toward the falls. It slammed into and over him creating the white water and spray that was larger than anything else nearby. He miraculously clung to a submerged rock near the top of the falls.

The man had been in the fifty-degree water for close to forty minutes. The Coast Guard rescuers guessed he was hypothermic and barely holding on. They could see the water rushing by him with excessive speed on its natural highway.

Hollinger circled the helicopter overhead while Lott and Mueller made preparations in the cabin to deploy the rescue swimmer.

It was Hollinger's first case as "pilot at the controls." Hinchion trusted him and provided guidance as the aircraft commander. In addition to overseeing the mission, he monitored the radios, which were "out of control" with chatter from the other rescue teams working the case.

The aircrew had been trained to use a decision-making process called Crew Resource Management. "We talked about what we wanted to do and how to do it safely. If the swimmer felt it was beyond his capabilities, he could refuse to go in the water," explained Mueller. "I've never heard of anyone doing that. I will admit that I did have a lump in my throat and my heart was pumping as I got my gear ready."

In no time, the team had agreed to rescue the man using a "swift water rescue" method. This direct-deployment technique, taught at the Advanced Rescue Swimmer School, meant that Mueller would stay attached to the hoist cable when he entered the currents.

"He was like a little kid he was so excited," recalled Mueller of Hollinger's first rescue. With great care, Hollinger flew toward the stranded man in an attempt to maintain a twenty-foot hover directly overhead. Aware of the dangerous forces created by the helicopter's own powerful push of air and water from its spinning rotors, he knew the rotors could "wash" the man right off the rock.

Lott, in his first year of flying as a flight mechanic was working his second case. In a pivotal job, he would control the aircraft's hoist cable, the lifeline for both Mueller and the man, while directing Hollinger into an exact position for the hoist. He would serve as the pilot's eyes in the backseat. The pilots sat too far forward of the hoist area to observe what was happening below and behind them as they attempted to maintain a hover.

Mueller was the glue that made it all stick. He planned to deploy attached to the hoist cable. He would use standard hand signals to communicate with Lott regarding where he wanted to be moved. Mueller's objective was to secure some rescue strops around the man, without knocking him off the rock and before the man's hold weakened.

They were ready to execute the mission.

"Lott put me down in the water far enough upstream so I could use the currents to draw me towards him and straddle the rock he was on," said Mueller. "But the twenty-five-knot rapids were swirling and I shot right around him."

The first attempt failed to get Mueller close enough to carefully grab the man, but Mueller was able to see that he was holding on to the rock with only his bare hands. Water rushed into his face. "I was scared I might knock the guy off the rock or else he would be swept off the rock at any moment!" said Mueller. "The water was only about five feet deep, but it was moving so swiftly that he could not even stand up."

Determined, the aircrew knew without a spoken word to set up, try again. "I told Hollinger that his hover was not steady enough. We were moving around too much," said Lott over the ICS. Hinchion suggested Hollinger use the trees, a fixed object, on shore to give him fixed positions. It would be a tool to help him steady his hover. "The water which moved under the helicopter played tricks on his mind giving an illusion that he was not holding the helicopter steady," said Mueller. "It had caused him to readjust continually."

Lott guided Hollinger into the "sweet spot" he wanted the helicopter to be in before deploying Mueller. Within a second, the helicopter was over the target and Lott lowered Mueller.

Mueller now fished for the man from the end of the stainless steel hoist cable. Lott released more cable as Mueller advanced. This would enable Mueller to be carried forward using the force of the raging waters instead of fighting it.

"When I finally got to the rock, I straddled it to break the force of the water which rushed around my body and kind of bypassed him, taking the water off of his face," Mueller stated. "Then I immediately stuck one of my hands up through his belt so that if the man did let go, I'd have him around my forearm. With my other hand, I put a 'quick strop,' or horse-collarlike device, around his chest and then grabbed his coat," recalled Mueller. "Then I put a crotch strop between his legs to keep him from sliding out of the quick strop. While I was doing all this the man wrapped the slacked cable around his forearm!

"The man was panicking—he saw the cable and wanted to get wrapped up into it," exclaimed Mueller. "I didn't want to say anything to him, fearing he might let go. He was very incoherent. He was rigid with hypothermia and had tunnel vision too. He just wanted to get into the helicopter."

The man's action had in an instant created a life-threatening situation for the rescuer, too. Lott saw what was happening and remained calm just as he had been trained to do in a justifiable panic situation. He articulated new positioning instructions to Hollinger in a controlled voice, hoping not to alarm him.

Mueller had to clear the cable before he could send Lott a thumbs-up, or ready-for-hoist, signal. He had no other option but to force the man to release. To free their lifeline, Mueller gave a couple of swift blows to the man's forearm hoping he would let go. The man did not release; he had a deathlike grip on it. Mueller opened his nonskid, lined-gloved hand and pounded his palm onto the man's hand. The man must have felt sharp pain because he let go. Mueller looked up into the sky for Lott who saw what he was waiting for: a thumbs-up. With that permission, Lott hoisted the men in less than a minute to the safety of the helicopter's cabin.

Ready for forward flight, the pilots prepared to leave the perilous hover. Because of the weight-load limitations of the helicopter, the pilots could not safely climb up and over the trees that provided a natural fence on both banks of the river. The only way out was directly over the falls.

At twenty feet and with fifteen-knot airspeed, Hollinger commanded CG 6558 forward over the falls. Using the gorge's drop as a cushion, he had room to increase power and altitude. The helicopter throttled ahead and out. Around seventy knots airspeed and above the gorge Hollinger banked the helicopter left over the American Falls. They flew toward the national park's parking lot where an ambulance and emergency crews were awaiting their arrival.

During the short flight, Mueller and Lott treated the man for hypothermia in the rear of the cabin. They carefully removed his wet clothing. "While I was taking off his layers of sweatshirts, he reached under the last one and pulled out his Marine Corps pin and demanded that I take it from him. He was expressing his gratitude," said Mueller. "I insisted that I couldn't take it from him before he again became combative, a sign that he was going into shock." Mueller and Lott used blankets and dry clothing to warm up the man's body.

Five minutes later they landed in the parking lot. When Lott opened the cabin door, an excited crowd greeted them. Some of them were rescuers who had attempted to reach the man from shore and others were throngs of tourists who had lined the riverbanks to watch the spectacle.

The ambulance crew made room and helped Mueller and Lott place the man on a stretcher. As he was being wheeled away, he sat up and saluted Mueller with tears in his eyes.

"A lot of people who are in the rescue business told me how cool it was that I got a rescue on the falls," said Mueller. "I later learned that the man was suicidal and apparently had changed his mind about dying that day!"

Aviation Survival Technician Second Class Eric Mueller was awarded his second Coast Guard Air Medal for his extraordinary heroism. The pilots and crew of CG 6558 each received Commendation Medals. In October of 2002, the Coast Guard Foundation in its annual ceremony recognized the crew of CG 6558 as heroes during its New York City Salute to the Coast Guard. Mueller made a point to recognize the aircrew he flew with as enabling him to accomplish the mission.

"ERIC MUELLER IS SOMEONE I'VE FLOWN WITH a lot. If you're going to pick your best to represent you, or a person that shows the corp's values of honor, respect, and devotion to duty, Eric shows all three," said Lott.

"I look up to him. Once we get into a situation, I know he's going to do it right and not make it worse."

The summer of 2003, Mueller, his wife Barbara, and daughter Mikayla moved to Oregon where he was assigned to Air Station North Bend. His son, Jacob, was born in October of that year. Mueller did not plan to reenlist when his commitment ended in September of 2004.

He had one very unlucky day two months before he would leave the Coast Guard and apply to serve as an Ohio fireman. During a lunch break, Mueller and others at the air station played street hockey. The command-endorsed "sport lunch" included wearing safety gear, no skates, and clearing the helicopters out of the hangar to make room for the sport.

"My foot just grabbed a really clean piece of floor and it stuck," recalled Mueller. "I swung around my leg. At the kneecap, the calf or bottom portion of my leg stuck to the ground and my thigh spun around it. My heel was in the front and my toes were in the back." Being a trained EMT, Mueller took action. "I reached down and realigned the lower half of my leg so that my toes were now facing forward," said Mueller. "The resulting maintenance of blood flow may very well have prevented the need for amputation."

Mueller pushed through his recovery like a rescue swimmer would. Initially, doctors felt if he had lost circulation to the lower part of his leg, they would have to amputate it. He had what he refers to as a "lame leg," or limited use of his right knee.

With his drive and determination, the athletic Mueller progressed a lot further than doctors ever expected he could for the injury he had suffered.

After about a year of rehabilitation and working out in the weight room, he regained strength and movement in his knee. Because nerves in his leg remain irreversibly damaged, he can no longer lift his foot when he walks. He uses a spring-activated brace to assist him. "I'm not complaining, but it is still a pain in the ass. Little kids notice when I'm walking with shorts on."

Recently medically retired, Mueller was credited with eleven years of service. Of all the awards and recognition he received during his career, the one thing that would have meant more would have been to receive a thank-you note from one of the people he saved. "That is the only thing I did not receive."

He is a stay-at-home dad for the couple's two-year-old son and eight-year-old daughter in Bowling Green, Ohio. His wife works as an English teacher at a Penta Career Vocational Center, one of her many different jobs during her career as spouse of a constantly relocating Coast Guard petty officer.

Of caring for his son, he says it is one of the toughest things he's ever done.

In the future, he would like to go back to school to earn a bachelor's degree in construction technology from Bowling Green State University. "I'd like to manage construction sites and finances for large corporations, firms, or even homes." He likens his future goal to being an apprentice for Donald Trump.

8

BOW MARINER

DAVE FOREMAN

A life lived in fear is a life half lived.

"BOW MARINER, BOW MARINER. We are on fire, we are on fire! Mayday, mayday, mayday. This is *Bow Mariner*, *Bow Mariner*, we are on fire! Mayday, mayday, mayday, this is *Bow Mariner*, we are on fire, we are on fire!" a frightened voice on board the stricken vessel called out over the marine radio. (From "Tanker Down," *Coast Guard* magazine, December 2004)

"I HAD JUST FINISHED eating pizza when the SAR alarm sounded announcing something like 'Tanker explosion, twenty-six people aboard!'" recalled AET2 Sam Pulliam, a flight mechanic for Air Station Elizabeth City in North Carolina.

"We never get calls like that, so I knew immediately this was pretty serious," said AST3 Dave Foreman, a twenty-five-year-old rescue swimmer also assigned to the air station.

As Foreman and Pulliam rushed out together on February 28, 2004, to board the HH-60 Jayhawk helicopter that would carry them to the scene, they thought about what they would need to bring. How do you prepare for such a catastrophe? They emptied the helicopter of unnecessary gear so they could carry more people to airlift from the ship. It was likely too that numerous crewmen would have severe burns and injuries.

Lieutenant Commander Eric Bader and Lieutenant Junior Grade Steve Bonn, the pilots Foreman and Pulliam were assigned to fly with that evening, met them by the helicopter. The team prepared for the worst despite not having a lot of information about the tanker, its crew, and what it was carrying. *Was it hazardous cargo?*

Before they launched, Foreman ran back to the rescue swimmer shop to grab additional burn kits and oxygen cylinders in anticipation of having to care for a lot of burn victims. He knew that the rescue litter, used to stabilize a severely injured person, and other emergency equipment and pumps had been prestaged on the aircraft. As he jumped into the cabin for takeoff, he took a moment to pray for the safety of his team and himself. He believed that a life lived in fear is a life half lived.

The helicopter's rotors turned with increasing velocity as the aircraft powered up. In an instant, the force created by the blades' rotations would stir hurricane-strength winds damaging to anything within a one-hundred-foot radius.

Bonn input coordinates for the sinking ship into the helicopter's navigation computer, then switched the radios on. They came to life with animated chatter about the accident that cluttered the emergency VHF frequency, Channel 16. "We heard that there was a five-hundred-foot ring of fire around this boat and that the boat had exploded. Even that it had split in half," recalled Foreman, who realized that they would not know until they got on scene what was true and what was exaggerated. "I wasn't sure if I was the only swimmer that was going to be there so it was kind of overwhelming." Although he was scared by what he heard, he tried not to get too worried. He rationalized he would do all that he could to save the people. If some died, it would not be his fault.

A native of the North Carolina outer banks, Foreman had surfed there frequently and often watched Coast Guard helicopters working in the area fly overhead. He was close to his uncle who had retired as a chief warrant officer boatswain. He knew it would be rewarding and exhilarating to be a rescue swimmer. He decided to join the Coast Guard after graduation from high school in 1998.

Coincidentally, his assignments were never far from home and family. A seaman after completing boot camp, he was assigned to work at the Elizabeth City Support Center before he transferred to Coast Guard Station Georgetown in South Carolina to work on small boats. After a short six-month tour of duty, he was picked up for the airman program and turned right back around to live in Elizabeth City to attend the prestigious rescue swimmer program. He graduated in 2001. His first assignment as a rescue swimmer was Air Station Elizabeth City.

Seasoned with three years of experience from work at one of the busiest air stations in the Coast Guard, he was ready for the most challenging evening of his life.

A WATCH STANDER AT COAST GUARD GROUP Eastern Shore in Chincoteague, also designated the SAR Mission Controller (SMC) for the disaster, had pieced together information from the Mayday call with numerous informational calls from other marine vessels. This prompted the Coast Guard to order the launch of a C-130 Hercules fixed-wing aircraft and numerous helicopters, boats, and ships to make best speed to the five-hundred-seventy-foot tanker's position. The *Bow Mariner* had been sailing from Linden, New Jersey, to Houston when it exploded fifty miles east of Chincoteague.

THE COAST GUARD C-130 HERCULES airplane lifted off ahead of the Jayhawk from Air Station Elizabeth City. It was equipped with pumps and life rafts, which could be deployed into the water. First to arrive at the accident, the fixed-wing aircraft's crew assumed the role of on-scene commander. It circled overhead while the crew surveyed the dangerous situation unfolding below. The aircrew reported back to the Coast Guard SMC, responding aircraft, and vessels regarding their observations, including verification of the tanker's exact position.

One of their many reports confirmed that the *Bow Mariner* was indeed on fire and only part of the ship's superstructure was still visible. The C-130 aircrew recommended not deploying rescue swimmers into the water because the chemicals released from the tanker's ruptured hull into the environs had not yet been identified.

Flying to the scene at best speed, the Jayhawk aircrew listened to the radio broadcasts and a list of possible chemicals that could have discharged into the ocean. "It was listed in scientific names. We were questioning them, 'What is that? What does that mean to me?' We asked them to clarify a little more. We were going blind most of the way," recalled Pulliam.

"We didn't know which of the chemicals on the list were biohazards. All we were told was that some of these could cause respiratory problems, burning, itching of the skin, and were highly flammable," said Bonn. "So right away the basic information piqued all of our interest— exactly how hazardous was this?"

The C-130, in addition to being a communications relay for on-scene resources, assisted with the search for survivors by using a powerful heat-seeking or gyrostabilized, forward-looking infrared imaging camera called CASPER (C-130 Airborne Sensor with Palletized Electronic Reconnaissance). "As they were circling the sinking vessel, the camera operator in the back could pick up any heat signatures for people that were in the water. They could easily depict the location of the oil slick and were able to pick out some life rafts that they directed the helicopters to go to," stated Bonn. A Coast Guard HH-65 Dolphin helicopter arrived from Atlantic City a few minutes before the Jayhawk did. It was directed to investigate a life raft. As the Jayhawk got close, the C-130 crew found another life raft and passed the positional information to Bonn and Bader for their action.

Still fifteen minutes away, the Jayhawk aircrew discussed the updates they had received about the situation and put together an informal plan of action. Amid the chaos of that first hour they were informed with certainty that in addition to fuel oil, the tanker's cargo was approximately 3.5 million gallons of industrial ethanol, a very flammable product.

Hearing this, the pilots held off before entering the hazardous and volatile area with the helicopter. The SMC had provided them with the flexibility to choose their path of action and they did. "We were told it was OK to stand off and assess the situation. Not that we could just turn around and go home, it was up to us to decide, not in so many words, if we needed to physically go in the water or go down and hover with flammable fumes all over your helicopter," recalled Bonn. "They gave us the option. It was in our best judgment as to what kind of risk we wanted to put our crew in."

The aircrew agreed on a couple of things. First, they would not hover too low and run the risk of causing an explosion. An explosion could be stimulated by the helicopter's own generated static electricity or from the engines that operated at over seven hundred fifty degrees Celsius and projected a fortified heat signature out the back. They would have to search for survivors at an altitude of about one hundred feet, much higher than normal. An average rescue hoist height was only thirty feet, sometimes quite a bit less.

"I've seen on certain nights static electricity arching sometimes twenty feet off the cable when it gets close to the water," said Pulliam. "We didn't want to put Dave into the water either, because of the chemicals. This would be a last resort."

The Atlantic City–based Dolphin helicopter crew members got on scene first. According to the *Coast Guard* magazine article, "Tanker Down," they witnessed the following upon arrival: "Lights still burned brightly inside the sinking ship, but soon the lights went dark. Searching for anyone who might be clinging to the ship, the Dolphin hovered nearby. The crew saw no one."

The Elizabeth City Jayhawk approached from the south on a course that held the assigned life raft in its line of flight. The C-130's CASPER had verified that there was life inside.

It was a moonless night. The ocean's waters had been laid flat by the blanket of heavy fuel oil. Foreman and the crew used night vision goggles to see in the darkness. "When we got out there I remember seeing strobe light after strobe light on the surface." These lights were attached to life preservers that escaped from the hull of the sinking ship. Every one of them was empty.

"I never did see the ship," said Foreman, "but I knew it was close by. There was an intense smell, like rubbing alcohol from the chemicals it was carrying. You could see sheen from the oil in the water too."

The pilots guided the aircraft into a slow flyby. Near the life raft they detected a small lifeboat with people aboard. The lifeboat turned out to be from a nearby container ship assisting in the search for the *Bow Mariner*'s lost men.

Bader then repositioned the Jayhawk high above the canopy-covered life raft in order to minimize the amount of rotor wash (the high-velocity air movement beneath the helicopter) on the fragile contents. At first it seemed that no one was in it. Then one of the pilots saw somebody move outside the entryway.

Before attempting the rescue, the aircrew decided to test the waters first. Would there be a reaction to the static electricity buildup in the hoist equipment? "We were very conscious of it. As we put the basket down, we were pretty high. If it would explode, we'd be so high in the sky that we could cut the cable," recalled Foreman who watched from the protection of the cabin. "I was afraid my radio could cause a spark too. We didn't know what would happen. My fins, which touch the water first when I'm hoisted down, could cause a spark and explode me."

After a successful test, "We descended to fifty feet to try to get the rescue basket to the people in the life raft. We needed to see if they would get into it by themselves," said Foreman. "There was an inflated canopy or roof over it so you could not see inside, just people leaning out."

"This guy was sticking his head out the door of the raft and looking right at the rescue basket. All he had to do was fall over," recalled Pulliam who had expertly positioned it for him to drop into.

"They did not move or even attempt to reach for the basket," said Foreman, who had shone a light on the raft to help the flight mechanic direct the pilots into position. Pulliam pulled the basket back into the cabin. The aircrew would need to have a group talk about this dilemma.

"I made the decision to ask the pilots if I could go down and investigate and help these people get into the basket. I knew they were going to say 'No,' so I tried to put it another way before I spoke up," said Foreman.

Foreman made a pitch that he would stay connected, using the direct-deployment method. If he felt that the chemicals would not incapacitate him, he'd disconnect, swim over, and see what he could do to help. "Otherwise I could just give a signal, and you could pull me right back up."

"Swimmers are very aggressive by nature, and they wouldn't be in this job if they weren't. They are ready to go at a moment's notice and are eager to get out there no matter what the conditions are," said Bonn. "Usually it comes down to the pilots reeling them back in and saying, 'No, I know you want to go, but we're not putting you in because it is just too dangerous.'"

The rescuers had realized that because of the forty-three-degree Fahrenheit temperature of the Atlantic Ocean, the survivors could be hypothermic and unable to move. After seeing the situation from this lower altitude, they had identified something else of great concern.

"There was this eerie fog dancing above the surface of the ocean," stated Foreman. "Like this mist-type thing. We couldn't see how much of it was coming inside the cabin of the aircraft."

"It was a very creepy night, like out of a horror movie," said Pulliam.

The pilots hesitated, knowing it might be a lethal situation. "Everyone spoke his mind. One of the pilots said if we do not put Dave in the water, these people die," recalled Pulliam of the pressure they were under. "We all agreed to put Dave in the water, but the original plan was to put Dave down as close as we could to the raft."

Foreman was deposited about fifty feet from the raft. "We didn't want to get too close, afraid the aircraft might blow it over because of the power of the rotor wash." Still feeling fine, Foreman disconnected and swam over to peek inside.

"When I looked in the raft, it was ohhh, this black goo everywhere, people screaming, reaching out into the air, then going unconscious then reaching out into the air for help, then falling back into unconsciousness. It was a sight. I think they must have been in the highest concentrations of diesel fuel oil and ethanol that had leaked out of the tanker."

Foreman climbed inside the raft. He had to take an even closer look to assess the situation. He knew too that he was racing against time and he could succumb to the chemical vapors that were intensified by the raft's cover.

Following procedure, he conducted a quick survey of each person's condition. Everybody had first-degree burns, hypothermia, and was affected by the chemicals. One man spoke some English, but because of the noise from the helicopter Foreman could hardly hear him.

He decided to rescue first those who were hurt the least and had the greatest chance of survival. Foreman feared he would suddenly become unconscious and could not rescue anymore, so he wanted to get as many people out as quickly as possible.

"He called over the radio and said there were six people in the raft, one of them had complained of back injuries, and another might already be deceased," recalled Pulliam. "So we decided to do four hoists with the basket and save the litter hoist for the man with the back injury for last.

"The first guy was brought up freezing and covered with oil," said Pulliam. "He looked pretty bad so I gave him blankets and a sleeping bag to cuddle with."

During the second hoist, there was just so much oil on the metal cabin floor that Pulliam did not have traction to pull the basket in. He propped himself up by putting his leg on the frame near the door to gain leverage and pull the basket in.

"Immediately when I dragged them out of the raft to the water and then put them inside the basket, they curled up into this fetal position because they were trying to conserve their body warmth," recalled Foreman, who was protected by his dry suit. Only his face and neck were exposed. Repeatedly after the lengthy swim to the basket with a survivor, Foreman returned though the gooey substance to the raft for the next one. At one point, he slashed the cover off the raft to release the trapped vapors. This initiative turned out to complicate matters for Foreman. Half of the life raft immediately began to sink.

"The fourth guy that came up looked the worst," recalled Pulliam. "He was completely black and had no white color in his eyes from all the oil. He was very stiff."

Pulliam carefully placed him with the others in rear of the cabin before he tried to assemble the litter, which was in two pieces. "I was just so scared I was going to slide the litter right out the cabin door." He managed to assemble it despite the layer of oil on the deck and hoisted it right down onto the raft. Foreman detached the hoist hook and sent it empty back up to Pulliam. Pulliam knew he had a few minutes to wait; it would take Foreman some time to secure the man into the litter.

"We knew Dave was getting a little groggy because some of the radio calls he was making back to us were a little confusing. I told him he needed to hurry up," recalled Bonn. "We were worried about his condition and knew he was working his butt off down there."

Foreman briefed the pilots, who had maintained a continuous hover without using any visual references to fly by. He carefully proceeded, step by step, to move the man onto the litter. "He was pretty slippery so it took forever to get him in there," said Foreman. "I was triple checking my steps because I'm not trusting myself anymore and knew I was being affected by the chemicals. There was some time when I was pretty much still, I don't know if I blacked out."

While Foreman worked below, Pulliam turned his attention to the survivors. He talked to them and asked how many people were on the boat? How many people were in the raft? Were they doing all right? "They all said they were fine, just very cold," recalled Pulliam. "About that time one of the pilots said over the internal communications system, 'Hey, I think Dave has passed out, can you shine a light on him?'"

Bader held the helicopter in a low hover while he watched Foreman. By using searchlights mounted on the front of the helicopter, he saw what was happening in the darkness. Pulliam, at the cabin door directed a huge spotlight, the night sun, down on Foreman. "From our perspective it looked like the litter was under Dave. He was just lying right on top of the guy. So we thought Dave had passed out," stated Pulliam. "I just started thinking, *How am I going to get him back up into the plane? He's not hooked up, there's no basket, and I can't send anybody down for him.*"

The aircrew intensely watched the rescue swimmer. After a few minutes, Foreman turned and gave a little hand wave. "We knew he was all right," said a relieved Pulliam. He immediately sent the hook back down to Foreman. The pilots evaluated the situation.

"We were still confident enough that we only had two people left for Dave to bring up. Dave was able to push through it very well," stated Bonn. "In that split second, right in the middle of it, it's hard to make that 100 percent decision. If we bring Dave back up, we knew we would seal the fate of those people. We knew that they would end up dying."

With the fifth man up, Pulliam knew he was just as bad if not worse than the fourth. "I haven't seen anybody that bad, ever. He was covered in black, eyes were black, his mouth was black, and he was just screaming. It was very loud in the helicopter, and I could hear him screaming over that noise like somebody had chopped off his leg or something." Pulliam had no choice but to leave him in the litter.

Foreman entered the life raft a final time to check for any signs of life in the sixth man. He tried to stir him to consciousness after he checked for a pulse. "I gave him a sternum rub by taking my fist and rubbing it vigorously on his chest, along the breastplate. That hurts pretty badly. If the person is alive, he'll come to pretty quick," recalled Foreman. "I also tried this thing, where I take my fingernail and push it down on the nail bed of one of his fingers. That hurts pretty good too." Foreman watched for the man's reaction. He reported to the pilots that the man was alive. He had even pointed toward his back as if he were injured. Foreman quickly thought, *What am I going to do? I don't have another litter.*

By now, the raft had sunk lower into the chilling ocean. Fortunately, it assisted Foreman in moving the suffering man into the basket. He was protective of the man's instinct to curl up into the fetal position because of his hypothermic condition.

"I had made a conscious decision to tell the pilot I did not want to use direct deployment for these people," said Foreman. "When a body goes from a position in the raft to a position in the water, and that person is really cold, all the chilled blood in their body starts to flow. When they go into a vertical position like during direct deployment, this cold blood moves into their heart and could instantly kill them."

Guiding the pilots into position, Pulliam brought the man up. His first thought upon seeing him was that Foreman had sent up a piece of luggage. "He looked just like the birds from Exxon Valdez. I couldn't tell he was a person," said Pulliam. "I didn't want to get him out of the basket because he was just so cold and frozen I didn't want to disturb him. He was very hypothermic."

Pulliam placed the basket, with no other room in the cabin, on top of the litter. He asked one of the other survivors to help keep the weight of it off the legs of the man strapped into the litter. Fortunately, the basket rested on the frame of the litter, above the man's legs.

"The sixth man opened his mouth and the oil would just drip down from the top," observed Pulliam. "I don't know how he was breathing he had so much oil inside of him."

The hook was once again sent down, this time for Foreman. "It was right there in front of him. It seemed like it took him thirty seconds to realize it was there," said Pulliam. "I almost had to hit him in the head with it."

Foreman had to search for a spot to sit in the cabin. He staggered over to a cubby near the pilots, who asked how he was doing. "He said, 'I'm all right,' and started checking the survivors," observed Pulliam of the rescue swimmer's emergency medical technician role.

Pulliam noticed Foreman was talking funny and sat down kind of hard. "He was almost intoxicated, mumbling. So I asked him to come sit by the door near a small air vent to get fresh air. We didn't want to open the door because I was scared the people would slide right out. It was so slippery, like standing on ice."

Foreman ambled over to the door, sounding strange and talking funny. "I stuck his face right into the little vent there to make sure he'd get some air," said Pulliam of the tiny three-inch opening. "The smell of the ethanol chemical had penetrated our air conditioning system and made us all pretty woozy." By then, the entire helicopter crew was nauseated. The pilots, distanced from the full effect, were in better condition. Flying home, fresh air circulated inside. "We definitely were not performing the way we should have," said Foreman.

The fumes were intense. "I had to shut the door and the smell stayed inside with us, I felt like I was going to throw up," recalled Pulliam. "It was very nauseating and gave us tremendous headaches, migraines."

Bader who had maintained the critical, no-reference hover during the entire forty-five minute rescue of the six survivors flew toward the East Coast. Bonn coordinated with the C-130 and shore-based units to determine where they would take the survivors for emergency care. He also communicated with the pilots of the on-scene Dolphin helicopter who had reported that their swimmer had pulled a man from a life raft. The man died a short time later.

A triage center in Ocean Center, Maryland, had been established for the incident. Bonn, a former Pennsylvania paramedic and former Army helicopter pilot, discovered that the center did not have a helicopter pad. He knew the survivors would spend a lot of time being initially evaluated, given initial treatments, and then be transported by ambulances to a hospital. He was not happy with this prospective delay. He recommended a hospital they were familiar with in Norfolk, Virginia. He knew it was equipped with a critical care unit and an adjacent helicopter pad. "Knowing how critical our patients were and the fact that it would easily be another half an hour before they even saw the inside of a hospital, I did some quick calculations with our flight computer and found that the difference between the two locations was only eight miles further," said Bonn. "We decided that we would go directly back to Norfolk and that way we could land at the pad and literally be a hundred yards from the front door of the emergency room."

Pulliam and Foreman did what they could to keep the survivors alive, awake, and comfortable for the trip back. "We tried to keep them from hitting us too," said Foreman. When the man in the litter passed out, they would rub his sternum as they were trained to do to keep him conscious. When he would awake, he would be very aggressive toward his rescuers. He would punch at them and even try to bite. When he'd open his mouth they could see the oil just dripping down. It leaked out of his nose because he had ingested so much."

"They needed oxygen and we didn't want to give it," said Pulliam. "Dave needed oxygen, and we didn't want to give him any either."

"Oxygen would have helped clear their heads. We didn't want to use it because on our way out Dave had said oil and oxygen don't mix, it's very flammable," said Pulliam. "We were very conscious about not mixing the two and of creating any sparks and explosions."

THE HELICOPTER LANDED AN HOUR LATER at Norfolk Sentara Hospital in Virginia. "I remember getting out and looking back at the plane. There was oil everywhere, it was completely covered. I can't believe we put Dave down into something like that and we got him back," recalled Pulliam. "It was just incredible for him to volunteer like that, knowing what was down there."

Foreman staggered over to the waiting emergency room personnel. He tried as best he could to give them information about the condition of the survivors. "I was crazy drunk when I hopped out of the helicopter," said Foreman from the affects of the chemicals. "I told them I needed to be admitted too."

"We found out after we shut down the helicopter that they were extremely hypothermic. Their body temperatures were down into the eighties," said Bonn. "They didn't have much longer to live at all. So, hopefully, that worked out rather well that we saved a half an hour by taking them directly to the hospital down there with a trauma center as opposed to dropping them off at a triage center."

Pulliam was released from the hospital around 4 A.M.

Foreman, though, spent the night in the hospital. "I spent the entire night next to these people I had just rescued listening to their screaming," joked Foreman. "They all lived."

In all, the Coast Guard saved six crewmen, recovered three deceased, and eighteen remained missing.

Foreman and Pulliam were monitored for cancer or lung damage by medical personnel because of their chemical exposure that night.

Looking back on this case, Foreman admitted his religion had a role. "I knew God was looking out for me. It was something I would do again. If I ended up having permanent brain damage or something, then I might look at it differently, but everything turned out fine."

AET2 Sam Pulliam, Lieutenant Junior Grade Steve Bonn, and Lieutenant Commander Eric Bader were each awarded Coast Guard Air Medals. The Coast Guard Foundation recognized the entire aircrew for its valor during its 2004 Salute to the Coast Guard in New York City.

AST3 Dave Foreman was awarded the Coast Guard Medal for his heroism. He received the *Rotor & Wing Magazine* 2004 Helicopter Heroism Award, and the USCG Combat Veterans Association honored him as person of the year. The Naval Helicopter Association named him rescue swimmer of the year and recognized the entire team as aircrew of the year for the region. The Department of Homeland Security honored Foreman with the Secretary's Award for Valor, and the Seamen's Church Association in New York City also recognized his heroism.

Foreman transferred to Air Station New Orleans in the summer of 2004. He was on hand one year later when Hurricane Katrina destroyed the Gulf Coast. During his first flight of this catastrophic event he flew nine hours with Captain Bruce C. Jones, commanding officer of Air Station New Orleans. He also flew with Lieutenant Junior Grade Bill Dunbar, Lieutenant Dave Johnston, Lieutenant Craig Murray, AET3 Warren Labeth, AST3 Lawrence Nettles, AMT3 John Jamison assisting with hundreds of rescues of men, women, and children during the hurricane's aftermath.

9

HURRICANE BABY

MARIO VITTONE

We do this job because every once in a while someone is out there without hope, desperately praying for their life, and we get to be the answer.

TROPICAL STORM GORDON WAS TRAVELING up the eastern seaboard of the United States approaching the North Carolina coast on November 17, 1994.

Early that morning, ASM3 Mario Vittone and fellow rescue swimmer ASM2 Scott Adlon were working out in the pool at Air Station Elizabeth City in North Carolina. Adlon, the more experienced of the two, was on call for any emergencies that might require a rescue swimmer. They had taken a break from their exercise and were talking about rescue techniques, towing, and moving people through the water. One of them questioned, "Man, what can you do if you had a baby?" They simulated a couple of techniques they could use to swim with a baby above the water. They knew they had to lift and carry the baby up over their own heads to keep it above the one-foot chop created by the rotor wash. The baby would be subjected to the stinging seventy-mile an hour spray created by the hovering helicopter. Vittone knew it to be an uncomfortable, painful experience to work through, one that swimmers had a hard time seeing through too. In a rescue, they try to shield the unaccustomed victims from it. With an infant, Vittone guessed it would be hard for one so little to breathe. Probably, it would panic in their grip, he guessed.

Vittone and Adlon finished up their pool time and showered before returning to the aviation survival technician shop. Everyone there was aware of Gordon's advance and prepared to be called into action. Its proximity would predictably cause duty aircrews to respond to multiple distress calls over the next twenty-four hours.

It was no surprise when the Coast Guard picked up a Mayday from the *Marine Flower II*, a Sundeer ketch. The air station activated the SAR alarm and announced the nature of the emergency situation over loud-speakers. A family of four, including two children, was in distress aboard the stricken sailing vessel, four hundred miles off the coast. The family was trapped in the clutches of the extreme winds and huge seas. With the announcement came the order for the duty swimmer to go on the mission, "Now, rescue swimmer provide."

Adlon, who had the assignment, had performed rescues in big water stirred up by the likes of this kind of storm. He understood what this rescue could demand of a person. He walked over to Vittone.

"He just kind of looked at me, like, 'You want it, youngster?'" recalled Vittone, who had qualified as a swimmer six months before. "You bet!" Vittone said with enthusiasm. This was the kind of thing rescue swimmers lived for. Vittone had promised his friend and fellow rescue swimmer, ASM1 Mike Odom, he'd take him to the airport. Instead, he grabbed his gear for the mission.

Vittone quickly put on his MAC-10, a one-piece flight suit with a wet suit sewn inside. Then he rushed to his wife's Coast Guard office on the base and told her he had to go flying. He explained he could be gone for a while. The case was 380 to 400 miles offshore and involved children, one of them a four-year-old.

VITTONE BEGAN HIS MILITARY CAREER in the U.S. Navy. Enlisting at the age of eighteen, he had served aboard aircraft carriers from 1983 to

1989 as an E-2 Hawkeye aircraft radar technician. The assignment was a strain on his family. The sea-to-shore rotation was getting longer and longer with more time at sea.

The first time he witnessed a Coast Guard rescue swimmer in action was while he worked aboard the USS *Coral Sea* in the Atlantic Ocean. The aircraft carrier had conducted joint operations with Coast Guard helicopter crews. Based on what he learned from them, he thought he'd be good at being a rescue swimmer and liked the idea of working around aircraft and the water. He knew it took someone with a "cool head" in a crisis, something he had developed over the years.

Vittone decided to change careers and joined the Coast Guard on his twenty-eighth birthday, October 24, 1991. "I wanted to be a SAR man," he said of the two-year wait after he enlisted to join the rescue swimmer profession. Determined to work in the field, he joked he was a little old to be getting yelled at again as a new recruit in the boot-camp-style training but stuck it out to achieve his goal.

But his home life became increasingly strained. He needed to be close to his family. In August of 1996, he decided to take some time off from serving in the Coast Guard because of the personal hardship.

Vittone proved successful at his own computer training business in Virginia and later moved to Florida. He was still not satisfied. "I can't stand feeling if I don't show up at work, no one will notice," said Vittone. "My friend Mike Odom would say if you tell someone you're a rescue swimmer, it's a three hour conversation . . . It matters if you show up or not." Lifesaving was in Vittone's blood. After five and a half years out of the Coast Guard, with the help of Master Chief Vincent W. Patton III and encouragement from his daughter, he rejoined the rescue swimmer profession. He was thirty-seven years old.

THE HUBBARDS DEPARTED LITTLE CREEK, Virginia, aboard the *Marine Flower II* for Bermuda on Monday, November 14, 1994. According to Coast Guard reports, the family consisted of Ira Hubbard, a U.S. citizen who lived in Colombia; his wife, Flora Ruiz; her thirteen-year-old daughter, Laura; and their four-month-old son, Ira.

Before this trip, only the father had sailed offshore or in the ocean. With his family aboard they primarily day-sailed in Newport's inland waters and the Chesapeake Bay.

In preparation for this ocean trip, Hubbard had consulted with a weather service about the forecast prior to sailing. "Based on what they told me, I advanced my departure date from Tuesday to Monday to avoid having a low pressure point hit us while in the Gulf Stream," said Hubbard during an interview with TAM Communications for an episode in the 1995 television series *Coast Guard*, created by Tam and Susan O'Connor Fraser. "It did hit us, but after we crossed the Gulf Stream." They sailed through that rough patch, and everything seemed to be going as planned. "We got hit by an unpredicted gale that continued on and increased in magnitude. It ended up in me finally asking for a rescue of my family, not, not for me, but for my family because I had also gotten a surprise story that Hurricane Gordon was heading right for me and nobody knew whether it was going to head right for Bermuda or left for the States."

While the boat was being tossed around by the rough seas, which exceeded twenty-five feet, and gale force winds in advance of Gordon, Flora made the first Mayday call, which was cancelled by her husband shortly thereafter, recalled Vittone. Hubbard believed they could ride it out.

When the Hubbards departed the Norfolk area for the Bahamas, Gordon's predicted track put it in the Gulf of Mexico. Hubbard was unaware Gordon had changed its course. After it entered the Gulf it turned right, crossed Florida, and pushed into the Atlantic Ocean on a northerly course.

To the south of the sixty-four-foot sailboat's position, the tropical storm, now upgraded to a hurricane, created a lot of barometric pressure that pushed the seas northward, said Vittone. To complicate the conditions, another weather system was driving down from the north. This set up the Hubbards to be caught between the two colliding weather systems.

Hubbard radioed the Coast Guard about 9:15 P.M. on Wednesday, November 16, reporting the rough seas were tossing his boat around. The weather continued to deteriorate throughout the night. By morning, he requested a Coast Guard evacuation. "It had gotten to the point where I decided, well, the first concern is the family, and that's why I requested the rescue, for them. I planned to continue by myself, but the way the sea deteriorated, I ended up throwing that notion away too."

HUBBARD TURNED ON THE *Marine Flower II*'s engine and reduced sail. "I maintained the main sail up a little bit just to give us some stability and keep us from rolling and shaking so much," he said during the TAM Communications interview.

By combining the engine's forward power and autopilot to control the ketch's heading, he managed to keep it facing into the waves. According to Coast Guard reports, "massive thunderstorms pounded the family and waves continually crashed into the battered sailboat." Hubbard had been awake the last forty-eight hours trying to single-handedly ride out the approaching hurricane. He was physically and mentally exhausted.

"It was difficult to handle the fear I saw in both my wife and daughter," said Hubbard of his family who sought shelter, huddling inside the cabin. "And that had a lot to do with my decision to finally ask for the rescue."

By 10:30 THAT MORNING, THE COAST GUARD launched an C-130 Hercules fixed-wing aircraft from Air Station Elizabeth City to assess the situation. It would locate the sailboat and circle overhead to communicate via the radio with the family. Their bird's-eye view of the conditions would help Coast Guard search and rescue planners at the District Operations Center in Norfolk plan a full, coordinated response.

Using the Automated Mutual Assistance Vessel Rescue System (AMVER), the operations center located *Northern Progress* about sixty-five miles away from the Hubbards. The Coast Guard asked the Bermuda-registered freighter to divert and stand by the sailing vessel in case the Hubbards had to abandon ship.

The duty helicopter crew hurriedly planned for the rescue. It was a complicated task and outside the three-hundred-mile operational range of the HH-60J Jayhawk helicopter. Lieutenant Commander David Gundersen would pilot the helicopter with Lieutenant Daniel Molthen as copilot, AM2 Bobby Blackwell as flight mechanic, and ASM3 Mario Vittone as the rescue swimmer.

Gundersen and Molthen decided that a rescue attempt was futile. The pilots had carefully considered the weather forecast and checked aircraft performance charts in their flight manuals to help make their decision. The distance offshore and an anticipated forty- to fifty-knot headwind on their way to the sailboat's last known position made it impossible to reach. The helicopter would not have enough fuel even with an additional fuel tank mounted on the undercarriage to make the eight-hundred-mile round-trip. Gundersen talked with the Coast Guard Fifth District Rescue Coordination Center controllers. "I told them that if they could get a gas station, like a boat, a Navy ship out there, then maybe we could do it."

At the same time, Blackwell and Vittone were busy working with ground crews installing an additional one-hundred-twenty-gallon fuel tank on the right side of the helicopter, which could hamper the hoisting area. They also checked for leaks and refueled the aircraft. To better prepare the helicopter for long-range search and rescue, they exchanged a dewatering pump for an additional six-man life raft.

When the RCC got back to Gundersen, they had good news. A Navy aircraft carrier was about one hundred miles off the coast. The USS *America* had remained there, unable to enter port because of Hurricane Gordon's approach.

The pilots recalculated the fuel requirements. "Yeah, we can do it. It's right at the edge, but it's worth a try," said Gundersen. "It was a family. If we weren't going to go out and get them, there was nobody else that could."

The helicopter crew launched at 11:34 that morning. The USS *America* was under way to rendezvous with the rescuers in a designated location, one that was in line with the mission's heading.

The crew flew at best possible speed toward the USS *America*. Fuel conservation was not a concern for that leg of the trip. They would refuel and proceed the next two hundred miles out to the sailboat.

WHEN THE HELICOPTER CIRCLED THE AIRCRAFT carrier in preparation for landing, they noticed an awesome sight. Gundersen, who previously served in the Marine Corps, had landed on a variety of ships before coming into the Coast Guard, but what he saw made him nervous. "I'd never seen blue water coming over the bow. The aircraft carrier was pitching in the waves and blue water was coming over the bow," recalled Gundersen. He turned to his copilot who had flown in the Navy and in fact landed on aircraft carriers. He said, "Dan, you've got the landing."

Vittone, who had also spent four years on an aircraft carrier while serving in the Navy, saw the waves breaking over the bow of the USS *America* as they circled the nine-story craft. *This was going to be ugly.* He had not seen such a sight before either.

Molthen agreed to make the landing. From a distance the carrier looked relatively small. As they got closer its size became apparent. "As we got closer, I could see it going up and down," said Molthen. A tiny figure on the flight deck guided them in. He thought, *I don't want to get too close because I might squish him and I don't want to be too far back, I might fall back in the water.* He made an excellent center-deck landing, which was the best place to land because the helicopter would be the least affected by the pitch and roll of the one-thousand-foot-long fortress.

Recovered from the tense landing, Gundersen and Molthen exited the cockpit. They stepped across the deck toward the aircraft carrier's control tower. "What I noticed when I got out of the helicopter was just the wind. It almost knocked me down. It was probably blowing around fifty-five knots which is about sixty miles per hour."

"It was pretty intense," said Molthen of the rain and strong winds, which had pounded him too.

The operations personnel in the tower discussed the situation. "The captain of the ship was getting a little nervous," stated Molthen. "In fact, he asked, 'You want us to stay out here? That hurricane's coming up. We were thinking about going back into dock.'" Molthen replied, "Just stay here a couple of hours. We may need you."

While they refueled, the Coast Guard rescue team received updated information about the *Marine Flower II.* "The initial call was a family with a four-year-old which turned into a four-month-old infant by the time we landed on the aircraft carrier to get gas," said Vittone. "It's always different, it's never what they say it's going to be. It's weird."

This would be the first time a Coast Guard rescue swimmer would attempt to save a baby, something no one in the profession had even trained for. "The odd thing was we had just discussed in the pool what to do with a baby," said Vittone of his morning swim with Scott Adlon. This baby, though, was in a hurricane.

During next couple of hours, Gundersen, Molthen, Blackwell, and Vittone discussed how they might conduct the rescue of the family. They planned to get the baby first. Of critical importance was that they act quickly. Fuel was the limiting resource. Only twenty minutes could be spent on scene attempting the rescue and still provide enough fuel for them to return to the aircraft carrier.

Vittone had not yet attended the Advanced Rescue Swimmer School in Astoria where swimmers train for the toughest cases and work in Hawaiian-like waves. "I did not have time to play in big water," recalled Vittone. His plan was to board the *Marine Flower II* and evacuate the family. There was great risk involved with rescuing an infant in such conditions and he felt he could use the one-man raft he carried to put the baby into. From there he could get the baby into the rescue basket for the hoist to the helicopter. Vittone knew he had one shot. The family would either make it or they wouldn't.

During the three-hour flight out to the sailboat, the aircrew got bounced around pretty good by the air turbulence and thunderstorms they were flying through. The pilots adjusted their altitude between three hundred and five hundred feet to get underneath and around the stormy clouds. There was a fifty-knot headwind, which limited the helicopter's advance to only ninety-five knots over the ground.

The C-130 fixed-wing aircraft, which had been orbiting overhead the last few hours, radioed to the Hubbard family that the helicopter was to arrive soon. The family was instructed to put on their life jackets.

After a stressful three-hour flight, the helicopter arrived on scene. Daylight faded into dusk. Gundersen hovered the helicopter alongside the *Marine Flower II*. Vittone observed thirty-foot seas with six-foot breakers rolling by on top of them. "The boat was pitching back and forth and the mast was swinging. All kinds of cables, ropes, and lines were scattered all over the place," recalled Gundersen. The back of the boat was cluttered with an assortment of gear making delivery of the rescue basket impossible.

The pilots and crew discussed the situation. They decided it was best to deploy Vittone. He would swim to the stern of the boat, inflate the one-man raft and put the baby in it in preparation for hoisting to the safety of the helicopter's cabin.

Gundersen prepared the family for the possibility of having them jump into the water. "We say, 'Since we're right at the edge of our fuel range, we have to do this quickly.' We just don't say jump in the water. Before we get there we try to have a radio dialogue with them: 'We're going to be putting a swimmer in the water that's highly trained. Wait until he gets right up to your boat before you jump in.' We stress, *don't jump in beforehand*. We calm them down and try to alleviate their fears. I haven't had anybody refuse. It's pretty much we're their last ditch effort," said Gundersen.

Vittone knew he had the option to say the situation was beyond his capability. "I've never heard of someone saying, 'I'm not getting in,'" he said. "It never crossed my mind to not go." They were in the only helicopter out there. He was their only chance for survival.

BLACKWELL SENT VITTONE DOWN from a height of fifty feet to avoid getting the helicopter too close to the pitching mast.

Vittone touched down into the surf and quickly released himself from the rescue strop attached to the hoist cable. He began his Herculean swim toward the sailboat. Between strokes he looked for the boat. In the trough of the wave he could not see it or the helicopter. "At the time, the waves seemed a thousand feet tall," recalled Vittone. He labored to avoid the breakers, which could push him down into the ocean's depths. At one point, a breaker broke on top of Vittone, and he lost his grip on the life raft. To him it was obvious that he was not closing the gap between himself and the sailboat.

The vessel, which was under power, was moving away at about three knots.

"I think all Coast Guard aviators ought to go to sailing school," said Vittone. "I started swimming after the boat, and it kept moving away from me. We didn't realize there was no way in the world they were not moving. Otherwise, the boat would be rolling over."

Vittone realized the situation had to change. He signaled "ready for pickup." Blackwell sent the rescue strop down to him. Vittone spun into it and then the flight mechanic took out some of the cable slack.

"He slid down a wave, kind of surfed right down about a twenty-five footer," observed Gundersen.

Within the next second, "The water ripped out from under me," said Vittone. The wave rolled by and the absence of that wall of water created a huge space, which Vittone dropped into.

"He started swinging pretty wildly, and as he came back, he smacked into a wave again," said Gundersen.

Every vertebra in his back seemed to pop. It instantly took the wind out of him. Now, whatever nervousness he had at first turned into fear. He realized that he could get hurt doing this, something he didn't *really* think of before. The fusion of emotion got Vittone's adrenaline pumping.

The aircrew brought Vittone back up and asked him if he was OK. "He gave a thumbs-up, 'Yeah, I can go out there, I think I can do this,'" Gundersen recalled him saying.

They devised another plan to get the swimmer closer to the sailboat. Vittone said, "Put me beside it, and I'll catch it as it goes by." With Vittone on the hook, the pilots and flight mechanic repositioned to deposit Vittone about fifteen feet away from the boat.

"As the flight mechanic was conning me in, the mast was swinging pretty good and the rescue swimmer was halfway down on the cable," observed Gundersen. "The mast came pretty close to him, about three feet, and almost impaled him." The pilots backed off a bit and finally got Vittone in the water near the boat.

Vittone again swam for the stern. Hubbard watched him approach. He held a lifeline. "He was just watching Vittone swim, swimming really hard," said Gundersen. "Vittone was giving it his all." Finally, Hubbard threw Vittone the lifeline. Vittone grabbed it and started to pull himself toward the stern of the boat. He put two or three wraps of line around one hand then reached out with the other to grab more line ahead of his wrapped hand.

Hubbard started to pull on the line, which then tightened and squeezed around Vittone's open hand. "Now, the line has got me!" exclaimed Vittone. He pulled up enough with his other hand to release the line and continued to pull himself toward the stern. When he was within six feet, a huge wave picked the boat up and revealed the props, churning.

"I can't get on the back of that thing," muttered Vittone, who still held onto the line and was dragged behind the boat. "They are going to have to jump in."

The wind blew so strongly it created a steady, noisy hum. Combined with the waves that rumbled by, it was too noisy for Vittone's shouts to be heard by the family. Vittone motioned repeatedly with his hands indicating they would have to jump in.

The mother understood. She had tethered the baby to her chest and carefully moved back to the stern. The baby wore an infant life jacket, one that strapped under his legs to keep him in it. The collared neck would keep his head above the water under normal circumstances. She stepped carefully down on the sailboat's swim platform.

No one had any perception of how this should work. It had not been performed before by anyone in the Coast Guard, and training scenarios did not include this. The pilots and flight mechanic were very nervous about the great risk they were undertaking to rescue a baby. Fifty feet above Vittone, they voiced their concerns and thoughts to each other and even thought about calling it off. Blackwell said, "I was thinking, *God, that could be my kid*. I have a two-and-a-half-year-old boy. That's all I could picture down there in the water. I love kids and seeing them in danger like that is something that tears me apart. Adults I can handle, they have a choice. Kids don't."

VITTONE KEPT A CLOSE WATCH ON THE MOTHER and child. He was ready for them. "She's real hesitant to jump in," said Vittone. "Then one of those breakers came up along the side of the boat and took her in."

Vittone lunged forward. He used the power of his fins to kick toward them and tackled them. He instinctively grabbed for the infant. Gundersen, who looked down from the cockpit while hovering the helicopter, noticed Vittone reaching for the baby. The mother grabbed Vittone, held his arm to stop him. Waves broke over their heads. The mother fought to keep her baby, keep him close. Sometimes that meant the baby was under the water. Blackwell observed, "She had a death grip on him."

Vittone thought and decided, *Keep the baby out of the water*. So he forced the mother and baby apart and held the baby up out of the water by its life jacket with one hand, and with the other, held the mother's life jacket.

Vittone looked up at the baby, which could not have appeared any calmer. "He looked at me like 'What's up, what are you worried about? Get me in the plane,'" Vittone said. It was a blessed moment. Vittone felt a sharp sense of relief between how nervous he was and how calm the baby appeared.

Blackwell positioned the basket for pickup. "I put the basket within arm's reach of him, so he didn't have to try and swim with it," said Blackwell.

Vittone yelled to the mother, "Get in, get in!" She pulled herself in and then grabbed for the baby on the narrow side, or wrong side, of the basket's crab-traplike openings.

Vittone thought of the water dropout experience he had just been through and feared that the water might drop out under the basket at any moment. With conviction and fear of losing the baby in the ocean, he fought the mother again. Vittone won and quickly put the infant in through the wider openings on the other side of the rescue basket. Just as soon as Vittone put the baby into his mother's arms, they started to crash down the side of a wave. The wave completely washed over them.

Blackwell saw this and hoisted them as quickly as possible into the cabin. "I got her strapped into a seat holding the baby," recalled Blackwell, who then wrapped a blanket around her to prevent the onset of hypothermia.

Vittone had no choice but to hang out in the ocean. Blackwell had to take care of the mother and child and secure them inside the cabin. Vittone knew when the hoist cable dropped down to him again he would attach himself and would be deposited near the sailboat. It had traveled completely out of sight.

Gundersen asked Molthen to look back and see how the baby was doing. Molthen reported that the baby's eyes were closed. The pilots were now not sure that the baby had survived the ordeal. Molthen looked back a second time to find the baby still had his eyes closed. "The third time he looked back, the baby had opened his eyes and was smiling," recalled Gundersen. "We were real happy then!"

Vittone looked up at the helicopter just in time to see Blackwell pointing behind him. He turned around to witness a towering, incoming wave. It hit him square in his face and pushed him under. When he surfaced, he was no less than fifty feet behind the helicopter.

Blackwell hoisted Vittone again. The pilots repositioned so that Blackwell could deposit him in the water near the boat. Blackwell had fine-tuned his sense of timing the waves with the execution of his hoists. "We have external fuel tanks and keeping the cable out of the area between the tank and the airframe is a real job. It takes a lot of strength to do it," said Blackwell. "I was using both hands to keep it out of there and fighting it to where I could hoist them up with it. The winds and seas didn't help."

Vittone grabbed the trail line then motioned to the teenage daughter to jump in the water. "She backs up and runs," said Vittone. "She clears the boat by like ten feet." Vittone cradled her while reaching for the basket Blackwell delivered.

The teenager got into the basket while Vittone held it. Together they dropped down a wave. He released his hold on the basket as she jettisoned up the other side. "What it looks like to me is she goes from zero to fifteen feet in half a second," said Vittone of her immediate launch skyward, leaving him behind. She was fine even though the basket was swinging wildly during her hoist.

Blackwell carefully situated the daughter in the cabin next to her mother and baby brother. Then he conned the pilots into position for Vittone's last rescue, the father.

The pilots opted to not hoist Vittone up into the cabin to save time. They taxied over to the sailboat with Vittone dangling below, further straining his sore back.

Alongside the sailboat the pilots notice that Hubbard had shortened the rope from fifty feet to about fifteen feet. In order to place Vittone close enough to grab it, the helicopter pilots would have to maneuver even closer to the mast. Vittone noticed this placed him really close to the crossbeam of the mast. Certain he was going to get hit, he quickly devised a mental plan that if it did get close, he would grab onto it and slide down to the boat. "Thankfully I didn't get a chance to try that," said Vittone.

Gundersen had another idea. "He does this tail-end of the helicopter into the seventy-knot winds, hovers, and got me into position," said Vittone. "This is Gundersen, what an animal!"

"Swimmer away," announced Blackwell over the internal communications system. With that, Gundersen turned the aircraft back around, into the wind.

Vittone caught the trail line and looked up to see Hubbard standing on the stern of the boat clutching a briefcase. "Well, if the case makes it, it makes it. They tell me in school they can't take anything," said Vittone, who motioned for Hubbard to enter the water. "Ira jumped and now we're messing with his life jacket, which was not zipped up all the way." Once it was secured, Vittone got him into the basket and watched him soar away. "Hubbard got the best ride of the day," observed Vittone, "even with his briefcase."

Once everything was situated in the cabin, the strop was sent down the last time for Vittone. He rode up toward the helicopter with ease. This time it was fun. Blackwell announced with relief over the internal microphone:

"Mario in the strop."

"Mario surfing."

"Mario ten feet above the water."

"Mario coming up."

Vittone, nearing the cabin, yelled at the top of his lungs, "I'm out of here!" Mentally he was finished too.

Their work was still not complete, though. A trained EMT, Vittone checked each of the survivors for any injuries or symptoms of a problem. They were all OK. The pilots computed their course and speed back to the USS *America*, which was about two hundred and eighty miles away. Blackwell buttoned up the cabin for the trip toward home.

"The hard part was coming back at night," recalled Molthen about their nighttime approach to the USS *America*. "It was pitch black, what you do is come in for a precision approach. They pretty much tell you where to go, and then you get lined up with the back of the aircraft carrier." Molthen followed a glide scope, which positioned the helicopter at the correct angle during the landing. "You don't want to be too low, or you'll go in the water. Too high . . . I guess you'll miss it," described Molthen. "We picked that up as we were coming down, that was real eerie."

The pilots could not see the water, only the huge carrier's lights going up and down with the seas. "We finally got down, and I kind of eased it in and lumbered on down and *boom*, we were there," said Molthen.

"Dan Molthen did an outstanding job. He just flew it right there, landed right in the middle of the carrier," said Gundersen. They refueled and took off again, this time for Elizabeth City.

"We were right on the edge of the hurricane. We were getting severe winds, driving rain, low visibility, low clouds, and we had to dodge thunderstorms again flying back," described Gundersen. "Besides the rescue, which was extremely tedious, the flight back and forth was pretty demanding also."

The entire mission took seven and a half hours to complete. Everybody was fine. It was a happy ending.

"You're riding pretty much a high," said Gundersen about completing the mission successfully. "I mean this is what you're trained for. This is what you do. We do search and rescue, and probably 90 percent of it is search and 10 percent of it is rescue. So, when you do make a rescue of this magnitude, you feel pretty good. You feel pretty good for a while. It keeps you going till the next one."

Each of the rescuers was awarded the Distinguished Flying Cross for their extraordinary heroism.

Captain Dave Gundersen retired from the Coast Guard and lives in North Carolina.

Lieutenant Commander Dan Molthen is the assistant operations officer for Air Station Elizabeth City.

AMT1 Bobby Blackwell is stationed at the Coast Guard sector in San Diego.

AST1 Mario Vittone, assigned to Air Station Elizabeth City, still serves as a rescue swimmer.

Following this rescue, January 26, 1995, was declared "Mario Vittone Day" by the mayor of Norfolk and Virginia Beach. Vittone received many awards for his heroic rescue, including the Association of Naval Aviation's Award for Outstanding Achievement in Helicopter Aviation; the Coast Guard Fifth District Enlisted Person of the Year, 1995; the Port Authority of New York and New Jersey 1994 Severe Storm at Sea Rescue Award; the 1994 Department of Transportation Military Valor Award; the Zachary and Elizabeth Fischer Award for Heroism, presented by the Coast Guard Foundation; and the Helicopter Heroism Award 1996, presented by *Rotor & Wing Magazine*.

In 2004, Vittone and a helicopter aircrew were sent to rescue three fishermen from their burning boat. When the helicopter team arrived, the men were hanging from the back rail trying to avoid the flames. The Coast Guard rescuers pulled them from the boat into the safety of the cabin. "We dropped them off at a heliport, and as I was walking back to the plane, the young Vietnamese captain grabbed my hand and stood up. He said to me, 'I was asking God to please let me live . . . I need to see my kids, please God, please let me live so I can see my kids. Then God sent me you.'" This moment fulfills Vittone and encourages his devotion to keep doing his work. It's one he will never forget.

The entire Air Station New Orleans officers, technicians, administrative support, and technical staff. One of the air crews from this station made the first recorded rescue— of any agency, including other military services—in the wake of Hurricane Katrina.
U.S. COAST GUARD

Former rescue swimmer Mario Marini awaits pick-up by the Coast Guard HH-3F helicopter. MARINI COLLECTION

Students at the Advanced Rescue Swimmers School in Astoria, Oregon, practice direct deployment maneuvers to rescue survivors from sheer cliff faces. GLENN GROSSMAN

Two rescue swimmers practice a rescue basket hoist battling hurricane-strength rotor wash winds—and waves—kicked up by the spinning rotors. GLENN GROSSMAN

Rescue swimmer George Cavallo is lowered by a hoist cable to rescue survivors.
CAVALLO COLLECTION

Coast Guard air crews rescued over 7,000 children, women, and men in the aftermath of Hurricane Katrina. Thousands more were assisted on the water by Coast Guard small boats, and cutters. U.S. COAST GUARD

During Hurricane Katrina, stranded families created roof top notes as well as used flash lights, candles, and yelling to get rescue workers' attention.
U.S. COAST GUARD

Rescue swimmers endure intense physical and mental stress during the chaotic task of saving lives. GLENN GROSSMAN

Air Station Detroit HH-65 Dolphin helicopter flies over site of rescue swimmer Eric Mueller's Niagara Falls rescue of a Marine Corps Veteran. USCG/MUELLER COLLECTION

U.S. Coast Guard personnel survey a HH-65B Dolphin search and rescue helicopter that crashed in the surf during a rescue operation near Eureka, California.

MARK McKENNA/THE TIMES-STANDARD

The first five men to become rescue swimmers in the USCG. Front row (left to right): ASM3 Kelly Gordon and ASM2 Steve Ober (the first two Coast Guard graduates of U.S. Navy Rescue Swimmer School). Back row: ASM3 Butch Flythe, ASM2 Matt Fithian, and ASM1 Rick Woolford.

USCG/O'DOHERTY COLLECTION

Rescue swimmer Dave Foreman (fourth from left) was awarded the Coast Guard Medal for his heroism in rescuing survivors from the Bow Mariner. *Rear Admiral Sally Brice-O'Hara (far right) officiated the ceremony. Also in the picture are (from left to right) North Carolina Senator Richard Burr, Coby Foreman, Mildred Foreman, and Micki Foreman.* U.S. COAST GUARD/FOREMAN COLLECTION

From left to right: Rescue swimmer David Yoder, flight mechanic Dave Barber, pilot Lieutenant Bruce C. Jones (currently commanding officer Air Station New Orleans), and Lieutenant JG Randall Watson. These four men rescued the captain and two sailing members from the Malachite *sailing vessel during a winter gale in the "Graveyard of the Atlantic" on December 12, 1993. Ironically, Barber saved Yoder's life when he noticed the hoist cable holding Yoder began to part.* CAPTAIN BRUCE C. JONES COLLECTION

10

OBSTACLE RICH

They are going to be swept away and gone, and I'm going to see those faces for the rest of my life! What is the land rescue team going to do that we can't?

WHILE MARIO VITTONE STRUGGLED four hundred miles offshore to save the Hubbard family aboard the ketch *Marine Flower II* during Hurricane Gordon, Mike Thomas, aviation survivalman second class, worked an equally punishing case as rescue swimmer. Three crew members aboard the sailing vessel *Pilgrim*, located one hundred miles east of Elizabeth City, were also battling Hurricane Gordon's punishing winds and seas as it stormed up the eastern seaboard. The USS *America* had intercepted the sailboat's Mayday call and assisted in determining its location.

Thomas volunteered to enter the dangerous ocean. He relinquished his protection inside the HH-60 Jayhawk helicopter cabin for a valiant attempt to recover the survivors. Each attempt was demanding and increasingly exhausting. He fought the extreme conditions spawned by Hurricane Gordon to tow the individuals one at a time toward the rescue basket. On the third hoist attempt, a screaming survivor swept well past

Thomas. Only his strobe light revealed his location in the darkness. Thomas lunged for it, grabbed the man, and in that instant accounted for a third life saved. For his courage, forty minutes of intense physical exertion only matched by the extraordinary aeronautical skill of the pilots and flight mechanic operating above, Thomas was cited for extraordinary heroism. He was awarded the coveted Distinguished Flying Cross.

It would be a mere seven months later on June 27, 1995, that Thomas would again be tested. He was called into the Blue Ridge Mountains.

A major storm that should have moved through the area remained stationary. It deposited an abundance of water in too short a time, exceeding human expectations and preparation. Floodwaters ravaged the land, destroyed homes, toppled vehicles, and threatened the lives of many in Madison County, Virginia.

Thomas was called to action. Joining Lieutenant Commander Bruce C. Jones (see chapters 11 and 14), aircraft commander; Lieutenant Junior Grade Mark L. Collier, pilot at the controls; and AM1 Glenn Jones, flight mechanic, they were all dispatched to the flood zone aboard a Coast Guard HH-60 Jayhawk helicopter from Air Station Elizabeth City.

"The initial call we responded to was that a three-year-old child had been swept away in the floodwaters," said Thomas. "We had heavy hearts thinking that maybe we were going to find the body of the three-year-old. It wasn't sitting real well with us to think about that."

As the aircrew sped to the reported location, about one and one-half hours' flight time away, they were diverted by another radio call. Multiple urgent matters in a variety of locations required their assistance. The aircrew asked the rescue squad, which had received many of the 911 calls, to advise them on which involved the most imminent danger. They would respond to this priority first.

Unfamiliar with the geographic terrain of the area and unaware of local landmarks used as reference points, their initial response was made more difficult. "One of the calls was that somebody was trapped at Jim's farm," recalled Thomas. "We didn't know where Jim's farm was so we literally hovered down in a farmer's field to ask for directions. From there we could follow road signs to the location."

The rescue team was accustomed to flying over the ocean. This was a different kind of mission. They had to quickly adjust to a diverse search and rescue environment, one that was obstacle rich, loaded with dangerous elements that could cause the helicopter to crash. They maneuvered in close proximity to treetops and power lines, abundant in the foggy, mountainous terrain. Equally daunting were the unusual predicaments adults and children were stranded in, left to struggle for their lives.

"The floodwaters were just raging, carrying huge propane tanks, uprooted trees, cars, pieces of houses, and dead livestock," said Jones. "It was really unbelievable."

As they continued to assist trapped people, the pilots frequently experienced poor radio communications. To combat the loss of communications, they would gain altitude to increase the radio frequency reception for updates and additional tasking.

One of the calls they responded to was a report of a red pickup truck and a nearby garbage truck stranded in the rising waters. In the truck bed were a ninety-two-year-old woman, Maud; an eighty-year-old woman, Nancy; and a twenty-one-year-old man, Adam, who had tried to help the women and became a victim himself.

The full-size pickup's front end was down in a ditch. Floodwaters rushed over the hood. To survive longer, the threesome had punched out the back window and escaped as far as the truck's bed. The floodwaters had continued to rise and were now circumventing the broken windshield.

Not far away, inside the garbage truck, two women were temporarily elevated above the floods.

The rescuers took little time to assess the situation. "I knew we had to act right then and there," said Thomas with conviction.

The team quickly discussed rescue procedures. Their plan was for Glenn Jones to lower Thomas close enough to the truck to allow the flooding currents to carry him toward it. From there, Thomas could extract each survivor with a surgeon's precision. The flight mechanic would then hoist each individual into the safety of the cabin.

With unanimous agreement, Jones prepared to lower Thomas using direct deployment, which keeps the rescue swimmer attached to the hoist cable at all times. Thomas would be lowered with a rescue strop, which would wrap around the survivor under the armpits and clip into the hoist cable for evacuation within seconds.

As Thomas was lowered, all Jones could see from his bird's-eye view was the cable descending through the tree branches and Thomas disappearing below. If Thomas had hand signaled directional orders about where he wanted to be moved, Jones could not see them.

"I got within inches of the survivors . . . Our fingertips almost touched," said Thomas. Then the flight mechanic made a sudden decision that caught Thomas by surprise.

"Abort! Abort! Abort!" yelled Jones to the pilots.

Thomas was snatched up. As he was pulled away, he watched the survivors' facial expressions change into that of horror. They reached for him and yelled, "No! No!" Thomas urgently hand signaled his command to be put back.

It went unanswered.

Instead, he sailed upward, cleared the treetops, and was deposited into the helicopter's cabin.

"What are you doing?" yelled a hotheaded Thomas. "Why did you pull me away? I almost had them!"

Jones explained it was a safety issue. He had lost sight of Thomas, who was hidden under a canopy of treetops and branches. He could no longer see Thomas's directional hand signals, which provided position instructions to keep the swimmer safe. If the cable had fouled in the trees, the flight mechanic would have to sever it. Thomas would be left, swept away by the currents, or worse.

"It was the right decision," admitted Thomas, who quickly apologized for his outburst. "There was a wild river rushing by us down there. I could have easily been killed."

The pilots started to fly away. Seeing what had happened, they planned to get a land rescue team to the scene to help the people below.

Thomas was very concerned about them. He urged the aircrew, "Fellas, we've got to do something now or those people are going to die." He continued to be assertive. He was committed to act quickly to help them. He relived the scene. Their horrified faces flashed in his mind. He was unwillingly pulled away. They clutched for him and begged him, "Don't leave."

Full of emotion, he appealed to his team, "They are going to be swept away and gone, and I'm going to see those faces for the rest of my life," he shouted. "What is the land rescue team going to do that we can't?"

Finally the pilots asked Thomas, "What do you suggest?" Thomas believed that the tree branches were not thick enough to really foul the cable. He decided to roll the dice. He said, "Put me down there again, and I'll direct you with my handheld radio."

Thomas was so determined to give it a second try he had developed tunnel vision. His plan involved assuming the flight mechanic's responsibility to provide directional commands to the pilots. Thomas thought he could correctly guide the pilots by using his radio. He did not really think about his own risk at the time, he was focused on saving those lives. He knew he would have a tough time the rest of his life if they died. Their faces would haunt him.

Jones's prowess enabled him to lower Thomas into an ideal position in front of the truck. Thomas then began the dangerous and intricate work of guiding the pilots so that they could in turn deliver the helicopter to the proper position.

"Forward and right five feet."

"Forward and right five."

"Easy right."

Using his fins as rudders, he steered into the truck. He grabbed the truck's side mirror, simultaneously grounding himself to release the static electricity that had built up within the cable and around his body.

"I've got it, give me slack," commanded Thomas to the flight mechanic.

He forced his legs up and over the truck. The slack cable minimized the force of his body being slammed into the side of the truck. It made the entry difficult. He had to pull his body inside.

"The survivors were pretty level-headed," said Thomas of his return. They did not rush him. "Maud, the woman in her nineties, was in a fetal position in the truck bed surrounded by water. She was borderline hypothermic and shivering, so I decided to get her first."

He introduced himself to her, "I'm Mike Thomas, rescue swimmer for the U.S. Coast Guard. I am also an EMT. If there is a medical problem, please let us know."

Just one week after the implementation of this direct-deployment technique as part of required Advanced Rescue Swimmer School training, Thomas would apply his knowledge to the situation at hand. Thomas also used a new lasso-type device called a "quick strop," which he placed around the woman's shoulders then under her armpits before cinching it tight. Next he pulled her close to his chest to connect her strop to the hoist cable.

"I've got her," Thomas informed the flight mechanic. "Take up the slack." With the cable taunt he ordered, "You have the load." With great care, they were hoisted above the truck and cleared the trees into the open sky above.

The pilots taxied the helicopter toward a nearby neighbor's house. During the rescue the locals had watched and, in fact, had videotaped it. With precision, the crew carefully transferred the frail woman to the neighborhood folks. With Thomas returned to the scene, all in all it took no more than ten minutes to pull off that rescue.

Thomas again assumed the directional commands when he was below the treetops. He guided the helicopter into position and got on board the truck.

Approaching the second woman he introduced himself to her. "I'm Mike Thomas, a rescue swimmer for the U.S. Coast Guard and emergency medical trained. If there is a medical emergency, please let me know," he said. "You're next."

Nancy was a bit nervous and quite scared but ready to go. Thomas calmed her and helped her into the quick strop. Face to face, he secured her harness to the hoist cable for rescue. Nancy was dropped off in the same location.

Thomas returned for the last survivor, Adam. He was obviously in the best shape, being in his twenties. He was physically fit and ready to go. Thomas introduced himself once again and readied Adam for the hoist.

As they were trained to do, the flight mechanic assumed the load. Up and off they went to deposit Adam with the others.

The rescue of the two women in the garbage truck, who happened to be lifelong friends from New York, proved to be uneventful. Thomas recalled a lighthearted moment during their rescue. He had instructed the first woman he approached in the garbage truck, "You've got to help me out. Hang on to me as I get you out," to which she replied, "Oh, baby, I've got you!"

"Don't you know you're in danger?" chuckled Thomas.

"Yeeessss," she replied.

With all survivors safely ashore, the helicopter started to fly from the scene. It was low on fuel, and the pilots estimated they had about fifteen minutes left. They notified the rescue squad of the successful rescues and their intentions to refuel in nearby Culpepper, Virginia.

As they flew to Culpepper at a low altitude, they searched for any distressed people. On the ground waving them over was a group of people directing the helicopter toward a tree.

The pilots maneuvered in to investigate. Two little boys were trapped in trees surrounded by the rushing floodwaters. One of the boys clung to a leaning tree, which perilously held him just a couple of feet above the floodwaters. The second boy had climbed up about fifty feet into a tall pine tree.

The pilots and crew evaluated the situation and noticed the trunk of the bent tree was giving way. Its roots were visible; it could go at any time. Without question, they would have to act quickly to save this boy first.

Attached to the cable, Thomas was lowered into the stampeding water. Using his fins he steered his body toward the bent tree. All the while he was deliberate in his hunt for any debris in the water, which could snag him. As he approached, he squinted to identify why the river gushed differently ahead. As it came into focus, Thomas saw the culprit. It was a barbed-wire fence. Immediately, he signaled the aircrew with an open palm facing down: Stop!

He waved across his chest to the left with haste. The flight mechanic repositioned him four feet above the water while the pilots leveled off and moved the helicopter and a dangling Thomas leftward.

With the danger out of the immediate path, the pilots slowly approached the tree from this new angle. Thomas was lowered two feet above the water as they continued the approach.

The boy saw Thomas close in on him and became hysterical.

"He's sees me and began screaming for help," said Thomas. "He was also praying that the tree would not break."

Thomas instinctively knew that the aircrew did not have time to bring him up inside the helicopter to discuss the rescue plan. He pulled out his handheld radio and requested, "Get me close enough to where I can grab him!"

Collier taxied the helicopter into position. Thomas was just above the flooding waters when he grabbed the tree. This grounded him and removed the static electricity that had naturally built up within his body and equipment.

Like a master, he slipped one arm around the boy and began configuring the quick strop under his arms and hooked him securely into the hoist hook. The boy put his arms around the rescue swimmer's neck. Now, face to face, the boy was extremely happy to be there.

"Hang on, we're going for a ride," yelled Thomas as they took off skyward.

Pressed for time, the pilots repositioned the helicopter for the last boy's rescue. Jones relayed Thomas's level-off signal to the pilots as he neared the tree.

"The pine tree was very thick with a lot of branches. This was hardly a way to get to him," recalled Thomas. He explained to his team, "You're not going to like this and I'm not going to like it either, but you've got to throw me into the tree."

Collier was up for the test. He demonstrated his clever proficiency in the next few moments. "He banged the helicopter left and then right, which swung me right into the tree," said Thomas, who was wearing a helmet. He covered his face with his hands as he went smashing into the branches to reach the child. "The pilot's skillful maneuvering enabled them to crab or move the helicopter sideways. I thought, *We've never done a land rescue like this before!*" Thomas said.

Thomas grabbed a thick tree branch and pulled himself next to the boy. Using the quick strop, he secured the boy to the hoist hook and said, "Don't worry, you can make this a ride at Disney and make money off it!"

They were pulled through the branches and surfaced above the treetops. When the Coast Guard rescuers returned the boys to their family, they discovered that the eleven-year-olds were brothers.

On their flight to Culpepper for fuel they were notified of more people in many different locations needing assistance. After they refueled they would return to the calls and help.

By the end of that first day of pioneering rescues, they had saved a total of twelve men, women, and children. They only stopped when daylight ran out.

The next day they resumed their efforts to help more people. They saved three more people, including a baby.

In addition to the aircrew Thomas flew with, the Coast Guard had launched additional resources to help other flood rescues.

For his heroism, ASM2 Michael P. Thomas was awarded the Coast Guard Medal. Only after the rescues did Thomas admit that he would not have been able to survive the river if the circumstances required for him to be cut from the hoist cable to save the helicopter and crew. He would have been forced to swim into the crazed river. It was out of control, swollen with cars, trees, and other debris, and he knew it would likely deliver a fatal one-two punch.

Recently promoted to chief, Thomas has the distinction of serving for one of the longest periods of active service, over eighteen years, as a Coast Guard rescue swimmer.

Lieutenant Junior Grade Mark L. Collier was awarded the Coast Guard Commendation Medal for his performance as pilot at the controls of the helicopter. He recently retired from the Coast Guard having served at Pacific Area Headquarters in California with his wife, Ellen, and their sons, Billy and Sam.

Lieutenant Commander Bruce C. Jones was cited for meritorious achievement during the aerial flights while serving as aircraft commander. He was awarded the Air Medal, his third. Currently he is the commanding officer of Air Station New Orleans. One of the most decorated helicopter pilots, Jones earned the reputation of being a "SAR magnet" for the many dangerous search and rescue missions he has flown wherever he has been stationed. He moved to New Orleans and helped lead one of the largest search and rescue operations in United States history.

II

POINT OF NO RETURN

David Yoder

The most difficult part for me was thinking about if we'd have to
ditch the helicopter or not.

ON THIS, THE THIRD DAY OF STRUGGLE for their lives against the sea, the
captain, along with his two crew members, had given up hope. They
were aboard the sailing vessel *Malachite* in an area of the Atlantic Ocean
known by mariners as the "Graveyard of the Atlantic," four hundred
miles east of Cape Hatteras, North Carolina. The men knew that the
boat was in danger of sinking, they just didn't know when. Sadly, one of
them had already written his last will and testament and tossed it overboard in a bottle.

The AT&T high seas operator took the Mayday call from the crew
of the floundering *Malachite* during the winter gale of December 12,
1993. The operator forwarded the distress information to the U.S.
Coast Guard, which interceded. The three men on board were preparing to abandon ship into the frigid Atlantic Ocean without a life raft or
survival equipment. They would leap to a ten-foot black-and-yellow
Avon dinghy. The Coast Guard radioed the men instructions to remain

with their vessel and keep a thirty-minute communications schedule. They were also directed to activate their 121.5 MHz emergency locator signaling device.

This call for help set about a chain of events that led the way to a struggle between the value of the lives of the men on board the *Malachite* asking to be saved and the value of risking the lives of those in the U.S. Coast Guard called to help them. One of them, rescue swimmer David Yoder, would attempt his first aerial rescue and find himself clinging for his own life to a parting steel cable above thirty-foot seas that rose on occasion as high as an eight-floor apartment building.

Yoder quietly sat in the rear of the cabin of the Coast Guard HH-60J helicopter, tail number CG 6008, while it flew toward his first rescue. He was not nervous about that fact. "The most difficult part for me was thinking about if we'd have to ditch the helicopter or not," recalled Yoder. "On our way out the C-130 pilot recommended we not do the rescue because the seas were so rough out there." He was thirty-two years old and qualified during the past summer as a rescue swimmer. He was an athletic, black-haired, blue-eyed, six-foot man who was eager to be put to the test.

Yoder had always looked for a challenge and variety when it came to his job choices. His standard, opening question of the military recruiters was "What do you have that's a challenge?" Yoder served one year in the Air Force as a law enforcement specialist and four years in the Marine Corps as a combat engineer before leaving the service to work for two years as a boat mechanic for an offshore racing team. In his spare time, he gave scuba diving lessons.

"I was looking for something exciting," said Yoder about turning to the Coast Guard for his next employment and adventure. He had considered the Navy Seal program and even returned to the Marine Corps in 1988, where he had received orders to enlist, but by that time the Department of Defense was no longer accepting men and women who had served before. His orders were pulled. The Coast Guard did not have such a restriction, he learned.

While living in Daytona Beach Yoder learned about the Coast Guard rescue swimmer program and decided it suited him. It was exactly what he wanted to do, something exciting and he could save lives at the same time. Single and twenty-seven, he enlisted in the U.S. Coast Guard.

It took two years of work, assigned aboard an eighty-two-foot patrol boat from Station Cape Cod, before Yoder would be accepted into the rescue swimmer program. He was sent to Pensacola to attend the Navy's rescue swimmer school along with a class full of twenty-nine men who had served in the Marine Corps, Navy, and three from the Coast Guard. Yoder was one of only nine to graduate. Of the grueling, four-week experience he said he kept reminding himself to keep going, "Tell yourself you're not going to die. They are going to pull me out and revive me if I drown," said Yoder. The last thing Yoder wanted was to fail and be forced to return to the patrol boat.

Heading out to the *Malachite*, he didn't question himself or his inexperience. He was focused on his job, rescuing survivors.

THE RELENTLESS SEAS AGITATED BOTH boat and men. They were powerless to defend themselves against the forces of nature lifting their boat and tossing it about. It seemed like a death sentence. They had suffered beatings from their unstoppable ride, which resulted in bruised bodies and minds as they were flung around the *Malachite*'s cabin and against the mast, boom, and anything solid. The intensely cold and harsh saltwater-filled winds burned their eyes and penetrated their clothing.

The forty-one-foot ketch had capsized twice—each time, it righted itself from three-hundred-sixty-degree rolls. On one occasion, the forty-one-year-old Canadian captain and owner, Nicholas Hull, while strapped to the helm, was taken completely under the water. Hull's left side had also been slammed by the boom, which immediately crushed a rib on impact. Mark Termint, a forty-one-year-old crewman who hailed from the United States, suffered from a lacerated finger. Ron Reggev, the eldest on board at sixty-one and another U.S. citizen, had multiple bruises on his back from the boat being hurled up and tossed down the crests of monstrous waves, which came packaged with the raging storm.

The ketch's engine room was on fire. What was left of the engine provided little power needed to operate essential equipment for navigation, communication, lighting, and steering.

When the New York-based U.S. Coast Guard Atlantic Area RCC was notified that the *Malachite* was in very heavy weather and breaking up, officials quickly plotted the coordinates. It was then they discovered that the *Malachite*'s position was nearly 275 miles west of Bermuda. Search and rescue experts at the RCC knew that to complete this mission with a helicopter would likely be a one-way trip. They inquired of Air Station Elizabeth City, the closest airbase, if it was possible to fly the HH-60J Jayhawk helicopter to Bermuda, a 632-nautical-mile flight. The helicopter had an operational range of three hundred miles. This range had been established to enable aircrews to depart and safely return home with a minimal reserve of fuel as long as they stayed within three hundred miles. If successful, this would be a record-breaking distance mission and one that had not been attempted by a Jayhawk crew.

According to Coast Guard files, by noon on December 12, the Coast Guard had directed multiple resources to help. Twenty-two minutes after the launch order, a C-130 fixed-wing aircraft, tail number CG 1503, departed Elizabeth City to locate the *Malachite*. The Coast Guard cutter *Forward*, having completed another rescue in the region, was assigned to proceed to the *Malachite*'s last known position at best speed. Additionally, the Coast Guard planned to divert the closest merchant ship to assist.

The duty pilots were asked to consider flying the mission. They would pilot the HH-60J Jayhawk helicopter, tail number CG 6008, from Air Station Elizabeth City. Aircraft commander, Lieutenant Bruce C. Jones, and his copilot, Lieutenant Junior Grade Randall Watson, consulted with search and rescue planners to consider the odds. Would they be able to hoist the men one hundred miles farther out at sea than ever flown before and land in Bermuda without running out of fuel?

At 1:55 P.M., after an hour of searching on scene, the C-130 aircrew located the *Malachite*. The vessel at first had appeared to be just another whitecap. Then they observed the ketch confronting enormous seas. When a swell approached, the vessel rode up the wave crest about halfway. The wave's height extended another forty feet or so above the top of the vessel's fifty-five-foot mast.

To assist search and rescue coordinators in tracking the on-scene speed and drift of the boat through the water, the C-130 team inserted a data marker buoy into the ocean.

In an effort to assist the men, the plane also dropped a series of sea rescue kits containing multiple life rafts and survival gear. Shortly thereafter, though, the kits had been "rendered unusable during attempts by the vessel to secure it to the vessel in heavy seas," according to the Coast Guard case report.

While circling above the *Malachite* and reporting back to Coast Guard operators regarding the on-scene conditions, CG 1503, a C-130 fixed-wing aircraft, established communications with a merchant ship, MV *Giovonni Della Gatta*. The vessel was sixty nautical miles away. The radio operator aboard the aircraft directed the merchant to proceed to the *Malachite*'s location at best speed. Because of the seas, the merchant radioed back that it would take them about ten hours.

For the greater part of the early afternoon, the pilots of the duty helicopter consulted with the operations center and aircrew members, flight mechanic AD2 Dave Barber and rescue swimmer Yoder. They checked weather conditions against the vessel's charted position to determine if it was even possible to respond. Their calculations revealed that if there was a ship in the vicinity they could land on to refuel, or if they could carry enough fuel to land in Bermuda, then, perhaps.

In preparation for the mission, they took the unusual step of mounting on the Jayhawk's undercarriage three external fuel tanks, which looked like missiles, in addition to a starboard-side one-hundred-twenty-gallon fuel tank. With the extra fuel and blessed with a favorable tailwind, they calculated they would be able to make the 632-mile transit to Bermuda. This journey would include a half-hour on scene for the rescue before continuing on to Bermuda with a forty-five-minute fuel reserve.

The commanding officer of Air Station Elizabeth City, Captain Norman Scurria, concerned about the mission demands, questioned each member of the rescue team. "This was the first time I had a CO come in on the weekend to pull each of us aside and say, 'If you do not want to go, you do not have to,'" recalled seasoned flight mechanic Barber. "I wanted to go. I was going to get to go to Bermuda after this rescue. In my mind, because I had trained in Alaska . . . anything else was gravy."

After further discussion and consultation with the commanding officer, the RCC, and his flight team, Jones decided to fly the mission. Two hundred seventy-five nautical miles offshore had been selected as the "go/no-go" point, or point of no return. From this imaginary mile marker in the ocean, Jones and his team would reevaluate their fuel reserve, winds, and conditions to determine whether the mission could be continued safely.

At 3:22 P.M., the four Coast Guardsmen jumped aboard the helicopter and launched from Air Station Elizabeth City. Flying above them providing cover and communications relay was a second C-130 aircraft, CG 1500.

For Yoder and the others, once they decided to fly past the go/no-go point, they had no other option but to continue on to Bermuda, the closest point of land.

Watson was responsible for calculating and recalculating with life-threatening accuracy the remaining fuel on board. Barber, having experienced Alaskan rescues, believed this case would pale in comparison. He focused his mind on making this a successful rescue. "I just wanted to do the rescue and go on to Bermuda, make a record case," said Barber.

Just after 4 P.M. the on-scene aircraft dropped the *Malachite* a second sea rescue kit containing two more life rafts, which also became unusable.

Around the same time, Watson reported to Jones that their fuel burn rate would leave them with less than fifteen minutes of fuel to land in Bermuda. The pilots adjusted power to conserve as much fuel as possible. Watson remained diligent in his calculations. When the Jayhawk was close to 175 miles offshore, the tailwinds that had blessed them by pushing them along, had slowly shifted to a direct crosswind. Watson, noticing this change, reported that it resulted in a further reduction of their "negligible margin of error."

Shortly before 6 P.M. the C-130 marked the *Malachite*'s position with flares. It was then relieved as on-scene commander by a C-130 based out of Clearwater, Florida, tail number CG 1719. Upon relocating the *Malachite*, this aircraft dropped additional sets of sea rescue kits. The extreme nature of the sea and wind conditions prevented the men from retaining ten life rafts attached to trail lines that were expertly draped across the ketch from the rear cargo bay of the of C-130s by the dropmaster crew. The lines that held the rafts snapped in the heavy seas.

Yoder and the helicopter rescuers were still flying toward the *Malachite* as the sky darkened. They were provided updated position data from the circling C-130 aircraft. The weather remained severe and began to disintegrate as they flew into a squall. The ceiling dropped from one thousand feet to five hundred feet with rain. Visibility was down to one-half mile. Lightning bolts descended from the night sky, surrounding the helicopter, and erratically illuminating thirty-foot seas. It occurred to

Barber that a lightning strike near the helicopter's General Electric T700 jet engine just might trip it offline.

Jones, Watson, Barber, and Yoder had other things to be concerned about too. Twice during the journey, they were startled by a loud warning horn that sounded in the helicopter followed by the illumination of a master caution light signaling that the stabilator had tripped offline. The stabilator, an airfoil or small wing in the rear of the aircraft, is designed to control the pitch of the nose. "If it drives down, it could make the nose drive down too," said Barber. Fortunately, it was a false alarm they were able to reset manually.

About forty-five minutes away from the *Malachite*'s reported position, Barber prepared for the rescue. "I checked the DMB frequency and the rescue swimmer's radio, PRC 90, for proper operation," wrote Barber in his case summary. Next, Barber, who had trained Yoder at the air station, discussed rescue procedures with him. They decided to use a bare hook with a weight bag attached as the ideal method for recovery because of the high winds and large seas. They wanted to avoid using other equipment, such as the unprotected open end of the rescue sling, which could cause injury to Yoder while he was in the dangerous ocean alone, or the rescue basket, which would act like a metal sail.

At 6:20 P.M. CG 6008 arrived on scene. "We found the boat pretty quick," said Yoder. "Up until now, I'd been sitting in the back of the cabin. When I looked out the door to see the boat, it was an amazing sight . . . the waves were at least eighty feet high and that boat was being tossed around and over the tops of them."

Jones carefully positioned the helicopter in a fifty-foot hover and about one hundred yards off the *Malachite*'s starboard side. The aircraft's floodlights and a directional spotlight illuminated the condition of the vessel. The *Malachite*'s sail was torn into ribbons, and six of the mast stays that held the mast upright were broken and swinging outward from the mast or trailing behind in the surf. Even though the crew had deployed a sea anchor to slow its speed, the *Malachite* was forced along at eleven knots.

As the flight mechanic, Barber needed to devise a plan to safely hoist the men without putting the helicopter in danger. "The seas caught me off guard," said Barber. "On the stern of the vessel, where a rescue basket delivery could have been made, a boom was swinging wildly from port to starboard with a five- to ten-second delay." Barber brought this to Jones's attention. "From that point the pilot and I knew that a trail line hoist to the boat was impossible and out of the question." Barber, a seasoned flight mechanic, suggested another option, something he had done before during Hurricane Charlie in 1986. The three men on the *Malachite* could secure themselves together and go overboard as a group. Then the rescue swimmer would attempt to help each of the men into the rescue basket, which Barber would hoist to the safety of the cabin. "I was confident that our crew could pull it off with no problem," Barber wrote in his account of the mission. "If I would have had any doubt in the rescue swimmer's ability or the pilot's ability to fly the aircraft, it would have gone different."

After discussing the procedures with his crew, who all agreed that it was highly unlikely the *Malachite* would stay afloat much longer, Jones contacted the *Malachite*'s Captain Hull, on the marine radio. Jones said, "Well, fellas, here's your choice, you could wait for another resource to get here, or jump into the water, but I can't hoist you directly from the boat." According to Jones's report summary, "the Captain immediately replied that he and his crew wanted off."

"I can't say that I wasn't surprised," Jones reflected. "You're out there almost four hundred miles in the ocean and the seas are bad and you're thinking to yourself, *Good God, they must really want to get off that boat.*"

Watson recalculated the wind speed and direction, the distance to Bermuda, and the amount of fuel remaining. They had precisely thirty minutes on scene before they needed to depart for a safe landing in Bermuda. Jones proceeded with the next step, coordinating the men's jump with the rescue swimmer's deployment into the gale-driven seas. "I asked Dave Yoder to confirm he was ready and wanted to deploy. He was like, 'Oh yeah, send me in, Coach.'"

When Jones directed the *Malachite* men to go, they jumped over the side and into the ocean without hesitation.

Yoder remembered vividly the very next moment. Barber was given the go-ahead to hoist him out the door. Yoder recalled, "I said my prayers before I left the cabin." From that moment on, he was only focused on rescuing the survivors. He did not think about his own risk as he entered the chaos below.

Barber lowered Yoder. "When I placed the rescue swimmer in the water he was only five feet from the three survivors," Barber wrote. Expecting the power of the thirty-foot rotors to kick up the seas, Barber noticed that the rotor wash had zero effect on them. The combination of the sea's strength and wind speed overpowered and flattened any chance of rotor wash kicking up off the surface.

It was a struggle for Yoder to swim toward the men even with the use of his fins for extra power. He was repeatedly forced under the surface by the rush of huge seas collapsing over his head. He was not aware of the massive height of the waves, he just concentrated on the area two feet in front of him as he proceeded.

The pilots also had challenges just keeping the aircraft airborne. Because of the darkness and no visible horizon, Jones used the night flares previously dropped by the C-130 to assist him as a visual reference. Soon the flares were swept away and he was forced to attempt to maintain a steady hover by referencing the foam-covered seas partially illuminated by the Jayhawk's lights.

Describing the situation, Jones said, "It's dark, dark sky, dark water. You can see what's in the illumination of the searchlight—that's really all you can see. You can't tell which way is up—are you leaning to the left? Are you leaning to the right? Are you going backward or forwards? It's unbelievably . . . constant struggle to focus on what's in the searchlight. Then repeatedly scanning, flicking your eyes to the left on your instrument panel to see your radar altimeter and vertical speed indicator to see if you're climbing or descending. You're trying to hold a steady altitude ,but the seas below you are moving up and down twenty-five to thirty feet at a time, you get a sensation that you're falling. Your altitude may not have changed much, but relative to the seas it may have changed as they pass by so its very disorienting."

Barber meanwhile had his own troubles. In order to see Yoder and steady the hoist cable with one hand to maintain a basket position near the swimmer, Barber kneeled and leaned way out of the cabin door, strapped to the deck by a safety harness around his waist. Because of the continuous rise and the twenty-five-foot, or more, drop of the seas from under the basket, Barber constantly hoisted the cable up or down with his other hand, impossibly trying to keep pace with the seas. Additionally, he had to provide visual and directional information for the pilots over their ICS mounted in their helmets. He became their eyes and ears during the rescue because the pilots could not see what was happening behind and below them.

Watson continued to monitor fuel gauges while communicating with the C-130, which circled overhead. Despite the decreasing time and fuel reserves, he calmly called out approaching swells to Jones and provided updates about how much time they had left on scene.

Yoder reached the men with great effort. He directed one man to unhook and swam with that first survivor, Mark Termint, toward the rescue basket by holding onto his life jacket.

Yoder neared the basket and prepared to assist Termint in getting to it. "My hands would get within four inches of it and the problem is, I could see the basket under the water, then all of a sudden it would disappear," described Yoder. The basket would slingshot away from Yoder. "It was like, 'What are they doing?'" he would ask.

Trying to hoist the men was extremely difficult. Jones recalled, "Every time we thought we were in position, within a second, the next thing you'd look up and they'd be one hundred feet in front of the helo and at the same level. Then a huge wave would go by and knock them behind us . . . Now we couldn't see them anymore."

Barber continuously spoke into the internal microphone, providing directions to the pilots. Jones recounted Barber's directions:

"Forward, right twenty . . .

Forward right ten . . .

Hold, hold . . .

Back twenty . . . *Back forty!* . . .

Back forty! . . .

OK, hold . . . You're drifting . . .

Target at one o'clock . . . OK, hold . . .

Back! . . .

Forward fifty! . . .

Right sixty, right sixty! . . .

Right thirty! . . .

Right ten . . .

Hold, hold . . .

Back and left fifty! . . . *Back and left fifty!* . . . *Back!*

"Trying to hold a steady position on an object illuminated in the spot-light in the middle of a black void, and the object itself keeps moving past you and up and down with the seas is very, very difficult," said Jones.

Tensions started to rise. Jones, Barber, and Watson took a breather and agreed to try and stay calm while doing what they needed to do to get the job done.

Yoder had a self-realization about what was happening to him. "The swells would drop twenty, forty, sixty feet, and it was me going down after them. By the time I got to the basket the swell was going up and the hoist cable would have twenty feet of slack—which would go through the bail on the basket and then pull tight when the swell would go down again." During one of these cycles, Yoder managed to get Ter-mint into the basket, rear end first, just before the cable pulled tight and "snatched him up and he was gone."

With Termint deposited in the helicopter, Yoder turned around to look for the other men and the boat. "The boat was long gone," stated Yoder. He did not see the men either. He was fatigued. He had not re-alized earlier, from his perspective from inside the helicopter, how big the waves actually were. In fact, the seas were rolling by with regularity close to sixty feet. Occasionally a rogue wave exceeded his estimate.

"Fifteen minutes," Watson forced himself to calmly report of their allowable time left on scene.

Jones noticed after this first rescue that Yoder was tired.

"I was having second thoughts about this mission. I looked at the clock, looked at our fuel, and thought, *If they all take fifteen minutes, we're never going to make it.* Did I do the right thing putting Yoder down there?"

Jones knew there was a very real chance they would not have enough time to hoist everyone. Someone might be left behind as the helicopter was forced to leave and refuel.

Barber knew Yoder was looking for the remaining survivors. First he located Yoder by identifying him by a green chemical light attached to his snorkel mask and another in his gloved hand. Both lights faintly glowed in the darkness. Barber flashed the spotlight on the remaining two men and then on to Yoder to show him where they were—about seventy-five yards away.

Yoder planned his swim upstream so that he'd be washed down on them as he got near. He knew if he swam directly for them he'd be washed away from them as he closed the gap. Barber said, "He got right up to them; then they all disappeared under a wave. Seconds later one popped up, then another popped, then Yoder."

When Yoder approached them again, Hull said, motioning toward Ron Reggev, "You're taking him—I'm staying for last."

Yoder and Barber went through a similar ordeal trying to get Reggev into the basket. With one significant exception, the approaching swell was closer to one hundred feet. Barber started to hoist Reggev up. Yoder recalled, "As the basket came up, the swell came up, and it put me so close to the helicopter I could feel the heat and probably could have grabbed on to the tire and climbed into the helicopter. All I could think about was that the rotor blades were going to hit the water!"

Barber observed this too and said strongly to Jones over the hot mike, "Up! . . .

Up! Up! . . .

Up! . . . "

Jones reacted by pulling up on the collective, which controls the angle of lift or descent, to power the helicopter above the point of collision. "I remember we shot up like a rocket," said Yoder. "Now, that scared me. I thought the helicopter was going in the water." Jones managed to recover the helicopter from the close call.

Yoder washed up behind the helicopter and began looking for the remaining survivor, Captain Hull.

Hull had lost his shoes in the turbulence. One of the shoes became a visual reference for Jones to fly by before it drifted out of the searchlight and out of Jones's sight.

The hoists were a violent and physical battle for everyone on the Coast Guard team. Yoder was smashed against the rescue basket repeatedly before it dropped a couple of car lengths beneath him into the ocean. Barber tried to maintain cable control. "I had the cable snatched out of my hands twice, violently straight out." A stressful force that repeatedly weakened the cable.

Jones had to fight off vertigo, a condition that affected his equilibrium as he piloted the aircraft. Vertigo was caused by the lack of adequate visual references, or a horizon, to fly by and Jones's constant adjustment of his hover position to stay in line with the horizon. The water and sky were one line, a blur. For Jones it was "a sensation of rushing forward and back. Constantly in a state of getting off course and correcting for it using any visual cues I could see in the searchlights. It was very hard work."

"Ten minutes," Watson uttered, a forced-calm announcement.

Unknown to any of them, while they worked to rescue the last man, the cable had been heavily stressed from the continued slack then sudden snatch and strain of the loads placed on it over and over again with great force by the ocean and hoists. At any moment it could unravel.

About fifty feet from Yoder, Captain Hull swam to meet him. Their eyes met with understanding of what had to be accomplished. Yoder helped him into the basket with all his strength. He was a tall, heavy man, over six feet.

According to Barber, the captain must have weighed 275 pounds dry. "Just as I was bringing him up out of the water, a large wave crashed on top of him. I thought he was going to be dumped back out of the basket by the way he was positioned, sitting sideways in the basket; this was the only way he could fit in the basket due to his size and the clothing, life jacket, and his state of fatigue," Barber wrote.

"Five minutes remaining," Watson said, forcing his voice to sound unruffled.

Yoder watched the captain enter the cabin of the helicopter above. Based on his preplanning with Barber, Yoder knew for his own recovery, the flight mechanic would send down a bare hook with a weight bag attached to help control its descent. This he could "slap into and go, done deal," said Yoder. "If I were to get into a basket or horse collar in those seas, I'd break my neck!"

Barber gave Jones conning instructions to position the helicopter as he lowered the hook to the ocean's surface where Yoder could see it. Then he paid out additional slack to compensate for the rise and fall of the seas. This sank the hook about five feet. In anticipation of Yoder grabbing the hook and pulling it toward him to connect it to his rescue harness, Barber started to take back the slack slowly as Yoder approached.

Yoder hooked in, removed his glove to reveal the green chemical light, which he needed to signal "ready for pickup." Just then, a large wave crashed over him. It submerged him and buried him deep inside the dark waters. Flipped end over end, Yoder felt the submerged cable wrap between his legs. Barber, unable to see the situation beneath the surface, had started to take in the slack seconds before the wave hit. When Yoder pulled through the wave and cleared the surface he was as close as twenty-five feet beneath the helicopter.

Barber continued the hoist. Suddenly he felt a broken strand of cable, or "spur," hit his gloved hand. He quickly stopped the hoist, an emergency procedure he used to prevent his caught gloved hand from going into the drum. "I watched the strands break right in front of my face . . . One, two . . . , as the third was about to break, It was like 'Oh my God this can't be happening!' It unraveled in front of my eyes!" Barber recalled with dread. He knew too that at any moment Yoder would drop into the ocean and they would not get him back.

Barber made a split-second, nonreversible decision, hoping to save Yoder's life. It was one that they would not even try in a training scenario because the hoist would become unusable after the fact. "I was betting on all of the remaining cable going into the drum, I had three-fourths of it to go and I didn't think it would snag." With no time to inform the pilots, Barber took what he had, three to four seconds, to instinctively take care of the situation by two-blocking the cable, or feeding it, into the drum at full speed. During that short time, Yoder was pulled up too. He was now in a position less than twenty-five feet below the cargo door. The cable held. Barber noticed that Yoder had been blown farther back and under the right auxiliary one-hundred-twenty-gallon fuel tank due to the fifty knot winds. With great difficulty, Barber managed to pull Yoder, who had no idea what had just happened, up to the doorway of the cabin.

"He would have died, it was a call I would not want to have to make again!" exclaimed Barber. If Yoder had fallen into the ocean, he would likely have been killed by the impact of his body slamming against the wall of water. The relief was short lived when, as he pulled Yoder toward him, Barber noticed his hands were up by his neck. *Oh my God, he's not moving, he's hurt his back,* thought Barber as he moved Yoder as gently as possible inside. "Are you all right?"

"Yeeeaaaaaoooowwww," yelled an exhausted Yoder. All his gear had come up around his neck, choking him. He released himself from the bindings.

"I had every confidence in Dave Barber because he trained me," said Yoder. "But, I have never been so happy as when I saw the door of that helicopter."

Barber completed the rescue checklist as he thought with relief and joy, *He's OK, and we're going to land!*

"They gave me thirty minutes to do the job, I did it in twenty-nine," Yoder proudly proclaimed.

The helicopter with the three survivors landed at Naval Air Station Bermuda about an hour and a half later signifying the end of what was recorded then as the longest operation for a HH-60J Jayhawk helicopter crew. The mission totaled 5.1 hours.

Over a couple of beers, the crew talked and planned their trip home. The men they saved hugged them as they thanked them for saving their lives. Yoder, Barber, Jones, and Watson were each awarded a Distinguished Flying Cross for their courage and valor.

"Our biggest reward is rescuing them, knowing they had no other chance to survive. They were on their last leg," said Barber.

David Yoder retired from the Coast Guard and is currently working as a recruiter for Johnson & Wales University off-site in Alabama. He is married and has a daughter.

Dave Barber left the Coast Guard and lives in the Clearwater area with his wife Cynthia. He works as a computer network administrator for the Heart and Vascular Institute of Florida in Safety Harbor. Their son, Joshua, applied for admission to the Coast Guard Academy. Barber's nephew, AMT3 Mike Barber, is a flight mechanic flying out of Coast Guard Air Station Detroit.

Commander Bruce Jones is the commanding officer of Air Station New Orleans and has since been promoted to Captain. He was assigned there prior to Hurricane Katrina.

12

THE PERFECT RIG

John Green

Fear reminds you that you are still alive.

From a running leap, John Green appeared out of the smoke and darkness. He was not going to wait for the helicopter to land. He squeezed his six-foot frame into a very narrow space between the flight mechanic and the doorframe of the HH-65A Dolphin helicopter.

"*He's in! Up! Up! Up!*" shouted Petty Officer First Class Mike Bouchard, the flight mechanic.

"I'm inside the helicopter, thinking, *That didn't just happen*, and I'm looking at myself, *No, I'm not burned, I'm OK*," recalled Green of the explosion that knocked him to his knees and nearly killed him. He picked himself up and ran.

Minutes before, Green had completed supervising the evacuation of fifty-one workers from a burning oil rig. Alone, he was awaiting his own rescue when the unexpected happened.

It was a couple of hours before midnight, twenty-five miles offshore, south of Grand Isle, Louisiana, on July 5, 2000. The men aboard the Ocean Crusader, a jack-up rig used as an oil platform, were large, strong, fearless adults who knew their way around an oil rig. That night they had been rousted from their station by an explosion.

Somehow a fire had been sparked and a fiery blast had followed. Flames were fed by natural gases escaping from the wellhead—the top end of the pipe they were checking. The pipeline penetrated the floor of the Gulf of Mexico.

This fire could not be extinguished. To keep it at bay, the crew had sprayed the salty Gulf waters on the fire along with any other extinguishing agents they could find. Their efforts, as long as the men remained on board to continue them, kept the natural gas from collecting inside the steel skirt surrounding the area. If collected, it could form a dangerous, volatile concoction, unknown and unseen by rescuers.

Trapped and suspended a hundred feet above the Gulf of Mexico, they waited for rescue. Grown men anxiously crowded around the helicopter pad. No fireman's pole, elevator, or fire escapes guided them to safety. Jumping the length of a football field into the waters below was an option, though not one that ensured survival.

Searing flames, within a hundred feet from where they huddled, reached upward for them. The flames' brightness illuminated the night sky, which had been blanketed by darkness over the waters of the Gulf.

A distress call had been sent to anyone who would answer. How long before another explosion? Could they evacuate before then? Who would rescue them?

First Class Petty Officer John Green, an aviation survival technician, was thirty-five years old. He had spent the last sixteen years of his life as a Coast Guard rescue swimmer. He was fond of saying, "Fear reminds you that you are still alive." His perspective may have contributed to his gray hair and mustache. He was tall, athletic, and weighed two hundred pounds. His presence was commanding, enhanced by his sharp blue eyes yet tempered by his good-humored manner. His reputation preceded him as one of the best in the business.

Green sat in the cabin of the HH-65A Dolphin helicopter and talked with Mike Bouchard.

For Bouchard, it was his first day of duty. Having recently transferred to Air Station New Orleans, he knew little about the area but made up for it with knowledge and experience as a flight mechanic.

The pilots, Lieutenant Commander Brian Moore and Lieutenant Troy Beshears, had mastered their trade from years of experience in the Coast Guard as well as prior service time flying for the U.S. Army.

Before taking off from the air station for the first case of the evening near Mobile, Alabama, the pilots noticed the humble giant, Green, running out to join them aboard the helicopter. He was late. He carried his gear instead of wearing it. He looked disheveled. "There's John," they laughed, glad that he would be aboard. It was rare that they would all fly together because of rotating duty schedules, and they enjoyed the few times they could.

This highly talented team was released from monitoring the fire in the marshlands near Mobile. Another Coast Guard crew aboard an HH-60J helicopter from Mobile had already evacuated a couple of people to a burn trauma unit.

"I was a little bummed that we didn't get a little part of the action," recalled Beshears, who flew from the right seat as pilot at the controls. Earlier, excited about the opportunity to fly, the pilots flipped a coin to see who would be the aircraft commander and subsequently fly the mission. The senior pilot, Moore, didn't win. He was relegated to the left seat in charge of instruments, assisting with navigation and communications. Overall, he still maintained final authority for decisions as aircraft commander.

Now, after two hours of circling the marshland fire they were available for the next emergency. Beshears maneuvered the helicopter westward toward New Orleans. Moore relayed their intentions to a watch stander at Coast Guard Station Venice, sixty miles south of New Orleans on the Gulf of Mexico. Venice was their communications relay with Air Station New Orleans because of the poor radio communications common in that region.

"Look, we're going to leave the area," Moore reported to the station watch stander who, according to Moore, was "typically an eighteen-year-old teenager." Distracted by another call, the watch stander's microphone was still pressed, or keyed up. This enabled the pilots to hear conversations coming into the station radio speakers in the operations center.

The pilots overheard an emergency call:

"*Ocean Crusader* . . . oil rig . . . on fire . . . "

"Did you hear that?" Beshears asked Moore.

"Yes," said Moore.

So did Green and Bouchard. Moore changed the frequency to the distress channel and they listened in directly.

"*Ocean Crusader* had radioed a Mayday. They had fifty-one people on board, an uncontrollable fire, and they were running out of firefighting equipment," said Green.

"The bad part was this guy didn't give latitude or longitude, which we use on the maps to identify his location," said Beshears. "All the oil platforms out there use a grid system where each name is specific to something they know . . . Apparently this guy on the rig's radio didn't know anything but that." The pilots didn't have a geographical map with the grids to find the rig's location.

Assigned to a second tour of duty in New Orleans, Brian Moore, an avid deep-sea fisherman, knew the grid names by heart. Moore created a geographical location that they could input into the flight computer to navigate toward. Adding to the pressure of quickly locating the rig, the helicopter was running low on fuel.

The pilots knew they would need to refuel from an oil rig on the way. Though not officially dispatched to the rig case, Bouchard and Moore made the decision. "Let's go," they said.

As they flew toward the estimated position, Moore monitored the radio and received assistance from the Air Station Venice watch stander to get more information about the nature of the distress and people on board. He also inquired about other helicopters and vessels that could render assistance.

Beshears was faced with many obstacles. The oil platforms in the Gulf routinely expended their pipeline pressures by burning off the excess that created plumes of fire. The light from these flames brightened the night sky. The pilots searched the horizon using night vision goggles, specifically designed to pick up sources of light.

"The night vision goggles were honeycombing . . . going from pitch dark, where you really need the goggles to so much light the goggles are really ineffective," said Beshears. "You try to pop these up, off your eyeballs so that you can still see to fly. It's a little disorienting because you have to refocus. It may make it a little hard, but by the grace of God and Brian Moore, we found the rig."

In all it took about twenty minutes to find it. "The *Ocean Crusader* was apparently attempting to start a new pumping session off an existing oil head that had been capped off years in the past," said Green. "So what they do is go out in a ship and jack themselves up on these giant legs, so it looks like an oil rig, about a hundred twenty feet off the water."

Beshears had the helicopter circle the rig so they could inspect the situation. "Once we've done a pass along the bottom of it, we saw that the fire was coming off the supply line coming out of the water, which is probably about the worst circumstance you could have for a fire," said Beshears.

With this information, the pilots and crew discussed the situation and orchestrated what everyone's job would be as soon as they touched down on the helicopter pad.

Beshears made the approach for the pad, a tiny piece of steel jutting out from the rig and located the farthest away from the fire. Complicating the approach, which required landing into the wind, smoke blew into the windshield, reducing their view of the landing site.

"At night, you can't tell how fast you're moving or if you're turning left or right, because you don't have those visuals you would have during the day," said Beshears. The helicopter pad had a surface area of about ten by fifteen yards. From the pilot's perspective, they did not see much of it at all. The flight mechanic hung out the side door informing them how fast they were moving over it and directing them left or right.

Safe with the wheels on deck, they looked out to find they had to concentrate on new issues.

"Anytime that you land, the first instinct is for survivors to run toward the aircraft," said Green. "Same with this case, we land and here are all these guys wearing life jackets rushing the plane. You might not think there is anything wrong with that, but the helicopter's blades are spinning around so fast you can't see them and you don't realize how low they dip down. One or more of them might have gotten hurt by the rotor's arch."

Bouchard and Green ran out to stop the men who approached dangerously close. Green had to disconnect from the ICS, an electronic cord he raced out with to herd them back down the stairwell. The stairwell became a choke point where he could control the mass of people and limit their access to the helicopter.

Green noticed a foreman holding a clipboard. He enlisted his help in keeping the men back.

Green joined Bouchard who had returned to the helicopter and plugged into the ICS system.

"What are we going to do with these guys?" Beshears asked Moore. "How are we going to do this?" With the summer's high humidity another issue, they were limited by how many men they could take on each trip. The humidity also made flying the Dolphin helicopter more difficult. "It didn't want to fly," said Beshears.

Green said, "The pilot was thinking that we could take three guys at a time. So I piped up and said I'll stay behind and you can take four."

"Well, if you're comfortable with that, we can do that," Moore responded.

"Well I'm comfortable with it," Green replied. "Plus it will help speed things up. By the time you come back, I could have the next four guys ready. We'll just get them on the plane."

"Green realized that the second we take off with four guys and leave the other forty-seven behind, it was not going to be a calm moment," Beshears said. "These guys don't know if we're coming back, they have no idea where we are going. And all they were thinking was that any second now this thing is going to blow itself apart and we're all going to die!"

Green hurried back to the waiting foreman. He directed him to select the first four men and have them wait on the helicopter pad. Green asked him where the closest rig was located for transferring the men. He also watched to ensure the foreman wrote down the names of the men being evacuated. Four were ready. Green showed them how to walk toward the helicopter, head crunched down low to avoid the spinning rotors, then slide into the cabin.

"Guys were dressed in everything, jeans, bathrobe, and coveralls, and one guy, one of the biggest guys there, had pink fluffy slippers," recalled Green. "Any other time, you would have chuckled, but in this case I thought, *Wow, they were really caught off guard.*"

Green had learned from many other rescues that his presence officiated his role. He was the leader. He looked official wearing the Coast Guard uniform, and people started to relax and listen to him. Survivors expected to hear from him what to do. His guidance would keep them alive. "In reality, I didn't know what to do either, except to help them stay calm, not panic, and tell them who would be next to fly," said Green.

"It was like I was seeing a bunch of life jackets with big eyeballs on top of them, wondering 'What's next?'" Green said. "That's part of why I stayed back and away."

"OUR PLAN WAS . . . HOW SCIENTIFIC IS THIS?" Beshears asked. "To locate the brightest light on the horizon and that's what we're going to fly to."

The helicopter took off, heading for the closest oil rig about ten miles away. Green was able to communicate with the aircrew using his handheld VHF radio.

Green readied the second set of four men. When the helicopter returned he looked down at his watch. The evacuation of the first group took thirty minutes. "Man this is going to take a while," he muttered. The evacuation could take another couple of hours at this pace. The danger was the rig could explode again at any moment. Green started looking for another way as he worked.

The second group of four men boarded the helicopter and departed. The helicopter was now running critically low on fuel. The pilots informed Green that during this trip, they would shut down temporarily, get fuel, and return. They would not be able to communicate with each other while the helicopter shut down.

"The first few guys were pretty excited," said Bouchard of the evacuation. "But after the first couple of passes, they realized we were going to get them off in an orderly fashion."

"On my radio I heard that there was a motor vessel trying to hail me," recalled Green. The Coast Guard radio operator ashore relayed additional details about a nearby ship.

The *Madeline McCall* was asking if there was anything it could do to render assistance. "It was an oil rig supply ship with a really flat back end for gear, pipes, and equipment," said Green. "It was like a really big dump truck, about one-hundred-and-thirty-feet long."

Green turned to the foreman with a hopeful suggestion, "Is there a way we can rig a ladder so that we can just all go down to this boat? 'Cause that would be great!" The foreman answered, "Nope. There is no way we can do that. We normally just lower down on the legs and since we are a ship, just float away." Because of the fire the *Ocean Crusader* could not be moved.

"How else can we get off of this rig?" asked Green. The foreman told Green that they could use the supply crane. So Green instructed the foreman to get the crane ready.

Green had the crane operator swing a large netted ring, or string purse, outside the fire's arc and lower a few men at a time down to the waiting ship.

"They would hang on for dear life," observed Beshears of the procedure in process when they returned.

The *Madeline McCall* continually repositioned itself underneath the crane's load to counter the forceful currents and winds that were pushing it dangerously close to the rig.

Alternatively, when Green knew the helicopter was approaching to evacuate another group, he would return to the helicopter pad and conduct that evacuation. "I felt like an air traffic controller, talking to everybody on the radio." He used many of the rig's handheld radios. The batteries ran out one by one from continuous use.

"The thing that we were all unaware of at the time was that the rig personnel were keeping the fire at bay," continued Bouchard. "I think they were using some sort of extinguishing agent. And once they were evacuated, we really didn't have any idea what we were about to run into."

After evacuating forty-nine men, they were down to the last load, the crane operator and Green. "The crane operator told me that he was going to have to secure power to the rig, so that when the firefighters come they don't have to deal with electrical power," said Green. "As he went down to the rig's office, a steel box, where he was securing power, all the lights went off on the rig." He returned to Green standing on the helicopter pad in the complete darkness. He had a cup of coffee in his hand. *I love coffee*, Green thought.

Green calculated they had about twenty minutes for the helicopter to return and asked where the man got his coffee. Offered a cup, Green walked with the man to the coffee mess.

They went around a corner to the ship's office and went inside. To his surprise, Green noticed two other guys sitting in the room flipping switches and going through a checklist.

As Green poured himself a cup of coffee his anxiety and stress level peaked. He grabbed another fully charged handheld radio before casually turning to ask the crane operator, "Well, are these guys staying on the rig?"

"No," was the reply.

"I was kind of shocked and almost shouted at the guy. 'You told me you were the last one,'" Green said instead.

"Well, what's the problem? There are just two guys here," the operator said.

They're not just any guys, Green thought, noticing they were not skinny either. "Well, the problem is the helicopter is gonna shut down and get fuel before they come back. So, if they get too much fuel they are not going to be able to take all of us."

"Can you call them?" asked the crane operator.

Green knew the helicopter was in the process of shutting down and in seconds he would loose all communication with the pilots.

"The last thing we heard was from Green, 'Oh no, there's a problem,'" Beshears said.

Moore and Beshears decided to take on just enough fuel to get them back to pick up Green and land on the mainland with an appropriate reserve of fuel.

Returning to the foreman, Green informed him he could not get through to the pilots. "So we'll manage, hopefully it will be all right."

Together the four men went up to the helicopter pad. Green initiated the use of flashlights in an attempt to illuminate the painted *H* on the pad's surface. *Like that's really going to do something*, Green mused. "But you've gotta do something, you know. Of course, by now the fire was illuminating it pretty good too. A big fireball was going pretty good behind us."

The fire was intensifying. Green was somewhat relieved when he heard over the radio a Coast Guard helicopter was approaching. "It was not my helicopter," said Green.

He safely vectored this second Coast Guard HH-65A Dolphin aircraft onto the pad. Then he escorted the three men around to the helicopter's cabin door.

"They were all looking at me, like, you've got to be kidding!" said Green of the other Coast Guard aircrew. They unanimously knew they could not take four men. Their facial expressions backed each other up.

"The rescue swimmer on that helicopter said, 'Hey, I'll stay here with John and wait for the other plane to come pick us up so you can take these three guys,'" Green recalled. The swimmer, Ian Powell, worked with Green at the air station, and they knew each other well.

Green informed the pilots that his helicopter was not far away and it was all right with him if Powell wanted to stay.

"The pilots liked that idea. One of them said, 'OK, sounds like a good idea,' so we got them inside and went back over to the stairwell," stated Green. "We just waited and waited for them to take off, which was making me nuts!" Green intuitively knew that plane should *not* be sitting there!

Waving to the helicopter pilots and crew with his flashlight, Green's questioning signal was returned. He was directed to come over. "We ran back around to the plane, thinking maybe they did some calculations and they can take us all, you never know," said an optimistic Green.

The aircrew yelled with excitement out the cabin door, "We can take one more, we can take one more guy!" They had calculated on their flight computer fuel and weight loads and determined they could still lift off the deck with the additional weight.

"So, naturally, I put Ian back in the plane," said Green. "It's his plane you know." Powell wasted no more time and got inside. Because of limited room, he had to squeeze in backward for takeoff.

Green was somewhat relieved about being the last guy on the rig and not looking around at others who needed to be rescued. Right before this helicopter took off he noticed on the horizon the lights of his helicopter returning. *All right, they are going to take off. My plane's coming in, I'm outta here!* thought Green as he walked back to the stairwell to wait.

"We see the other aircraft taking off from the rig, realizing, right now, everything is great, all we have to do is go in and get John," recalled Beshears. "This is actually a historic case for a Dolphin rescue, the most people pulled off in any one case."

Beshears flew two hundred feet above the water. He set up a racetrack-like pattern to make his approach to land on the pad. When he was perpendicular to the pad, Beshears stared outside and down, looking for what he knew should be there. He saw Green being helpful, waving his flashlight. Beshears planned to properly orient the helicopter for the descent and landing on the powerless rig.

As Beshears lined up for the approach, he was concerned about a couple of things: one of the two engines had been damaged earlier that evening when he had unintentionally "oversped it," landing to take on fuel. And, he was worried about the fact that the aircraft was a little heavier from having refueled. This meant he was limited in the engine power available to him. "You have to be like a ballerina in the air to control the aircraft in the summer because the humidity makes it not want to fly."

FROM THE DEPARTING HELICOPTER Powell noticed Green fade into the distance. One second he was there and then in the next, an explosion!

"It blew up! It blew up!" Powell yelled.

An orange-gold fireball engulfed the entire structure. Thick, black smoke followed, surrounding the rig.

Beshears witnessed the explosion too. "I remember the pressure changes from the blast. I felt it in my ears. The fireball was so huge it bounced straight down to the water and bounced up to hit the deck," recalled Beshears. "They say when you have your adrenaline going in a situation like this, that time stands still. And it does. Only it was just a matter of seconds."

Beshears described what they all felt during those seconds. "Jesus, John's dead, all three of us were 'Oh my God, John's dead! What are we going to do?'"

"I didn't know him, it was my first duty day, and didn't think there was any way anybody could survive that," said Bouchard. "I figured he was gone. Nobody said much. We were just kind of stunned."

Green was knocked to his knees by the force of the explosion. He grabbed his radio and spoke calmly into it, "If you guys are going to come get me, this would be a good time."

He vividly recalled his trauma. "Soon after the helicopter took off with all those guys, the rig exploded. Knocked me to the ground. Really, I didn't know what had happened; just something had knocked me to the ground, intense heat. Instinctively, I covered my face with my gloves and tried to make myself as little as possible," recalled Green. "The office connex box [the container housing the office] was between me and where the explosion was."

"He was so calm. In an emergency swimmers could have a shark chewing on their foot and would say, 'Look, this is my problem,'" teased Beshears.

The pilots and flight mechanic were not able to see Green. There was a large plume of smoke. "I'm right here, right here on the helicopter pad," Green said.

Beshears continued to fly his planned approach. The problem was that now he couldn't see where the helicopter pad was supposed to be. Nervous, he reminded himself he had done it numerous times that evening. "I kept flying the pattern. And we're going through this discussion in the cabin. 'What are we going to do? We can't land there, we can't even see it.'"

Green heard Moore's assessment over the radio, "We can't make an approach to that rig; you're going to have to jump. We can't see you." The pilots thought they could fly underneath the pad to pick up Green after he landed in the water.

"When he tells me I have to jump, I kept thinking, *I can't jump from one hundred and twenty feet, I've jumped from pretty high before but nowhere near that. I don't think I could survive a one-hundred-and-twenty-foot jump.*" Green searched for other alternatives to answer his question, *What do I do now?*

With resignation and despair he muttered to himself, *There are no other options.*

"But, I kept noticing the helicopter kept getting closer and closer," said Green. *So the aircraft commander is telling me they can't make the landing, but the pilot is making the landing!*

"We're telling John to jump and we hadn't thought it all the way through," said Beshears. "When you're trying to figure it out and you're going to risk the rest of the crew in the same moment, it's a really hard decision."

"By the time Brian looked up from his calculations, I had finished the pattern," stated Beshears. "I had both Brian and Mike hanging out looking for it. I also said that after five seconds if I don't see anything, I'm going to pull out."

As the helicopter approached, Bouchard leaned out the door looking for any sign of the pad, anything.

"About the same second I was about to wave off," Beshears remembers, "Mike yells, I got it, I got it!"

"I was able to see just the outside part of the pad, the rotor wash had washed some of the smoke away," recalled Bouchard. "At that point everybody got pretty excited."

Acting as the pilot's eyes, Bouchard vectored Beshears toward the landing, "Easy left, easy right, left ten feet."

Green saw them get close. He wasn't going to wait any longer. "I ran out to the outside edge of the helicopter pad on the same side as the helicopter door." *I better jump in this plane as quickly as possible,* Green thought. *Even before I let the wheels touch down.*

"Here's Mikey, leaning out the door, talking to the pilots about the landing, and I just run right past him and jump inside the plane between him and the pole he's holding on to," recalled Green.

"*He's in! Up! Up! Up! Let's go! Let's go!*" yelled Bouchard. "Once he was in, we didn't waste much time."

Beshears quickly maneuvered the helicopter that was set up for landing into a takeoff position.

"I'm inside the helicopter thinking, *That just didn't happen,* and I'm looking at myself, *No, I'm not burned, I'm OK,*" said Green.

Everyone had felt Green's frame collide with the inside of the helicopter. He hit hard against the back bulkhead, rocking the aircraft.

Then a much greater force rocked it.

"We didn't clear the pad by much before the whole thing exploded," recalled Bouchard.

"All of a sudden we pop out the other side," said Beshears. "That extra fire and heat actually lifted us up and probably saved our lives."

They expeditiously landed at the first shore-based helicopter facility about 4 A.M. in the morning. The helicopter was "downed for maintenance."

Sitting down on the helicopter ramp to commiserate and relieve some of the stress of the experience, they talked. The team faced the reality of what they had experienced, drinking sodas and joking. Green laughed, "You know, it was the perfect rig," referring to the recent feature film, *Perfect Storm.*

"If we had been off by a second or two . . . it was one thing after the other, we probably would have all died," said Beshears. "Everybody trusted everyone else . . . With all our experience, we were blessed that we had the four of us together at one time. It's just one of those dynamics that we reacted the way we did. We were damn lucky!"

"John Green is a rare individual, one of the best examples of what a true Coast Guard rescue swimmer should be," said Beshears. "He holds himself to such standards of fitness and technical competency because he knows people's lives are at stake. He doesn't do the job for accolades, he does it for the job."

Green described the experience with his own analogy: "Have you ever tried to light a barbecue grill and the match doesn't work and the lighter doesn't work and finally the match works and you get that big poof? It's like that—only you're standing on the barbecue grill. Just like that."

"The oil rig fire was like propane, only it was natural gas and that's uncontrollable," said Green. "In the process of hooking on to the pipe, they know to inspect for this, there is a buildup of natural gas. For some reason they had a buildup of natural gas, so much of it, that they could not put the fire out after it exploded."

"We were lucky that night in that we had senior guys in the aircraft," said Beshears. "We had not flown together in a couple weeks. We had a bunch of guys who had been around the block, which I think probably contributed to how well we accomplished this mission. The fact that everybody was relatively calm enabled all of us to do our jobs."

Their story was entered into the *Congressional Record* by Louisiana Senator Landrieu. Green, Bouchard, Beshears, and Moore were each awarded the Distinguished Flying Cross, the highest award for aviators.

Promoted to chief warrant officer in June of 2005, John Green is a marine inspector for Coast Guard Sector New Orleans. In the aftermath of Hurricane Katrina, Green was extensively involved with damage surveys of American shipping vessels. "We also oversee some of the salvage operations for many of the vessels that ended up on land and now have to get back in the water," said Green.

AMTC Mike Bouchard serves at Air Station Houston.

Lieutenant Troy Beshears retired from the Coast Guard and lives in Louisiana.

13

GAME ON, GENTLEMEN, GAME ON

Never forget that it's a team venture. A man in the water is only as good as the guys in the air. Stay in shape and train for the game.

THE EMERGENCY LOCATOR TRANSMITTER (ELT) beacon activated automatically when the Cessna 180 slammed with heavy force into the steep, remote mountainside. The crash site was ten miles from Amber Bay on the Alaskan Peninsula. Four people were on board the small plane when the pilot could not clear the snow and ice-packed mountain peak the evening of August 23, 2000. The sixty-one-year-old pilot, Joe Maxey, from Anchorage, was returning passengers Allen and Ellen Daws and their friend, Linda Brooks, to their lodge. The vacationers, from Jackson Hole, Wyoming, were all in their fifties.

USCG Air Station Kodiak was alerted to the ELT distress signal and correlated reports of an overdue Cessna from Flight Center Kenai and the Coast Guard RCC in Anchorage. They immediately launched resources.

A C-130 fixed-wing aircraft and an HH-60 Jayhawk helicopter were given orders to determine the exact position of the 121.5 MHz distress beacon and render assistance. Additional crews were awakened in the early morning hours of August 24, 2000, called in to help with the ongoing search.

"I was at home when around two o'clock in the morning I got the call from Air Station Kodiak. It was Tim McGee who asked me if I had been called," said AST1 Robert E. Watson, an experienced helicopter rescue swimmer. "He told me he thought it was a plane wreck." Watson knew what he had to do. The thirty-nine-year-old, was one of the Coast Guard's most decorated men for heroism. He threw on some clothes and prepared to go to work.

"When my wife asked me where I was going, I told her, 'I don't know.' A typical answer we give our wives. They can hear the wind blowing outside and we're going to do what we love to do and they stay home with the kids."

Watson did not know where he would be going. He would not return home to his wife until much later. When he did, he would find comfort in her presence. "I recapped what I did. Did I do it right?" Watson reflected. "I'm not the one who created that mess, just the one to try and fix it, help them out, doing the best I can."

Watson knew a lot about living, hunting, and working in Alaska. An avid mountain climber, he was well aware that the weather in Alaska could be unpredictable and in an instant change your plans. "The mountains will hold clouds or fog, keep it from drifting. It was lousy when the Cessna 180 tried to go through the pass. Maxey had gotten so far into the canyon he could not turn around," Watson said of th epilot of the Cessna.

Watson was instrumental in saving many lives from situations in which he had endangered his own life. He had the reputation of being a part of some of the most difficult and challenging cases Coast Guard aircrews have ever flown. Watson was awarded the Air Medal for rescuing six crewmen in 1999 from the fishing vessel *Nowitna*, which was taking on water in heavy seas near Cold Bay, Alaska. He received another Air Medal for helping five survivors into the rescue basket in only fourteen minutes after their vessel, *Cajun Mama*, sank from taking rogue waves in stormy Alaskan seas in 1992. He was aboard an HH-3F helicopter flown by Lieutenant Harl Romine and Lieutenant Timothy Scoggins and aircrew AD2 Ronald Klassen and AE3 Kenneth Malocha.

In 1993 Watson was awarded the Meritorious Service Medal for his heroic achievement while on liberty for helping two severely injured people from an automobile accident after they slid off an icy road and over a one-hundred-fifty-foot cliff.

In the summer of that same year, he deployed during the night to help an epileptic climber, stranded at thirteen hundred feet near Whittier Glacier. The fifteen-year-old was also overdue on his medication. During Watson's descent by hoist cable into the dense alder trees, his harness caught on a branch and released him. Without his safety harness attached to his lifeline, he clung to the vertical surface with his hands, merely six feet from the boy. When the rescue basket was lowered from the helicopter, he coached the frightened teenager to get into the basket first. The helicopter pilot was once again Lieutenant Harl Romine. Romine, directed by flight mechanic Ethan Curry, maneuvered the aircraft so that they could swing the basket back in to the cliff for Watson, making it a "two for one" recovery. "I didn't think I would make it back; I was only twenty-eight years old and this was one of my first cases," recalled Watson, who later received a Coast Guard Commendation Medal for his effort.

One year later, he was honored with the Distinguished Flying Cross for his heroism in rescuing fifty people in the aftermath of Hurricane Rosa including a possible drowning victim from the overflowing San Jacinto River in Texas. In this rescue he had to avoid live power lines in addition to being swept away by the raging river's currents.

JOE MAXEY, THE LEAD PILOT OF TWO SMALL AIRPLANES, had navigated into the canyon to return the three vacationing passengers, the Daws and Linda Brooks, to Painter Creek Lodge. The group had spent the day fishing in Amber Bay with friends and Linda's husband who were aboard the trailing plane piloted by Jeff Meinel. Meinel piloted his plane into the canyon passage behind his longtime friend Maxey when he received his urgent radio call. Maxey advised Jeff to leave the area and return to Amber Bay. Up ahead, the weather had deteriorated quickly to an impassable degree, filling up the valley between the mountains and making passage impossible and exit improbable, even with the aid of navigational instruments. Jeff trusted his friend's advice and skillfully managed to make an immediate hard turn, aborting his flight plan and backtracking out of the danger. He radioed Maxey who had continued ahead, "Maxey, can't you turn back around?"

"No, I think I'm pretty committed," Maxey answered.

"I think it's better that you turn around—"

"No, I feel like I'm pretty committed!" exclaimed Maxey, who climbed out of the canyon demanding all the power the plane could provide in an attempt to clear the mountaintops, according to Watson. "He hit the side of the mountain at about three thousand feet."

AT 9:17 P.M., ON AUGUST 23, the C-130 arrived in the vicinity of the ELT beacon's signal. Electronic equipment in the fixed-wing aircraft tracked the 121.5 ELT signal, but thick cloud cover prevented the crew from identifying the source a few thousand feet below.

The HH-60J Jayhawk helicopter arrived twenty minutes later, piloted by Lieutenant Commander Scott Buttrick. This aircrew was able to fly at a much lower altitude and used night vision goggles to enhance their search. They hoped to validate the source of the distress and start the rescue. They, too, were unable to pinpoint the signal because of the freezing rain, sleet, and fog in the area.

By 5:30 that morning, Bob Watson walked aboard another C-130 aircraft, piloted by Lieutenant Commander Ruhde. He had attended an operations center brief at the air station with HH-60J Jayhawk helicopter pilots Lieutenant Commander Russ Zullick, aircraft commander, and copilot Lieutenant Andy Delgado, and flight mechanic AMT3 John Neff. They formed the second helicopter crew and would relieve the on-scene aircrew. Based on what had been reported to the air station, they discussed how they would attack the situation when they arrived. They knew the weather made the search difficult for the first aircrew that had searched through the night and into the morning.

Zullick, Delgado, and Neff joined Watson inside the cargo area of the C-130 aircraft, tail number CG 1707, for transport to the rendezvous site, King Salmon, a World War II Air Force landing facility with a medical building on the Alaskan peninsula. A skeleton crew maintained its operation.

The flight to King Salmon would take about an hour. Watson rolled out a survival suit as a makeshift bed in the back of the C-130. "I took a nap and thought about what we were going to do," said Watson. "What we'd gotten was that a HH-60J helicopter had made an attempt.

They could not get up to that plane. The weather was so bad, it was nasty, nasty, nasty."

About twenty minutes after Zullick and his team were dropped off at King Salmon, the helicopter landed with an exhausted crew. "They were all bagged," recalled Watson. "They shut down the helicopter and we talked about what they had tried and what they thought might work."

"They briefed us on the route they had flown. The ELT beacon was emitting a signal, but because of the high terrain, the signal skipped around," recalled Zullick. "They told us the highest probability of where they thought the aircraft might be located." The pilot of the second small plane and the owner of the lodge, Meinel, had briefed the first Coast Guard crew early on. He provided crucial details about the typical route the planes flew to the lodge.

Zullick and his team reviewed the charts and were shown which areas had been searched. "We decided where we would concentrate our search. They narrowed it down significantly for us," he said.

They took off aboard the helicopter, tail number CG 6036, around 6:30 A.M. for the one-hundred-and-twenty-five-mile flight. The Coast Guard C-130 orbited at an altitude of eight thousand to ten thousand feet. "They had the ELT signal pinpointed down to a pretty tight area," Zullick said.

The weather en route was perilous. The crew encountered turbulent headwinds and near zero visibility, freezing rain, and snow showers. On scene, the weather became "horrific."

"We flew real low to the ground, close to the terrain, to choose where we needed to go. We were taking ELT hits," Watson said. Meanwhile, the pilots determined which direction they needed to fly. "We couldn't get to the crash site without hurting ourselves" Watson said.

"It was snowing very heavily and then when the snow finally subsided we had a very, very low cloud base that had the top of the mountains and the valley we were trying to get up enshrouded in fog," said Zullick. "So we flew right up to the base of the fog and landed the aircraft."

There they were able to conserve fuel and use auxiliary power with a small turbine engine to run the generator, and to talk with the circling C-130 aircrew. "They let us know the weather they could see," said Zullick of the moving weather systems. "Basically it was a solid cloud deck, they could not see down below us. We were just waiting as the day got warmer, hoping that the warm air would push those clouds up."

While they waited in the uncivilized place for the right moment to go in, a herd of caribou walked behind the helicopter.

Very slowly the clouds rose up and down, up and down, between two high mountain peaks. "Then, there was a splotch of blue, an opening," exclaimed Watson.

The pilots powered up the helicopter. Delgado took it up to an altitude level with the cloud ceiling, around thirty-six hundred feet.

"We were waiting for the blue to come over us," said Watson. We could slide right up into the blue spot and drift with it across the mountainside to see if we could find the plane."

"We were working right on the very peripheral. Imagine the helicopter with the rotor blades in the fog and us hanging out below the fog as we were hovering up the side of this mountain," described Zullick as they entered the valley. "We were getting a very distinct tone now on our direction-finding equipment, and our direction-finding needle pointed right down this valley we were going into. We knew we were going down the right path."

The copilot, Delgado, who used the flight controls from the right seat, was the first to see the wreckage from his side.

The plane looked totaled, as if it had been in a bad car accident. It was on its side one thousand feet below a thirty-seven-hundred-foot mountain peak, resting on a narrow shelf. "It was completely demolished, the front of it was completely gone and it was on its side. The right wing was off on the other side and perpendicular to the plane, landing gear smashed off, and the front of the cockpit pretty much gone," Watson observed.

Delgado maneuvered closer so they all could get a better look. As the helicopter moved in to a distance of about one hundred feet, the rotor wash, as powerful as hurricane-force winds, started to lift the plane. The debris fluttered in the winds. The rescuers realized this might cause the plane to slide off the side of the mountain and quickly backed off.

"Bob, do you think anybody could live through that?" Zullick asked.

Watson remembered that moment, looking down from the cabin door and thinking, *Gee, I'd be hard pressed to believe anybody made it through that. That is really devastating.*

He told Zullick, "I want to check. I could not live with myself if I didn't."

"The plane was really compressed. We were really doubtful if we would find anybody alive in there," Zullick said. They proceeded with the rescue checklist. They would have to confirm that all preparations were complete before sending the rescue swimmer down.

Neff prepared to lower Watson on the hook to the side of the mountain, below the crash site. They could tell that the steepness of the mountainside would make it a challenging climb for Watson to reach the plane. The ground on the mountainside was covered with shale, a dark brown and black sedimentary rock, like large pieces of gravel. There was no vegetation, just shale and some patchy areas of snow and ice. Watson elected to take a small crash ax from the helicopter to use to gain some traction during his climb.

"I let them know that I would nod my head as the signal to have the helicopter back away from the side of the mountain," Watson said of the moment when he would disconnect from the hoist cable. "Normally I would use a hand signal." He needed both hands to keep his body from sliding down the side of the mountain.

"We put Bobby Watson down," said Zullick. "It was really loose shale. Every step he would take, he would go back two," Zullick observed. "It was a constant battle for him to work his way over to the aircraft."

As Watson climbed he found that the ax did nothing to help him gain his footing and advance to the plane's position. It was at least a sixty-degree grade, doable for Watson. "I'd been living in Alaska for eight years, hunting, chasing sheep and goats and everything else," said Watson. "I was used to throwing my body weight around on the sides of hills and cliffs." The physically fit blond-haired, blue-eyed, five-foot-ten-inch-tall rescue swimmer weighed one hundred and seventy pounds. He was as comfortable in the water as he was on a cliff.

Yet, as he worked his way up to the right side of what was left of the plane, he feared what he could not control. "The thing that was scary was once I got to the plane, I was worried it would take me down the side of the mountain." He carefully made his way up to the underside of the aircraft. Before he crossed in front and over it to look inside, he said his prayers. "Lord, keep my mind right for what I'm fixing to see— I could tell the front of the plane was gone—don't let the devastation overwhelm me."

"WE TRIED TO STAY AS CLOSE TO HIM as we could so we could watch him," said Zullick of the helicopter's proximity to the mountainside and their rescue swimmer. "I'm constantly trying to watch to give us a way out." The visibility at times was two hundred yards, then reduced to fifty yards or less as the fog continued to rise or descend with regularity.

"Bobby asked us to stay away from the wreckage because it was very unstable and he felt the rotor wash would take the plane right down the side of the mountain," Zullick recalled. "As we tried to maintain hover station, we got engulfed, the fog had descended upon us. We're visual creatures and now we can't see anything so you don't know where you're at." He understood why the copilot was distressed.

Zullick, forty, was a more experienced pilot who enlisted when he was seventeen years old and served as an airman before becoming a pilot. He had flown in the first Gulf War as an Army pilot then transitioned into the Coast Guard where he flew at Traverse City, Michigan, and Sitka, Alaska, before flying from Kodiak. Each air station was known for challenging weather and conditions.

Zullick understood his copilot's panic and tried to calm him. "Andy Delgado really had his hands full, and I think was getting pretty excited, rightfully so, trying to maintain a hover while he can't see anything," he said. "Bottom line we can't move anywhere, otherwise, we're going to crash into the side of this mountain."

Delgado started to move the flight controls around erratically. "I came onto the controls with him and remember looking down between my feet through the chin bubble [a small window], and just barely seeing the outline of a rock, the only visual reference that I had to maintain," Zullick explained. "I had configured my instruments for a no-reference hover, hoping that would not happen." He thought, *If I keep that rock in the same position, between my feet, life is good.* "In that eight to ten seconds a lot can happen," Zullick recalled of his decision to grab the flight controls and override the copilot to take over control of the helicopter. The aircraft's radar altimeter provided a vertical reference, not an indication of lateral distance from the side of the cliff face they hovered next to. "You only know before you go into the clouds. We were maybe ten feet; the margin of error was zero. If we were going to drift, we wanted to drift to the left, not to the right, right was into the cliff. Now, we can't see, we don't know where the wreckage is, we don't know where the swimmer is." Except for the visual on the rock, they could not accurately sense which direction they were drifting.

"He was just slamming those controls into my hands, so erratically. I really thought that if we don't see something soon, we're going to crash this helicopter," Zullick stated. "I felt those controls hitting the palms of my hands, and for a microsecond I thought about my hand being on my pregnant wife's stomach earlier that evening and that baby was kicking it. I thought, *I'm never going to see this baby.* Then I realized the way I'm going to see this baby is if I hold this helicopter in a steady hover. Between the two of us, we were able to do that."

Just as quickly as the fog descended upon them it was gone. "Delgado said, 'I can see, I can see, I can see,' and came back on the controls. We were all fat, dumb, and happy again," Zullick recalled. "It is an extremely, extremely demanding skill that Coast Guard pilots practice and are trained to transition to their instruments, usually over the open ocean. We were reverting to that in a mountain canyon. It lasted maybe eight to ten seconds, but it seemed like an eternity."

WATSON, HAVING FINISHED HIS PRAYER, came around the front corner of the plane. "The pilot and the guy who was flying in the copilot seat were demolished. I went around, trying to work my way back to the cabin area to see if anyone down inside was alive. Sure enough a hand was waving," exclaimed Watson. "I remember when I first saw the plane from the helicopter, I thought it was a piece of material flapping in the breeze. It had been a hand the whole time."

"We found life where we didn't think it would exist," said Zullick.

The woman's situation was dire. "It was as if you put your face into your knees and left yourself there for fourteen hours in snow and rain, wearing only neoprene waders, a sweatshirt, and windbreaker. She'd been trapped there, and I thought to myself, *Oh my God, there's somebody alive.*"

He asked the survivor her name.

"Linda."

Watson got on the radio and yelled, "Game on, gentlemen, game on. We have a live one!"

The radios were buzzing with activity and conversation, wanting the report repeated, confirmed. "Are you kidding me?" he heard back. "Nope, get people rolling," Watson answered.

His focus was now on figuring out a way to get Linda out of the wreckage. The door, a likely exit, was at the bottom of the plane and cut off. Watson decided he'd have to use the crash ax to cut through the plane and make an exit. He started working on that, nervous about hitting her with it. It was a precarious job, too close to her shoulder. Watson found a sleeping bag and gently stuffed it between her and where he needed to chop, six inches away.

He kept the radio nearby. "Everybody was trying to spool up and do the right thing. I heard them tell me that we could have a cliff rescue team out of Juneau here in four hours," Watson recalled. "I told them this will be over in two. These people don't have time."

He worked quickly and carefully, cutting a spare, or rib, of the Cessna's airframe by striking it hard. By the third strike, he busted through it and peeled back the skin of the plane like a can opener. He created a gap the size of a four-person dining-room tabletop.

"Once that area was down, the rest of the cabin was exposed and I could see another woman in there. 'What's her name?'"

"Ellen," Linda said.

"OK, Ellen, we're going to get you out," Watson said with confidence, despite the fact that he heard her moaning and could tell she was in critical condition.

He turned his focus back to Linda. She would be the first survivor he could evacuate.

"At first, I thought her eye was missing, the orbital looked smashed. Her left leg looked snapped, spun around inside the waders, pretty nasty looking. But, thank God for the waders, they kept everything in place," said Watson as he worked gently to remove her. He noticed a stable area above the plane, ideal to keep her safe until he had help to take her down the mountain.

"He carried her fifty feet up the near vertical face, well clear of the wreckage and placed her in a small depression," according to a written report from Captain E. D. Nelson, commanding officer of Air Station Kodiak. "He then descended back to the wreckage and recovered seat cushions and a sleeping bag that he used to provide the survivor additional comfort and stability on the cliff and protection from the freezing rain and sleet, staving off the early stages of hypothermia."

"If the plane did take off down the side of the mountain, at least one would have made it," Watson said. After he checked Linda to ensure she was warm and safe, he returned to extract Ellen.

After he cut through the fuselage to get closer to her, Watson assessed Ellen's condition. She had pelvic fractures. "I had experience with it, and people with these injuries never seem to do well, don't seem to make it because the body tourniquets itself for a short period of time, then they bleed to death."

DELGADO LANDED THE HELICOPTER to conserve fuel at an altitude of two thousand feet on an outcropping of rock seven hundred feet below the crash site.

"We were very excited to hear somebody was alive and then a bit later hearing there were two gals," Zullick shared. "I asked Bob what was his game plan and what can I do to help? I realized it was going to take a while. My game plan was as soon as Linda Brooks was cut out of there, I wanted to get her to King Salmon as soon as possible."

The pilots coordinated over the radio with the help of the C-130 crew and Air Station Kodiak the next steps for providing the survivors with immediate medical care after they were evacuated. Zullick also requested a second helicopter's help. He did not want to leave Watson alone with Ellen when Linda was flown from the crash site to King Salmon. Once there, Linda would be put on a life flight jet, used to transport the critically ill or injured, to Anchorage.

The weather turned snowy and windy again. Watson continued to work in the intermittent fog. He could not see the helicopter nor could they see him. By talking over the radio, he provided continuous updates to Zullick and his team. Watson expressed concern that the fuselage was extremely unstable and in danger of sliding off the cliff. He wanted to treat the survivors, who were both in critical condition and needed help getting them down the mountain. He requested his EMT kit and a litter to use to secure the first survivor before she was carried down the mountain to the waiting helicopter.

Zullick responded. He informed Watson that Delgado and Neff were to climb up the mountain to assist. They would lug what amounted to seventy pounds of gear with them.

Just before they left, Zullick learned from the C-130 that two men from the Alaskan State Trooper Mountain Rescue Team, adept at cliff rescues, had volunteered to help. They would land about twenty miles away on a dirt airstrip. Zullick asked Watson if he wanted their help too. Watson knew of the trooper's credentials. "They are very acclimated to cliff rescues and do a lot of body recoveries," Watson stated. "I know we don't have time for the Juneau cliff rescue team, but if you could, I'd like to have those two state troopers give me a hand instead of the copilot and flight mechanic who don't have the same experience those two have."

Before Delgado left the helicopter with Neff to take the gear up to Watson, Zullick expressed his concerns. He might have to leave the crash site in order to pick up the state troopers who could arrive at the dirt strip before Delgado and Neff came back down the mountain. It was imperative that Watson was not left alone when Linda was flown to King Salmon. "I'm going to be faced with a decision whether I'm going to wait for you or not to go get those troopers and bring them back here. Delgado said to me, 'You've got to do what you've got to do,'" Zullick remembered.

Once the copilot and flight mechanic were up the mountain, Zullick was given an update from the C-130 that the troopers had indeed landed. Zullick radioed Watson. How long would it take his copilot and flight mechanic to come back down?

"Forty-five minutes to an hour," answered Watson.

Zullick recalled Bob calling back again saying, "I can't wait that long, this gal is going to die."

"Are you telling me no delays are acceptable?" Zullick asked.

"Basically he said, 'No delays are acceptable,'" recalled Zullick. "Roger that Bob, that's the answer I needed."

The next thing Watson saw was the helicopter taking off. He looked down the mountainside and the flight mechanic and copilot were still on the ground climbing up toward him. "Well, that's career ending for him. Mr. Lieutenant Commander just threw in the towel," Watson told himself. "The helicopters are not supposed to be flown by one pilot. When Zullick landed back at the mountain, he was gambling again that he would not hit a rock, smash the tail. By the grace of God, he did not ding anything up."

Zullick picked up the state troopers and Jeff Meinel, the pilot of the second plane, and returned to the staging area, about seven hundred feet below the crash site.

One Alaskan trooper went up the mountain to help Watson, Delgado, and Neff who had remained there assisting Watson in stabilizing Linda and placing her in the litter. Meinel and the other trooper remained with Zullick.

Making the seven-hundred-foot trek with a survivor down the almost vertical surface was another matter. The team rigged a rope to the litter to help gradually descend it over the ice- and snow-covered shale. At points, they were resigned to slide down on their rear ends.

"We got Ms. Linda Brooks in the litter. Then we had to drag her heels in the snow in a slow, controlled descent down the side of that mountain to Mr. Zullick's aircraft, and she was gone!" said Watson.

The second HH-60J Jayhawk helicopter arrived on scene just before Zullick, Delgado, and Neff prepared to take off with their injured passenger. They briefed the incoming aircrew and made suggestions about where to lower their swimmer. On board this helicopter was a Coast Guard flight surgeon, Commander Steve Kinsley, and a corpsman from the air station's medical clinic. They would treat the remaining survivor, Ellen, during the flight to King Salmon.

Watson, the state troopers, and Meinel turned and climbed back up the mountain. When Watson learned that Meinel was the pilot of the second plane, he asked, "Are you sure you want to be here?" Jeff said he was OK and continued to help.

The second HH-60J helicopter, piloted by Lieutenant Lisa Blow, approached the mountainside to deploy the swimmer and litter.

AST2 JASON BUNCH, TWENTY-FIVE, WAS THE NEXT GUY in line at Air Station Kodiak to be called in to help. "I went to the pool and was working out a little bit and felt pretty safe because it is rare that we have to send a third swimmer out on a case," stated Bunch. "While I was there, the phone call came that they needed another aircrew." Bunch rushed to get ready to go. "When Bob says he needs help, that usually means this is big."

"I prepared myself mentally for the case as we flew through the maze of mountains," recalled Bunch. "We were at the latitude and longitude given, but we could not see the other helicopter." He realized that the copilot, Lieutenant Chris Bish, was extremely busy coordinating with the C-130 and Zullick's helicopter over the radio. Bunch took the initiative to help find the staging area. "What I ended up doing was climbing up, putting my head into the cockpit, and throwing the chart up on the console. I showed the pilot without her having to look down, as she was watching her airspeed, trying to fly and search, where I thought we should be." Lieutenant Lisa Blow took his recommended left turn into the valley. They could only go so far. Working together, they figured out another way to get to the other side of the mountain despite the low ceiling. "That was a really cool and rare experience, she was so awesome to take my direction," Bunch said.

With the assistance of the flight mechanic, Joe Miller, Bunch prepared to be lowered down. "We saw Bob Watson. He was wearing the blue dry suit coverall to protect him from the elements—it's liquid death up there—and the red TRI-SAR harness, which has a CO_2 canister to inflate the life vest if we need it, radios, flares, and survival gear."

Watson wanted to know with whom he was going to work. "For two reasons I think he wanted to know. It was a very gruesome site, something I still think about on a weekly basis, and he wanted to know he would have someone that could prepare mentally for that. The second reason was that the terrain was very, very difficult. He wanted to make sure he had a swimmer who was used to the mountains. We are swimmers, not mountaineers. But luckily, I have climbed every mountain range in Alaska. Mountains are kind of like my hobby. I think Bob was pretty relieved, he would not have to keep one eye on the swimmer, he could concentrate on the survivor."

Watson conned the helicopter into the position on the slope where he wanted the swimmer deposited so he would not have to hike up seven hundred feet.

"They sent me Jason Bunch. That was a great deal. He's a mountain-climbing machine," Watson said. "Once he hit the deck, he's wide open, working at one hundred miles per hour doing what had to be done."

"The first thing he said to me was, 'Man, I'm glad to see you here,'" recalled Bunch. "The second thing he said was, 'It's kind of ugly, you need to mentally prepare yourself.' That was experience playing on Bob's part." Bunch, a seasoned swimmer, had dealt with similar situations in the past. The physically fit, one-hundred-seventy-pound, five-foot-nine-inch-tall, dark brown-haired, blue-eyed rescue swimmer started in the profession when he was twenty-one. His first thirteen cases all involved deceased people.

"As quick as we could, we got back up to Ellen," Watson recalled. "Time was ticking away now. By 11 A.M. we had the first survivor down the mountain. It took forty-five minutes to climb back up, that made it close to noon."

The state troopers, Meinel, Watson, and Bunch all arrived back at the plane at the same time.

THE PLANE WAS SITTING IN THE NATURAL DRAINAGE flow of the mountainside in a little V-shaped area. "I'm actually very amazed that that plane didn't slide down," said Bunch. "I took my helmet off and laid it down on a rock and it just started rolling; it was deceivingly steep. It was one thing to go up, another to go down, a real eye-opener for me."

Bunch assessed Ellen's condition after being introduced by Watson. "The only reason I think she was alive due to the extent of her injuries was because her head was angled down, her feet and the rest of her body were up, above her head. She had been in a shock treatment position for over fourteen hours," Bunch described. She was extremely hypothermic. She had a head injury, multiple spine injuries, and her pelvis was crushed and twisted. Her legs had multiple fractures. "She was tough, one tough lady. She opened her eyes a few times and remembered her name."

Watson and Bunch talked to her to help her keep her wits. Bunch would tell her, "OK, Ellen this is Jason talking, you have to hang in there, stay with us."

"She needed to fight. A lot of survivors, once the Coast Guard arrive, they crash. Her will to survive was strong," said Bunch. "Even when she wasn't awake, you still talk to her, 'OK Ellen, stay strong, we have five more minutes to get you to the plane, there's a surgeon down there waiting for you.' She didn't know where she was. She did know that her husband was dead because his foot was right there in front of her face. His boots were different from the others." Watson had covered his foot by putting a blanket over it.

"One of us had to step inside the shifting plane to get Ellen out and up in front of the plane," stated Watson. Wires from the wreckage were wrapped around her, preventing the extraction. Bunch went since he was the smallest. They made a human chain, holding onto each other, with the troopers off to the side of the plane. Bunch removed some of the wires and one of the other troopers reached around and got what was left.

Ellen was given oxygen and fitted with a c-collar to stabilize her head and neck when the crew slid her into a hypothermia bag prepositioned on the Stokes litter. "It was a very smooth transition," Bunch said. "She did know that we were there. She was alert enough to focus and look us in the eyes. She would go in and out, in and out. She was extremely fatigued, a very hurting survivor."

It was a critical time. How to best to transport Ellen and from where on the mountainside to get her into the helicopter as soon as possible? Once the rescuers got her into the litter, they faced a slippery descent of at least five hundred feet.

"I did not want to hoist her from right here," stated Watson, who had been asked about hoisting her near the plane. "We needed to find a better location before we do this. There was no way I was going to kill four of us for one."

"Bob and I looked at the whole plan and felt that the only option was to take her down the mountain," said Bunch.

The rescuers did all they could medically to treat her before they traveled rapidly but safely down the mountain. Bunch and Watson took the top position, behind her head to protect it from the falling rocks and to control the speed of the litter's descent. The troopers took the lower position.

"When we got near the bottom, she was at her wit's end. That was probably very painful and a lot of effort on her part. She was still conscious. She looked at me once. Then we hoisted her," said Bunch.

Ellen was delivered into the helicopter at the first possible hoisting site. The flight surgeon and corpsman worked on her during the whole flight back to King Salmon.

The rescuers had meanwhile returned to the airplane to retrieve the other two bodies, that of the pilot, Maxey, and Ellen's husband, Allen.

"Jeff worked all day to help us retrieve bodies. Maxey and Ellen's husband were torn up pretty good," Watson said. "I remember getting back into the helicopter, between the body bags, and Jeff was sitting in the rescue swimmer's chair. The weight of it all finally hit him. He put his head in his hands and started to cry. He'd known Maxey for quite a while."

WATSON RETURNED HOME, AND COMFORTED by his wife, summarized what had happened in the last eighteen hours. "You try not to second-guess yourself, you're there to help them and do the best you can," Watson admitted. "We are type A personalities and most critical of ourselves."

Hearing that Ellen had died, Watson wondered if he had made the right decision about where to hoist her, knowing that time was critical. He did not want the airplane to blow down the mountain putting all of their lives at risk. He wondered, *What if we did take the chance?* The Coast Guard flight surgeon who treated Ellen told Watson that besides her severe injuries, "Her time was her time."

FOR HIS EXTRAORDINARY HEROISM PARTICIPATING in the aerial flight on the morning of August 24, 2000, Watson was awarded his second Distinguished Flying Cross.

Of all that he has done and been recognized for, Watson is most proud of "my family. My wife, Lori Watson, she's the hero. When somebody loves you enough to let you do what you want to do . . . as long as you show back up," said Watson. Laughing and genuine, he said he never pushed his son, Nicholas, to go into the Coast Guard airman program. Nicholas, whose grandfather was a member of the U.S. Navy Underwater Demolition Team (UDT or Navy Seals), has started on his own journey to become a Coast Guard helicopter rescue swimmer. For Bob Watson, his philosophy is, "Enjoy what you are doing, this isn't a rehearsal, go ahead and live it . . . Wow, what a ride."

JASON BUNCH, SINCE PROMOTED TO AST1, was not aware until the day after returning from the rescue mission that Ellen had died. He had a hard time dealing with the news. He was awarded the Coast Guard Achievement Medal for his efforts to save her life.

Now he is an instructor at the Elizabeth City training facility where he trains prospective swimmers and includes a classroom lecture to provide students with awareness of this side of the rescue.

"I tell my students at the AST A School parts of this case so they can walk away with a lesson learned," said Bunch. "The lesson is about critical incident stress. Are you ready for this? Are you ready for the kind of emotions you could have after such a case? What are you going to do, fill your wife's brain with these kinds of stories? She can't fathom what you're telling her, and all you're going to do is scare her. Just give her the short and skinny of it and move on . . . You try to leave a lot of this at work; if you need to talk, you find your boys in the AST shop. We have your back; we'll be there for you. They have to know that it is not all glory or big medals; there are some things that are going to happen that are hard to live with."

Bunch explained that as long as you can say in your heart that you did every possible thing you could, all the "huffing and puffing"—you did your job, even if it did not pan out. "A lot of us can relate, we're here for you," said Bunch. "It is very burdensome to have to deal with people who are at the end of their rope with luck, good people. Those feelings are normal; it is OK that it is burdensome. Especially when they look you in the eyes with an expression that says, 'OK, you have me, I trust you,' and then you still let them down."

Bunch credits Watson, John Hall, Will Milam, and Tim Adams as some of the other rescue swimmers who were his best friends in Kodiak. Fellows who had experience beyond his and knew, understood, that some cases could bother or stick with swimmers, like this one. On active duty for thirteen years, seven of which were at Air Station Kodiak as a helicopter rescue swimmer, the most noteworthy award he has received was the Air Medal and Alaska Emergency Medical Service Provider of the Year for the rescue of an injured crewman aboard a vessel located 250 miles from Adak, Alaska. The rescue took over twenty-six hours.

Bunch has been involved in a variety of search and rescue scenarios, including stranded or lost hikers, overturned fishing vessels, vessels taking on water, vessels on fire, people in the water, bear attacks, and plane crashes. He has also flown as the EMT during helicopter medical evacuations with patients who suffered from ailments such as severe appendicitis, broken bones, severed limbs, heart attacks, and hypothermic survivors.

Bunch and his wife, Kimberly, have a three-year-old son, Dawson. One day they hope to return to Alaska and raise their son.

LIEUTENANT ANDY DELGADO AND AMT3 John Neff were each honored for their service with the Air Medal. "Watson is pretty well known throughout the Coast Guard; it was an honor to fly with him," said Neff. "He is quiet, does not appear to be or want to pass for a hero type. With all that he has done, I would not be surprised if he was one of the most decorated men in the service."

"The amount of physical exertion that was required of Bob Watson, the oldest swimmer in the shop, was intense. Nobody was in better condition than him, and he was drained. He was worn out from bringing Linda Brooks down," recalled Zullick. "'Hey, Bob, how are you doing? I'll be all right.' That's how he is."

Lessons learned? "It goes back to it's a team exercise until the swimmer leaves the plane. There is no more teamwork; they are on their own down there. The Coast Guard, we really hang them out there. They are a very young and adrenaline-pushed crowd of guys," stated Zullick. "I've had situations where I won't put them out there if—it's beyond my flying skills to get you back in this aircraft," Zullick said. "They say, 'Put me in, put me in,' and I'll say, 'No, you're not going out, I don't have the ability to get you back.'"

Zullick has exchanged Christmas cards with Linda Brooks since the accident. Annually, close to the August 24 anniversary of her rescue, he receives an e-mail from her too. Over the years he has kept next to his work desk one of his most treasured letters, one she wrote while still in the hospital with her jaw wired (excerpted with permission from Linda Brooks):

Dear Russ,

I know my family has been in touch but I also have wanted to write. But, wow, how do you ever find the words to thank someone for saving their life. I know that there were many involved and I am so grateful to all of you, your expertise, perseverance, kindness, extraordinary efforts and just for being there for us. In addition, I believe there was someone who said it just wasn't my time and I am convinced our oldest son, who died in 1990, was a helper. But, it was this incredibly difficult rescue that you accomplished that made it possible for me to be with my loving family again. Thank you from the bottom of my heart!!

Linda

"At that time and place in the Coast Guard, in 2000, I don't think I could have had any more talent put together at any one time. They had phenomenal leaders, Senior Chief Olav Leavelle and Chief George Cavallo," said Zullick. "I had the top-dog swimmer in the shop with me, and John Neff is an extremely competent flight mechanic."

"I had a newer copilot with me that had never been in those types of conditions. That's not by any means to say that Andy Delgado was a weak pilot; it's just that he had not had the Alaska experience at that time. What I tell kids, pilots coming to Kodiak, 'Welcome to the NFL, this is hands down the hardest flying you will ever do in your life. You will never be more challenged than you are going to be up here,'" Zullick said.

Commander Russell H. Zullick III grew up hunting and fishing with his father and grandfather who were part Iroquois. Since he was five years old, he had dreamed of living and fishing in Alaska. Zullick flew his last flight in Alaska accumulating 5,949.5 flight hours on June 17, 2005. He accepted orders to Coast Guard District 13 in Seattle to serve as chief of response for Sector Seattle. Zullick, his wife, Deborah, and their five-year-old son, Russell IV, live on Bainbridge Island.

On the potential loss of his career by single-handedly piloting the helicopter during the rescue, he said, "They didn't know if they were going to court-martial me or give me an award." Zullick was awarded the Distinguished Flying Cross for his extraordinary achievements.

14

SAINTS OVER NEW ORLEANS

You take people for granted in peacetime operations; then when a disaster strikes and they have to step up to the plate and step into the breach, you realize, wow, these are the most talented, dedicated people that America has to offer and somehow we got them into the Coast Guard. It makes you very proud.

—Captain Bruce Jones, commanding officer,
Coast Guard Air Station New Orleans

COAST GUARD HELICOPTER RESCUE SWIMMER AST3 Matt Laub, twenty-four, was about to save a career's worth of lives in just one day. His first two years in the profession he described as an unremarkable period of service, not spectacular or "hot" like that of other rescue swimmers. He had a couple medical evacuations to his credit, nothing he would bother talking about.

"I was the guy who was on duty and if I went home or traded my duty day, I would have missed it, the big case. Just always in the wrong place at the wrong time," Laub said. All that changed the morning of

August 30, 2005. Hurricane Katrina, at one stage a Category 5 hurricane, weakened before it came ashore the day before, obliterating Gulf Coast regions from Louisiana to Alabama. According to the Coast Guard, it created a ninety-thousand-square-mile area of destruction, larger than the size of Great Britain.

Laub worked at Air Station Savannah in Georgia. He watched with a few others in the AST shop as television images of Hurricane Katrina's wrath were broadcast across the world. They learned that the New Orleans levees had been breached. Overnight, neighborhoods were under as much as twenty feet of water.

The complete devastation of New Orleans and towns all along and inland from the impacted coasts was something he could not begin to fathom from television. As Laub watched, his concern grew for the people of the Gulf Coast and his fellow Coast Guard members working non-stop on scene to rescue thousands of displaced Americans. Suddenly the AST shop chief entered the room and bellowed, "Who wants to go down to Mobile today?

"I was on a plane two hours later," Laub said. He had volunteered to go to ground zero. With only enough time to go home, pack a bag of belongings and his digital camera, the one thing he really wanted to have with him, he returned to Air Station Savannah for the flight down.

Laub had joined the Coast Guard on September 4, 2001, right after graduating from high school. Refreshingly innocent, yet strong in his convictions, the brown-haired blue-eyed gentleman grew up in Front Royal, Virginia. He had never traveled very far. A hometown buddy, Shannon Brugh, graduated four years before Laub and now worked as a Coast Guard rescue swimmer. When Laub visited his friend and learned more about the job, it was enough to convince the five-foot-eleven-inch-tall, 155-pound high school senior that this was what he wanted to do. Laub signed up. During his first week in boot camp, the tragic events of September 11 happened. He believed with new conviction that he was in the right place and graduated. His assignment before going to the AST school was as a seaman aboard the Coast Guard icebreaker *Polar Sea*. Laub became a world traveler while aboard the ship, which made many port calls, including Antarctica, Australia, and Hawaii. In 2003, Laub qualified as a rescue swimmer. With this accomplishment and as was the tradition, he felt the long-awaited chill of victory. "They strapped me in one of the rescue litters and poured a bunch of ice on my head as a 'Welcome, good job,'" Laub laughed.

The Coast Guard Falcon jet arrived at Air Station Savannah around 3 P.M. that afternoon from Air Station Cape Cod. Laub joined two pilots and a flight mechanic for their mission to work in the damaged Gulf region. He did not know how long he would be gone nor did he really comprehend the extent of the ruins, waste, and hazards he would find within arm's length. He was a member of just one aircrew among thousands of Coast Guard men and women, boats, ships, and aircraft responding en masse to the region.

ON SATURDAY, AUGUST 27, 2005, two days before the hurricane made landfall, the commanding officer of Air Station New Orleans, Captain Bruce Jones, had evacuated all nonessential personnel. Colocated at Naval Air Station Belle Chasse, the Coast Guard air station was equipped with five HH-65B Dolphin helicopters and one hundred ten officers and enlisted personnel. Five "flyaway" crews remained with the helicopters to take the aircraft to safer areas before the hurricane hit.

Coast Guard families knew the drill. They had evacuated before for previous storms and did so for this one. Like many other spouses, Jones's wife, Linda, and their three boys took their German shepherd and a few personal belongings they had packed into their car and drove west. "We had the typical evacuation load, clothes for three days and dog food, some photos and papers," Linda said. They planned to spend the night at a familiar hotel in Lake Charles, Louisiana, a place they had evacuated to before with other Coast Guard families since moving to New Orleans in the summer of 2003. "When we got on the road, three o'clock Sunday morning, we had moved not even two miles in four hours," Linda said. "I had to make a quick decision, we just had to get off the road. We turned around and headed east. I called friends, a retired Coast Guard family in Opelika, Alabama, asked them if we could come to their house. They said 'sure.'" Everywhere across the South, the spread of families evacuating from the hurricane's projected impact zone was evident by congested highways and no fuel.

Jana Refowitz, twenty-nine, a graduate assistant and MBA student at Loyola University in New Orleans, was the wife of Lieutenant Craig O'Brien, thirty-two, a helicopter pilot at the New Orleans Air Station.

They were able to evacuate together because O'Brien was not a member of the flyaway aircrews. She knew he was likely to get recalled once the hurricane blew in. Married for two years, and living in their first home together, she worried that they would lose everything. Her home was in a flood zone. They scrambled on Saturday to secure their belongings on the second floor or in closets and evacuate. "It really is an effort mentally and physically to evacuate," said Jana. "I left with flip-flops, some stuff for the dog, and important documents. Half the time you're wondering if you're going to get damage or looted with the city empty." They drove through the night Saturday and arrived at their familiar evacuation hotel in Lake Charles. They would meet two other Coast Guard families. "This time it was a little more stressful, you actually saw the hurricane coming to New Orleans on TV and thought, *Huh, that's weird*." Not really wanting to turn off the TV, she went to bed wondering if she would have a house after the storm passed.

Sunday morning, August 28, Captain Jones and the flyaway aircrews discussed departure times. They would stay in the area as long as possible to provide prehurricane search and rescue response. He decided to send two aircraft to Coast Guard Air Station Houston early. The remaining three would leave midafternoon. Their goal was to stage the helicopters as close as possible to areas where the hurricane was going to hit yet as far away from its threat to minimize the potential damage to the aircraft and flyaway crews. Everyone would immediately return to the area and start search and rescue operations as soon as weather conditions permitted.

AST2 Chris Monville was the rescue swimmer aboard one of the two helicopters sent to Houston. The thirty-three-year-old had worked in New Orleans for the past year. He specifically requested the assignment to be closer to his six-year-old daughter, Hannah, who lived in Houston.

Monville grew up in the Great Lakes area in Bay City, Michigan. He spent four years in the Marine Corps as a head machine gunner and was mobilized overseas many times. He was stationed in Hawaii where he was a lifeguard on the beach. Comfortable in the water, he had been a competitive swimmer since he was eleven years old. After he left the Marine Corps he was interested in getting back into another military service. Monville talked to a Coast Guard recruiter and found out about rescue swimmers and immediately knew that was what he wanted to do. At twenty-six, he joined the Coast Guard. "I always loved the whole rescue aspect of being in the water. Putting that together with the military and jumping from a helicopter was exciting and rewarding at the same time," Monville said.

Monville's fiancée was planning a late September wedding in Michigan. First, he knew he would have to see what Hurricane Katrina's wrath would bring.

THE REMAINING THREE HELICOPTERS were prestaged in Lake Charles. Jones piloted one of them with Lieutenant Junior Grade Bill Dunbar, Lieutenant Commander Tim Tobiasz, flight mechanic AMT3 John Jamison and rescue swimmer AMT3 Dave Foreman.

The Coast Guard had closed ports and waterways along the Gulf Coast and evacuated its personnel and resources in preparation for Hurricane Katrina's landfall the next morning. "More than 40 Coast Guard aircraft from units along the entire eastern seaboard . . . 30 small boats, patrol boats and cutters are positioning themselves in staging areas around the projected impact area—from Jacksonville, Florida to Houston—making preparations to conduct immediate post-hurricane search, rescue and humanitarian aid operations, waterway impact assessments and waterway reconstitution operations . . . Extensive damage and closures to ports and waterways throughout the central Gulf coast should be expected," according to a Coast Guard press release distributed the evening of August 28.

Early Monday morning, August 29, Captain Jones reviewed the track of the storm with the other pilots. He directed the helicopters in Houston to return and regroup with the others in Lake Charles. Together, all five helicopters flew to Houma, Louisiana, a rural town thirty-five miles southwest of New Orleans. "We landed there with about sixty knots of wind, and we shut down to await enough time to pass before we felt it would be safe to head to New Orleans," Jones said. They had encountered tropical storm force weather and visibility was decreased ranging from two and five miles. After refueling the helicopters, the crews evaluated launching into the southwest side of the storm to begin recovery operations. "We launched about 2 P.M. our first two helicopters from Houma with instructions to go southeast toward Grand Isle and the mouth of the Mississippi River and work our way up from the mouth of the Mississippi towards the city, staying on the rear of the hurricane with safe wind levels and look for survivors along the way."

Jones, with the remaining helicopters, flew in to assess the condition of Air Station New Orleans. "We made phone calls to every number we could think of to get the status of the city and the status of our airfield to make sure it wasn't flooded and the fuel truck was usable, not in a ditch somewhere," Jones said. He had been unable to get answers; no one was answering phones or satellite communications, and they did not have access to television. They were on their own.

The flyaway crews did not know the extent of damage, only that the hurricane had made landfall. As they approached, they got their first glimpse of a portion of the annihilation. Katrina's winds had peeled back the hangar roof and flooded the facility with rain.

Commander Scott Kitchen, executive officer (XO) of the air station, disembarked to inspect it with Lieutenant Commander Tobiasz, operations officer. "As OPS I had to get the operations center up and running, and the XO had to assess the base for damage," Tobiasz said. "The air station had to be reopened if we were to sustain SAR operations after the first few flights. We would need gas, places to sleep, an operations center." It was a blessing that the mission's essential airfield and aircraft ramp were usable, and the fuel truck was fine.

They were able to immediately start rescue operations working from the powerless air station knowing they could refuel the aircraft. A ground inspection later revealed that most shop spaces were uninhabitable because of flooding. They would make do.

The two helicopters tasked with flying up the Mississippi River reported back to Jones. From Venice, Louisiana, northward along the whole mouth of the river from the Gulf Coast up to New Orleans was just devastated, Jones said. "They immediately started picking up survivors. The very first rescue recorded by any helicopter crew from any agency or service was around 2:51 P.M. in Port Sulphur, Louisiana. The Coast Guard helicopter recovered a mother, her four-month-old baby, and grandmother in a flooded skiff jammed under a tree in floodwaters."

Monville, aboard the second helicopter in the area, flew with AMT3 Mike Colbath a flight mechanic, and pilots Lieutenant Olav Saboe who was the assistant engineering officer for the air station, and Lieutenant Junior Grade Shay Williams. Searching at an altitude of approximately three hundred feet, they looked for anybody who needed help. "We weren't seeing anything, no movement, nobody," Monville said. "Every time we found a subdivision, the water was all the way up to the shingles. We were flying looking down at rooftops for people. We found our first house. There he was a guy and a dog and a big hole he'd cut through the roof. We commenced hoisting right then and there. It pretty much began and it did not stop. Other than for sleep, for the next four days we didn't stop."

"Sometimes we'd fly looking for anybody in the area we were assigned to cover or we'd get calls asking who's in this area and we'd call back and then they would give us a position," said Monville. "For instance, we had a call to help a lady on a shrimp boat with this six-inch gash all the way down to the bone and her femur was broken." The circumstances were precarious with a lot of rigging in the hoist zone. The woman was in a position underneath an overhang. Monville stuck his head out to give the flight mechanic directional hand signals. Colbath had anticipated how Monville would want the rescue basket hoisted. He understood the intent of the swimmer's really slow ready-for-pickup hand signal, and with diligence, slowly lifted the woman into the cabin without getting her entangled in the nets and rigging. "It was a perfect hoist in not so perfect conditions. It was really cool, because we know how each other works and know what to expect even in a situation like that; things went really smooth," Monville said.

"That was easy. It steadily got worse," said Monville of the first couple of rescues. That same morning the aircrew went to Saint Bernard High School where local firefighters and Good Samaritans were helping people needing critical care. The school's second floor was an ideal location for people to go to get out of the floods. When the aircrew arrived, about four hundred people had gathered inside.

Monville worked with the rescue personnel there to triage the crowd. "We'd carry them out of a window or off the roof to hoist them into the helicopter. People who could not walk, we'd carry them," Monville said. "This is the point where it starts to mentally get to us, the rescuer, how do you pick and choose from everyone who goes? You know that we'd take the injured, the elderly, women, and children first, but after that how do you choose?"

It was a bad situation. The bathrooms did not work. There was no food, and people were stealing from each other. "That was the first day. I think these guys were frustrated; they saw what had happened to their homes, and they had nothing to go back to. They just wanted out of there," Monville said. "I'd have to explain that we could only take so many at a time, you're walking, breathing, talking—you're fine. We have to take the sick first. Everyone comes to you, and they all have a story. You have to sift through all this, triage process, and take the worst out first."

The aircrew took the sick from the high school to a nearby hospital or other dry location. "They were taken out of a bad situation and taken to a place that was a little better, like Belle Chasse High School where EMS [emergency medical services] was staged," Monville said. He worked there until the pilots called him to go.

Simultaneously, other Coast Guard units' search and rescue response and capabilities grew in magnitude and force, saturating the region. Hundreds of people were saved when the first windows of opportunity opened as the storm passed that Monday afternoon and evening.

After the levees broke, water surged into already devastated areas. Tropical storm conditions continued blowing forty knots of wind with gusts to fifty-five the rest of the afternoon and into that evening.

During the evening of August 29, all five Air Station New Orleans crews, two Air Station Houston, and four helicopters from the Coast Guard ATC in Mobile were engaged in rescue operations.

By 11:30 P.M. the Air Station New Orleans helicopters had exceeded maximum flight time limits and had to land. "Without any fresh crews available to pilot aircraft, bagged crews slept as best they could and were airborne again beginning at 0705 on 30 August," Jones wrote. "Meanwhile, Houston and Mobile helicopters continued operations throughout the night."

The floods saturated every niche. Water flooded homes to rooftops and tractor-trailers sank, highways and byways were awash, and waters spilled into the third and fourth floors of buildings and apartment complexes. People scrambled to higher ground seeking shelter in their attics or on roofs.

HELICOPTER RESCUE CREWS CONVERGED on the disaster area from the Coast Guard, U.S. Army and Army National Guard, U.S. Navy, and U.S. Customs and Border Protection. The Air Force PJs worked from three PavHocs helicopters and the U.S. Marine Corps used an H-53 helicopter team from the USS *Bataan*.

Thousands of additional active duty and reserve Coast Guard service members and small boats were recalled to help from as far away as Barbers

Point, Hawaii. Coast Guard cutters and small boats were positioned off the coasts of Louisiana, Mississippi, and Alabama to join the search and rescue efforts and to provide communications and fueling stations for aircraft. Coast Guard Maritime Safety and Security Teams (MSST), Port Security Units (PSU), Marine Safety personnel, and Coast Guard Auxiliary volunteers joined forces along with Coast Guard Stations along the Gulf Coast to help people in need. Other Coast Guard members worked with petroleum industry representatives to survey damage to offshore oil platforms.

Jana Refowitz's husband, Lieutenant Craig O'Brien, was recalled to return to work in Alexandria, Louisiana, as Air Station New Orleans's representative. A temporary headquarters was set up at a hotel there for the Coast Guard relief efforts. "We get to Alexandria, and he literally goes to work that minute and through the night," Jana said. "Late Monday night he came up to our room and said, 'I'm leaving.'"

"I gave him all of our food and snacks. He shoved it into a flight bag," said Jana. "They were burning through crews, I had no sense of what was really going on with our house, and it still wasn't clear that you could not go back. There were so many unknowns, all I knew was my husband was leaving." She had no idea when they would get back together but thought it would be a lot sooner than it turned out.

EARLY TUESDAY MORNING, AUGUST 30, Monville was airborne again. For over nine hours he flew with the same aircrew he had worked rescues with the previous day before flying with Lieutenant Huberty, Lieutenant Dill, and flight mechanics AVI2 Augustine and AET2 Roberts later in the day. The aircrews were assigned to the Ninth Ward and other low-income neighborhoods. In these areas, the water was so high that from the air they saw only the roofs of submerged cars. They slowly flew over four identical apartment buildings and noticed men wading in chest-deep water. The pilots went into a hover, and the flight mechanic lowered Monville to assist. The men were evacuated by rescue basket while Monville stayed below to find others.

While he walked in the water toward one of the buildings, Monville could feel bushes and debris touching his legs in the water, things he could not see. Over about seventy yards away, a dad with his young son and teenage daughter waved to him from a second-floor window. He waded over toward them. Upon closer inspection he saw that the water was three-quarters of the way up their front door. He had to convince them to come down to the first floor, not wanting them to jump into the debris-filled water and risk injury. He does not know how they got the door open, but they did. "The daughter came out, she was the only one who wanted to leave. Dad said he would stay with the young son. He did not want to go. She kind of waded out, and I reached over and grabbed her. As I walked over to the rescue basket, she was petrified, clinging onto my neck like there was no tomorrow. We hoisted her up."

The pilots repositioned the helicopter a couple of buildings over to continue rescuing people. "There were hundreds of people on top of this apartment building. Once again, they put me down on the roof, and I just started plucking babies and moms, one after the other. On that first rooftop, there must have been twenty-six people, all babies and moms," Monville said.

Working in an urban environment was something very different for the aircrews. The swimmers were lowered to black tar roofs, drenched in sunshine, which raised temperatures above ninety degrees. The air was thick with humidity. They wore shorty wet suits, the TRI-SAR harness, knee pads, and leather boots.

"We very rarely wear knee pads, but with working on roofs and tearing apart shingles our knees were getting torn up," Monville said. "The worst part was the heat and not having enough water. I could not drink enough water, and [I was] sweating to the point that it was insane. Everybody wanted off and wanted off now. Young males were probably the worst. They would come up and were very aggressive. People were under the influence of drugs and alcohol, you could tell by looking at them; they didn't care about anybody in the world except for themselves. They would push kids out of the way to try and get in the basket. I held grown men back, telling them 'No,' and putting children in."

During such encounters, Monville was verbally threatened while trying to do his job. He had to think about his own safety now too. Like all rescuers working there, he was fatigued from not sleeping properly at night and sweated profusely all day. To help him maintain 100 percent control of the situation, he would ask the biggest guy in the area to help with crowd control. To help care for those they could not take into the overloaded helicopters, they brought some nourishment.

"We would always bring down a big case of water and MREs [military Meals Ready to Eat] to help the people who were left behind until we could come back," said Monville. "Some of these people were suffering from heat exhaustion, sitting on top of black rooftops with no shade for days."

"Probably the worst part about it was that as rescuers, we're up there risking our lives to save these people who we don't know, and we don't even know what our own houses look like, and we're thinking about our own families at the same time while they are being hostile with me," Monville said. "Until you get them up in the helicopter and they are flying away, these people say 'Wow, it's not just me and my neighborhood.' They see how severe the devastation is, how far it stretches across, and they realize it's everywhere. They see the other thousands of people and their jaws drop. It's just amazing to look at them. They didn't have any idea of how bad it was."

TUESDAY AFTERNOON, AST3 MATT LAUB; Lieutenant Steve Foran, pilot in charge; Lieutenant Ryan Allen, copilot; and AMT1 Bill Breiner, flight mechanic, arrived from Savannah and deplaned in Mobile. Laub's eyes widened with amazement. A chaotic scene was in progress at the usually subdued Aviation Training Center. ATC had morphed into a staging area for Coast Guard aircrews flying in from around the country to help. "It was crazy when we got there, helicopters all over the place, it had that energy going on like you're in the middle of Times Square, like wow," said Laub. The four men checked in with the operations center before making do with one room, cots, and two beds to try to get a few hours of sleep before they would be airborne.

Late that same evening Linda Jones heard from her husband for the first time since the hurricane hit. "I spoke to Bruce for about one minute. He basically said, 'Figure out where you want to go for the year because it doesn't look like you'll be coming back here.'"

Jana never knew when she might talk with her husband again. "I literally had my cell phone attached to me, I went to the bathroom with it, I never knew when I could hear from him," said Jana. "I was fortunate because the hotel was where the Coast Guard had set up and they had morning briefs."

Sometime early Tuesday she did get a short phone call. Jana was able to speak with her husband again for just a few minutes over the next four days. She kept busy staying current via the Internet, even connecting with her neighborhood watch list. With phones still out, she was able to provide her neighbors, who evacuated, with information she received from the hotel briefs and also exchange with the Coast Guard their concerns for loved ones left behind.

AROUND 1 A.M. WEDNESDAY MORNING, August 31, the Savannah aircrew awoke, not having slept much. They knew as soon as an aircraft was assigned, they would fly to the destroyed foundations of a homeland civilization. In hindsight, they would work like they never had before.

They walked into the Air Station Mobile Operations Center for assignment. They were tasked to go to Air Station New Orleans and assist in the massive search and rescue operation in progress.

Laub was excited to finally work his big case. He did not realize he was on the front lines of the Coast Guard's largest search and rescue mission in its 216-year history.

Before dawn the Savannah aircrew was airborne from Mobile for the forty-minute flight. Within the hour, they checked in with the operation center for tasking and an operational update. Unless assigned to a critical mission the mantra was "go out over the city and rescue people."

The rescue teams, immediately on scene behind the eye of the hurricane, had been running on adrenaline over the past forty-eight hours, picking up as many people as fast and as safely as they could by air, water, and land. Coast Guardsmen and women had already saved 1,120 people by Coast Guard helicopter alone from Monday afternoon to the break of dawn on Wednesday. That number would increase sevenfold over the course of the next eight days as thousands more were rescued.

The Coast Guard air station and other responding units from many different agencies and departments had received literally thousands of specific missions tasking from a variety of sources.

It would only take two minutes for helicopters launching from Air Station New Orleans to get over the city and find thousands of people needing rescue. From an aerial perspective even without specific prioritization, it was not hard to determine where to start. Based on situational awareness and experience from traditional search and rescue profiles, aircrews were able to respond first to those in greater apparent need.

Every day the situation changed. Early on, focus areas included Saint Bernard Parish (county) and eastern New Orleans's Ninth Ward. After the third and fourth days the housing projects near the Superdome were flooded too. Hundreds of people who didn't necessarily need help the first couple of days waved for it now. Those who rode out the storm realized that after about the fourth day the floodwaters were not receding; they were without food and water and suffered from dehydration. Now, they too wanted help. "Places you'd fly over one day, there was no one waving for help, you'd fly over it the next day and they needed help," Jones said.

"In a situation like Katrina, I was very comfortable as commanding officer sending my crews over the city knowing that we might have very difficult times communicating with each other and up our chain of command," Jones said. "I knew they would use their judgment and experience to assess the situation, determine what the most appropriate course of action would be in a deteriorating situation, and take it, and they did."

All Coast Guard units in District 8, essentially the Gulf of Mexico region, are required to go through a hurricane drill in April, two months before the hurricane season officially starts. They practice their unit hurricane plan to help everyone understand what they have to do, where they evacuate, and the procedures for returning and setting up operations. They practice the process several times during the hurricane season whenever a hurricane comes close. "We evacuate and breathe a sigh of relief as we don't get hit by the big one and come back to our units," Jones said. "The extent of the destruction and flooding and number of survivors was all forecast quite accurately by the Hurricane Pam Exercise [The FEMA exercise used realistic weather and damage information developed by the National Weather Service, the U.S. Army Corps of Engineers, the LSU Hurricane Center, and other state and federal agencies to help officials develop joint response plans for a catastrophic hurricane in Louisiana] in 2004. Anyone who had paid close attention to previous studies or Hurricane Pam would not have been surprised by extent of the devastation or the flooding.

"Now, having said that, when you see it with your own eyes, it still takes you back and is still a lot to comprehend," Jones said. "When you have literally thousands and thousands of people that are stranded, isolated, on rooftops, and injured, it still requires an unbelievably intense and resource-intensive effort to rescue them all, and having rescued them, to then provide them immediate levels of care and get them on to a final destination. The overwhelming extent of the need and the number of distress cases and the amount of rescue operations needing to be conducted, the volume of it all was the most difficult and challenging thing."

"IT TEARS AT YOUR HEART...because everybody needs to be rescued," said Monville. "Who am I to pick and choose who goes?"

A couple of cases Monville worked really took their toll on him, one of which was at a hospice hospital for terminal cancer patients. A caretaker had called for help saying doctors and nurses had abandoned twelve patients. "The PJ was on the rooftop and wanted another rescue swimmer to help him carry them out," said Monville.

The two men went down a hatch on the roof and climbed down the ladder from the fifth floor to meet the caretaker who took them to the second floor, lit only by candles. Monville and the PJ split up and started to triage the elderly in each room. "These people were laying in these beds, with their catheter and their IVs and a candle burning on the table. They were literally dying right there in front of me. I walked up to check the pulse on every single one of them," Monville said. "Some [pulses] were beating one time to three times a minute; they were basically on their last leg of life."

The rescuers decided they would get the people out of there. They talked about it and in a very short time they were faced with a troubling realization: there were no hospitals that could accept advanced-care patients. To complicate matters, Monville's crew was getting low on fuel. "It was the hardest thing I had to deal with the whole three days. I couldn't do a thing for them." Monville called the helicopter to discuss the situation further and was told he had to leave then. The helicopter needed fuel. Monville told the PJ he had to go.

Monville was picked up from the rooftop. "I broke down, I saw those twelve people, and I was probably the last face they will ever see. They were dying, and we could not do anything for them."

"We're up there and we want to save these people, but it's like what do you do when the hospitals are flooded, they have no power and these people are terminal?" Monville said. "It was one of those situations when there was nothing worse than feeling so helpless like that."

"I don't know how many times I'd be lowered from one hundred feet to a guy on the roof and ask, 'Is there anyone else?'" Monville said. In one case the man said yes, he had a wife, a four-year-old, a six-year-old, and a one-month-old baby. "A one-month-old?" Monville asked incredulously. "He had basically put a hole in his roof and put his family in the attic." While they evacuated the children, wife, and baby, Monville learned the man was a former Marine too. Because of weight restrictions, they could not overload the helicopter with one more person and it needed fuel. Frustrated, Monville had to leave the man on the roof with his father-in-law and go.

"Just like every time before, we had good intentions to go back to them. After we got fuel, we were called to go somewhere else," said Monville. "You know what's ironic about it, the day after that, I had got back from a long day of flying and walked into the air facility and there was this guy eating an MRE. He looked so familiar and I knew I had seen him before." Monville asked him where he was from. The man told him and said he was a former Marine. "I said to him I got your wife and babies. Somebody had picked him up with his father-in-law. They were just so low on fuel that they dropped him off at the air facility. Very few times are you reunited with someone you rescued.

"If you could put yourself in my shoes for a second, imagine yourself sitting in the door of the helicopter flying over the city where pretty much every large building has people on top waving blankets at you, some of them have refrigerators and coolers up there, living up there . . . You wish you had a huge net and you could just scoop them all up," said Monville.

THE SAVANNAH PILOTS LAUNCHED AND CLIMBED to search altitude. This was Laub's first visit to New Orleans. What he witnessed that morning was fanciful. "The sun was still coming up, when we got in the air over New Orleans. We saw flashlights all over the place, shining up into the sky. Thousands of lights everywhere from people on roofs or in their houses shining them out windows," Laub noticed. The sight was overwhelming. To get to work, they had to focus on their own postcard-size view of one of the worst natural disasters in American history. There was so much to do. At first, they tried to get into a couple of tight places to rescue people and could not safely do so even though they avoided downed power lines and treetops. Near a high-rise apartment complex, Laub was lowered on the hoist cable as the helicopter hovered in position.

"I just got caught in a wind tunnel and I could not see what I was doing when I started spinning real bad," said Laub. "The flight mechanic pulled me back up, there was no way I could do that one."

One of the pilots spotted a red T-shirt waving from a window of a nearby house. The water had risen to the third floor. "I got lowered to the roof and took a little ax that we have in our helicopter and I leaned over and screamed into the house, 'How many people do we have in here?'" Laub called. He heard someone shout back "Three."

Of his limited options, Laub's first choice was to enter through the window. Steel bars meant to keep out buglers stopped him. "I chopped a hole in the roof and jumped down. I ended up in their bathroom." Laub looked down the stairwell to find the water level had approached at least halfway up, flooding the inside of the home. Sequestered in an adjacent room he found a mother, her husband, and their twelve-year-old daughter. "It was like 105 degrees that day, so their house was like a sauna inside," Laub said.

The pilots radioed Laub to ask what he was doing and if everything was all right. They were holding the helicopter in a hover over the house, unable to see what was unfolding inside. Laub called for their assistance by asking them to look for a window he could work from to get the people out. He opened a couple of windows, all of which had bars on the outside. The aircrew saw where Laub was and helped decide which location was going to be the best to work the hoists from. The window with an installed air conditioner and a little patio-type area the family could stand on below seemed to be the best place. "I kicked the air conditioner out and took the ax and chopped out around the window. A bigger ax probably would have gotten it done a little quicker, but this one worked fine," recalled Laub. He climbed out and signaled for the rescue basket. He put the daughter in it first and off she went. The aircrew took the mom and finished this rescue off by hoisting the dad into the helicopter's cabin.

"When we dropped the family off, the little girl was crying, and the mom gave us a hug and stuff," said Laub. "They were probably pretty dehydrated because they downed bottles of water pretty quick. We gave them MREs too."

"We got fuel, took a small five-, ten-minute lunch break, MREs or granola bars, and got back into the air," stated Laub.

The rest of the aircrew's day and the many that followed were full of back-to-back rescues. Time after time, they packed the cabin full with as many people as they could before transporting them to a dry area. At one point, they rescued some nurses near what Laub thought was Memorial Medical Center, "stuck on their own little island."

Laub stayed on the ground as his helicopter, packed full of people, took off. "They were going to come right back for me," Laub said. "As soon as they took off, people saw there was a helicopter. I don't know where they came from but they just started coming, from nowhere, from the side streets, from boats. I ended up having a crowd to deal with. Women and children were there, infants . . . It quickly became a nightmare. Some of the men that kept coming out of the sides became kind of pushy, getting up in my face, using their manpower to overpower some of the people."

Laub tried to reason with the forceful men. "Look at this infant, are you going to push him out of the way?" The men had pushed women and their babies aside in an attempt to go ahead. "Go sit down," Laub said. They would not and threatened to go get all their friends and come back to be airlifted first.

The rescuers took as many people as they could from the site. "I called the helicopter and said, 'I'm coming with you this time.'" Despite their efforts, they had to leave about fifteen to twenty people on the ground. They notified officials of the situation. "As soon as you get in the air, there's people everywhere that needed help. You pick and choose where you can go, what you can do. We spread the word; hopefully a couple helicopters got in there to clear them out . . . It was a mess," Laub said. Laub said one man he rescued explained that he and his mother stayed because they didn't think the hurricane was going to be that bad. "He told me he and his mom watched Katrina pass through from some of their blown-out windows. Once it was gone, it was sunny, and a couple hours later water rushed all the way up to the roof of his house."

"That was day one for me," said Laub. He and the Savannah crew returned to Mobile for the night. A waiting aircrew was assigned the helicopter. It was a twenty-four-hour operation that would continue for days.

Of the landing sites available to drop off evacuated people, Laub had experience with three. "They started off with one place called Clover Leaf, a stretch of I-10, and they had ambulances there. Once it got too crowded, they opened up another section of the road at Lakeview or Lakefront.

The most convenient and the one I think went most smoothly was when they opened up at New Orleans International Airport," recalled Laub.

On Thursday, September 1, Laub worked with flight mechanic AET3 Brandon Hughes from Air Station Cape Cod and Mobile based pilots Lieutenant Commander M. Vislay and Lieutenant S. Cerveny aboard a HH-60J Jayhawk helicopter. The team would triple Laub's recorded number of rescues from the previous days, saving 104 people.

Overnight, the dangerous circumstances and threats directed toward rescuers required that rescue swimmers pair up. Laub partnered with AST3 Jonathan Ptak from Air Station Mobile. "We did that just because the crowd was pretty aggressive. It felt a lot better to have two guys to control the situation," said Laub. Their day began by dropping off eight hundred pounds of food and water in Clermont Harbor, Mississippi, for the stranded people there. "They needed supplies more than they needed evacuation," Laub said. "They were not flooded . . . New Orleans took the brunt of the news coverage, in Mississippi the entire coastline was just gone."

The Jayhawk helicopter completed the mission and approached New Orleans. Suddenly they were diverted to a call for help from one of there own, AST3 Robert Williams. Williams, a rescue swimmer from Air Station Corpus Christi, was on a rooftop, alone. He had been assisting a group of people at a Days Inn when the helicopter he was working with had to depart because of a maintenance issue.

Laub and Ptak were lowered to his location immediately. "It made it a lot easier, if you get on a roof and two guys could institute crowd control, it made it a lot better," said Laub. In this particular case, three rescue swimmers would work together.

As they approached they could see that the lower floors of the Days Inn were surrounded by fifteen feet of water. Laub and Ptak descended to the roof and joined Williams. They were able to work with the hotel owner to manage the evacuation. "We asked him to clear the hotel, go into every room, and have people come up to the roof," said Laub. "At first we had thirty people, and we thought, *Oh, this will take a couple of minutes.* Then all of a sudden lots of people started coming up to the roof, and we were like, 'Where are these people coming from?'"

Talking with the owner between hoists, the rescue swimmers learned that these people had planned on waiting there for the water to recede. It was hard for the rescuers to understand. Laub, Ptak, and Williams knew these hotel guests did not have air-conditioning, could not flush toilets, and were without power. "The water was up to the third, fourth floor of the hotel. It was hard to tell. There were school buses and trac-tor trailers on the outside of it that were completely covered in water," Laub noticed. "They really did not know how bad it was."

The Coast Guard rescuers picked up as many people as they could safely carry in the helicopter before flying to a drop-off site. With a large group like this, they tried to keep mothers with their children, so three or four were sent up in the rescue basket. "The pilot's log recorded ninety-two people saved on that rooftop alone," Laub said. This num-ber exceeded a career's worth of lives saved.

Next, with Laub and Ptak pulled away from the emptied roof and back aboard the helicopter, the pilots flew over to a bridgelike structure with stranded people on top. It was submerged on both ends in water yet there was enough of an area to land the helicopter in the middle. The aircrew picked up the six people there.

Up in the sky again, they located a mother and father with their daughter and son in an apartment complex waving at the helicopter. Ptak was lowered down. He used the direct-deployment method and stayed attached to the hoist hook and used a rescue strop. He wrapped it under one woman's arms to hoist her into the cabin with him and re-turned for the second. In turn, Laub did the same to hoist the two men.

"After that case, we were out of time and out of gas," said Laub. They returned to Air Station New Orleans, having rescued 104 people over a span of just eight hours. They flew back to ATC Mobile for much needed rest.

Laub was assigned to work from Air Station New Orleans for the next four days. Of the living conditions there, he described it as "like a bad camping trip . . . Half the hangar was destroyed, port-a-johns for bathrooms, there was an Army gym I'd say a mile and a half away if you had to get a shower . . . It was so hot, you almost had to. People would use the emergency eyewash station, to let some water rain down on them, cool off a little bit." For sleeping, it was a matter of finding a quiet place to lie down. "I slept with earplugs it was so loud," he said. For food they had boxes and boxes of MREs, tons of water, and Gatorade in the beginning. "One day a C-130 crew flew in 115 pizzas from a small town in Mississippi, which was awesome," Laub said. "They were gone pretty quick. Other than that it was you'd grab an MRE, put it in your bag, and find time later to eat it if your nerves calmed down enough to eat.

"When you're doing it you start to get nervous because you don't know what to expect and you knew the situation was bad; after four or five days you knew the situation was critical and that kept a lot of swimmers on edge," Laub said of the deteriorating condition of survivors. They were increasingly dehydrated, delirious, and many smelled of alcohol. "To see the people like that you wanted to help them more than you could," said Laub. "After four or five days, 50 percent of the people just wanted food and water, you'd try to explain to them, 'Look, there's fifteen feet of water outside your apartment complex; you need to get these kids out of here.'" Despite the horrible condition of their homes, the smell of raw sewage, and lack of sufficient food and water, these people could not be convinced by the rescue swimmers to abandon what was left of their homes. "Maybe they didn't know where they would go. That was probably one of the most frustrating parts of the whole trip," Laub said.

The following two nights, Laub flew aboard HH-65 Dolphin helicopters for rescues before being reassigned again to daytime rescues. "When you're flying around the city at night, it's just an eerie feeling. There is no power to the city, the only lights you have are burning buildings basically and flashlights from people's roofs. The city skyline is dark, I don't know if you'll ever see something like that, you get chills thinking about it, all you see when you look down is water covering houses, streets filled with water, like flying over something in the twilight zone."

On Laub's fifth day, September 4, he was assigned to fly with pilots Lieutenant J. Egan and Lieutenant Marcus Canady, flight mechanic AMT3 D. Cunningham who swapped out with AMT1 M. Currier from another crew, which was sent to the Ninth Ward. The pilots executed a really slow hover over the many buildings in the complex. They knew that the noise of the helicopter would draw people outside where they could be seen.

"We found some guys in the apartment complex. I got lowered down to the balcony, but I didn't want to touch that nasty water, so I stuck my foot out and the guy pulled me into the patio," Laub said. "I go inside, and there is this big pit bull with another man. I couldn't leave the guy, and the dog was all barking and frothing at the mouth, all dehydrated and sick looking." Laub convinced the man to hold onto the dog and keep him away from the crew and he would take the dog too. The men seemed to be brothers and had been there for a while.

"Right after that we saw a woman standing on the roof of her house. She'd been flown over for three or four days and why no one saw her was amazing," Laub said. "It was not like they weren't looking for her, it was just that there were just so many people out there at the same time that you can't find everybody." As he put the woman, who appeared to be in her midthirties, in the basket, he asked if she was alone. She pleaded for Laub to get her dogs. After Laub hoisted her up, he climbed down a makeshift ladder she had made to get inside her house. "There was this rottweiler sitting on the floor, looked really sick, breathing real heavily. I walked around the corner and this huge rottweiler charged at me and started barking . . . so I jumped out the window and climbed back up on the roof and got out of there." Laub apologized to the woman that he could not take her dogs after one tried to attack him. "I felt really bad," Laub said, "I'm not trained in dog-capturing techniques." The aircrew passed along the information hoping that someone was able to help the dogs.

Laub, like many of the rescuers, would never know what happened in this case and others like it. They would not be able to find out either what happened after they left a scene. "Guys were trying to convince people to leave their house. People had like five suitcases they wanted to bring. They would start crying . . . You had to tell them it is either your life or your luggage."

"Nothing can get you completely ready for a mass chaos situation like that, but the training you go through in 'A' school is a definite bonus, it helps you out," Laub said. "The bulk of the training is for water, but they do teach you how to handle a crowd regardless of being on water or land."

The number of people rescued dropped significantly by Sunday, September 4. The Coast Guard continued to fly around the clock looking for those in need.

"I'll never top this again. The situation was horrible, it was kind of like, throw the worst at us, and we did our best," Laub said. "Towards September third and fourth, they had more crews coming in who were ready and fresh and took the load off of us. We still had no power in the hangar, everything was running on generators, no running water until the day I left for Savannah, Georgia, on September sixth."

"After about the first five days our people were just totally done. ATC Mobile and Air Station Houston stepped up and took really good care of our people," said Jones. "We basically allowed everyone assigned to Air Station New Orleans to rotate out for a week. Then they'd come back and work for eighteen hours a day, seven days a week, and do it one more time."

THE AVIATION TRAINING CENTER IN MOBILE was the Coast Guard's large staging area for aviation personnel and aircraft. ATC Mobile also funneled people coming in from all over the country to where they were needed most. Often it was to help with Air Station New Orleans' search and rescue efforts, which focused primarily on southeast Louisiana.

Additionally, ATC Mobile had responsibility for coastal Mississippi aviation missions. The difference was that after the first couple of days in that area, anyone who needed to be rescued had been.

Operations continued around the clock for at least the first ten days. "On a daily basis we had up to fifty Coast Guard and DOD [Department of Defense] helicopters constantly coming in and out on my ramp," Jones said.

Coast Guard Vice Admiral Thad Allen assumed the role of principal federal official (PFO) for the multistate response to Katrina on September 7, 2005. He wrote a note to classmates, which was published in the Coast Guard Academy Alumni magazine October 2005 issue, and is excerpted here with permission: "I will tell you that there is an incredible effort underway by thousands of response and recovery personnel for which you and the nation can be justly proud. The incredible bravery and dedication of our air crews immediately following the hurricane has been matched by countless small boat crews who have saved thousands."

THE KIND OF SEARCH AND RESCUE THE COAST GUARD accomplished after Katrina could not be compared to its traditional work.

"In the typical SAR case, you'd transit offshore, be knocked around by the wind or heavy seas, and get on scene. In about thirty minutes to one hour almost every SAR case is wrapped up," said Jones. "You'd be pushing your skills to the limit, use all your capabilities, adrenaline pumping, then you're done and you'd get bounced around, moor back up at the pier, then its over and you breathe a sigh of relief."

He said that aircrews and ship crews regularly talk about a rescue with their coworkers and go home to sleep. Every once in a while, a crewman would remember it, but for the most part it was ancient history. In that period of high-intensity stress and adrenaline rush, fear was relatively of short duration, Jones said. "In Katrina, crews would get airborne and be already over the city starting to do rescues because it was only two miles from the unit. Working in one-hundred-degree heat, no wind, high humidity, which is the worst conditions for the underpowered HH-65B helicopter to operate in . . . hovering on top of trees, next to power lines where if anything were to happen to the engines, you're going to crash and burn . . . There were constant reports of people shooting at helicopters, some of which were verified, some of which weren't, but you didn't know that," Jones said. "You've got angry people shaking their fists when you fly over after the days wore on, and you had the state failing to bring in water and food and the medical supplies in the tent cities that were needed for all these tens of thousands of survivors. So we're picking up people off of rooftops and setting them down in fields and there is no one there to care for them.

"By the fourth day there were one hundred fifty helicopters total over the city and it was just a hornets' nest. There was a constant concern for a midair collision, we were all very concerned there would be a Class A mishap, a fatal mishap, and by the grace of God and good skills of all the crews and keeping their heads on the swivel and being very attentive, we avoided midair collisions."

"As the folks came back, every day from their flights, I'd try to greet as many people as I could coming off the helicopters, and they looked shell-shocked," Jones recalled. "Then they'd work for eight hours after their flights, loading food and water, unloading C-130s, fixing the helicopters, trying to rebuild the unit, then they'd sleep for a couple of hours on a cot inside a building with no power. They would get up the next day and do it again. They did that for a week, and the boat crews did the same thing.

"The situations the rescue swimmers found themselves having to deal with were unpracticed and unrehearsed," said Jones. "During one debriefing session, I talked with Dave Foreman, who was my rescue swimmer on the first day for nine hours. I brought up the *Bow Mariner* and asked him how this compared knowing he was exposed to a toxic environment to save six people during one of the greatest Coast Guard rescues in Coast Guard history, and he said that 'Captain, *Bow Mariner* was nothing compared to what we went through in Katrina.'"

During a rescue with Jones, swimmer Dave Foreman was lowered to the second story of a flooded house to try to help two elderly, bedridden people in the Lakeview area of New Orleans. "The window was three feet underneath an overhang so he had to grab onto the overhang with one hand and swing himself in," Jones said, "then break out the window with his gloved hand. In this case he could not get them out, and we spent almost a half hour there and finally he had to say to me, 'Captain, I just can't get them out.' That was a very difficult thing to do, leave people behind. But we just didn't have a choice."

Many rescue swimmers had to deal with tremendous risks and physical hazards over and over again, which was very different from a typical offshore rescue where they would fight heavy seas. "Every time you come into a hover, you'd never know what was going to start flying around, what kind of shrapnel the rotor wash was going to generate," Jones recalled. "And people were angry sometimes when you landed on a roof; after three or four days in one hundred degrees on a rooftop, people were just pissed. Even though they wanted to be rescued, they were hungry, dehydrated, and they felt abandoned. They would take their anger out on the rescuers."

AST2 Joel Sayers, from ATC Mobile, was faced with such outrage when he got to a roof with about twelve people. One of the men came up to him from behind and broke a bottle over his head. Sayers avoided injury because he had his rescue helmet on and thought quickly. According to Jones, Sayers grabbed the biggest guy on the roof and said, "If anyone does that again, we're out of here, we're not coming back." "The big guy established order over his peers," Jones said.

"The extraordinarily high-op [operations at their highest level] tempo, absolutely unprecedented in Coast Guard history, the number of sorties, and the intensity of the operation, despite that there were no significant injuries to personnel, just cuts and bruises, no broken bones or deaths. It was just phenomenal that there were no significant injuries," Jones said. "When you look at an individual rescue swimmer's stats, you could see they saved a total of seventy-five to one hundred people over the course of the week, which is more than you'd normally save in a whole career. Of the rescues, fifty of them would have been completely unique and individually stood on its own as a great rescue."

FROM THE FIRST COAST GUARD RESCUE AFTER Hurricane Katrina came ashore until September 8, the number of lives saved by Coast Guard helicopter crews working around the clock was 7,070.

In October of 2005, Air Station New Orleans marked its fiftieth anniversary of service. "In terms of our five helicopters from Air Station New Orleans, it was little over fifteen hundred lives saved during Hurricane Katrina. If you prorate that by what we had done in the previous fifty years, that's about twenty-two years' worth of lives saved in one week," Jones said.

The Coast Guard announced that more than 33,520 lives were saved and evacuated by its massive response—six times the number of rescues by servicewide air and surface components in all of 2004.

Included in that data are 9,400 patients and medical personnel evacuated from hospitals in the Gulf Coast region. "At the height of rescue operations, the Coast Guard had at least 62 aircraft, 30 cutters and 111 small boats assisting in rescue and recovery operations," detailed a Coast Guard press release. "More than 5,200 Coast Guard personnel conducted search and rescue operations, waterway reconstitution and environmental assessment operations and more than 400 Coast Guard reservists were recalled to active duty."

HOW COULD A LEADER DEAL WITH SUCH a catastrophe day after day? "I managed to handle it because I have absolutely magnificent people working for me from my executive officer, Commander Kitchen, and my ops officer. Lieutenant Commander Tobiasz, to the most junior member of the crew," Jones said. "It was just a phenomenal thing to see how these men and women stepped up to the plate and worked around the clock without a single complaint despite people working until they just dropped, curling up into a ball and sleeping for an hour." Jones further credited the talent, dedication, and devotion of the electricians, facilities engineers, aircraft mechanics, and all of the support personnel as phenomenal.

"IT WAS CERTAINLY THE MOST STRESSFUL, intense period in my life and the most challenging and exhausting," Jones said. "After the sixth day I was done, mentally tapped out. I was ordered out and resisted for twenty-four hours. Then I was picked up by a Falcon jet sent in by the 8th District commander, Admiral Duncan, to take me to ATC Mobile to rest in the barracks for thirty-six hours." Jones tried to decompress and made phone calls to his family to find out where they had decided to move.

"My wife is very strong and independent person who packed for three days and left town and found out later that she would not be able to return for the next year," recalled Jones. "With a very strong support network of friends at our last duty station, Traverse City Michigan, they were able to find a place to live and get started in a new home."

"All of the Coast Guard spouses are very resilient and strong. They relied on their own initiative to find new homes and decide what they would do next about jobs, schools, and establishing a new way of life," said Linda Jones. "We know when hurricanes come our spouses go to work—we know it is time to pick up the slack and take care of things. It is just amazing what these women have done, not one single family was left there, everybody was evacuated, everybody was safe, and in one day we were spread out all over the country. It was just so strange. It really makes you see things differently. When you see people suffering like that, your personal things are so worthless. But also, just being very concerned about the physical side of what the rescue swimmers and rescuers were being exposed to and the unbelievable stress they were under."

By the time Jana saw her husband again, two weeks after the hurricane, she had temporarily relocated to New York. "He was zonked, he didn't even know what was going on. They were so insulated, no newspapers, no television, they were living such a primitive life that he had no idea what the rest of the world was doing," said Jana. "When you don't have regular showers, just working twenty-four hours a day, can't really leave because there is no where to go. The city is empty or destroyed and there are military vehicles everywhere. . . . He asked me, 'Have people forgotten about us?'"

"In terms of his safety as a pilot, I had to get over that really fast or I never could have been a military wife," said Jana. "My way of dealing with it from the beginning is 'This is his job, he has to do it, I can't sit here and worry about every little thing or I'll go crazy'. . . . I was mostly concerned because I knew these men and women had to be in a certain condition it order to do their job safely in terms of being able to sleep, eat, and feeling well and clearheaded. His mom and I tried to figure out how to get care packages to them, with Gatorade, snack bars, Power bars deodorant, socks, underwear." She had learned that everyone wore the same flight suit and alternated between two pairs of underwear for the first two weeks.

Jana and her husband plan to rebuild their flooded New Orleans home themselves. She has returned to school, and her husband is back to working "normal operations" at the air station. "I've always really respected the fact that these men and women and my husband chose to do something they knew was helping people, every single day and putting their own lives in danger . . . ," said Jana. "I kind of would have expected nothing less. This is what they would have done anytime; it's their job and they are dedicated. I'm honored to know them."

"OUR BOAT CREWS AND AIRCREWS ARE AMONG the bravest and most dedicated, competent people you'll ever run across," said Jones. "It's a hell of an organization." Completing his two-year assignment as commanding officer the summer of 2006, he will transfer with his family to the 1st Coast Guard District in Boston, assigned as chief of incident management.

AST2 CHRIS MONVILLE MARRIED HIS FIANCÉE in late September. He continues to work at Air Station New Orleans. AST3 Matt Laub returned to work at Air Station Savannah. In October of 2005, he was the Coast Guard rescue swimmer representative for the Coast Guard Foundation's Salute to the Coast Guard fund-raising dinner, which honored those who served in Hurricane Katrina rescue operations.

Among the other thirteen representatives honored were Rear Admiral Robert Duncan, 8th District commander, who served as the operational field commander for the Coast Guard response to Hurricane Katrina; Captain Bruce Jones and MK3 Brian Bresnehan of Air Station New Orleans, small boat community representative. Also present was the Maritime Safety and Security Team (MSST) Representative Lieutenant Commander Sean Regan, Commanding Officer MSST 91112 in New Orleans; Cutter Fleet Representative, MK1 Charles Hunt, assigned to CGC *Spencer*, home ported in Boston, Massachusetts; Sector Mobile Representative, CWO Steve Lyons, Commanding Officer of Station Gulfport, Mississippi; Port Security Unit (PSU) representative Lieutenant

Teresa Hubbard, Logistics Officer of PSU 308 in Gulfport, Mississippi. A Marine Safety representative, Commander Roger Laferriere, Commanding Officer of the Atlantic Strike Team in Norfolk, Virginia, was also recognized along with Support (Maintenance and Logistics Command) Community Representative, IT1 Scott Campbell of ESD [Electronic Support Division] Detroit.

Coast Guard Auxiliary representatives, Mr. Dave Phillips of Flotilla 6-6 and Coast Guard Auxiliarist and Representative Mr. Chris Ware, attended the event as did Aviation Training Center (ATC) Mobile Commanding Officer Captain David Callahan.

EPILOGUE

RESCUING THE RESCUER

CRITICAL INCIDENT STRESS MANAGEMENT

You are able to off-load the information, and that is a part of the healing process. Rescue swimmers or firefighters are usually macho, type A personalities. The last thing they want to do is admit to someone that they need some help.

—Chief Warrant Officer George Cavallo, rescue swimmer

DURING THE EVENING OF JULY 12, 1994, Air Station Humboldt Bay in California responded to a distress call from two people aboard a grounded, forty-foot sailing vessel by sending an HH-65A Dolphin rescue helicopter. "While engaged in a nighttime search for the stranded vessel, the 6541 struck a shoreline cliff in heavy fog just south of Shelter Cove and was lost," wrote rescue swimmer and Chief Warrant Officer George Cavallo.

The rescue swimmer on that search and rescue mission, Senior Chief Petty Officer Peter A. Leeman perished, along with pilots Lieutenant Lawrence B. Williams, Lieutenant Mark E. Koteek, and flight mechanic, First Class Petty Officer Michael R. Gill.

The two people on the sailboat made their way safely to shore.

Then a First Class Petty Officer, George Cavallo was assigned to lead the Air Station Humboldt Bay ASM shop six weeks after Senior Chief Peter Leeman died. He worked with the men, one of whom was his brother-in-law, to bring them back, help them want to go out to save lives again. By paying attention to them, understanding their grief, and normalizing their emotional stress, they were able to overcome their traumatic experience and return to work.

Cavallo would find himself working as a rescuer in a similar trsgic case. He was the Coast Guard rescue swimmer deployed to the crash site of the United States Air Force Reserve HC-130 P aircraft on November 22, 1996.

According to Cavallo's written summary of the accident, the fixed-wing aircraft departed Portland, Oregon, on a routine, over-water navigation training mission to North Island Naval Air Station California, near San Diego. Two hours after it left that evening, all four engines flamed out and the crew declared an emergency. On its final descent, fifteen minutes later, the aircraft slammed into the Pacific Ocean at two hundred miles per hour. Ten of the eleven men on board died. The sole survivor was the radio operator.

What Cavallo saw during his rescue of the C-130 survivor was haunting. The rescue aircrew arrived on scene aboard a Dolphin helicopter and commenced a search for the C-130 crew. Lieutenant Kelly Larson, the first female rescue swimmer, profiled in chapter 4, was the copilot. "The problem was we only had seven to ten minutes of fuel before we had to go back," Cavallo said. "The first two guys we really couldn't do much for with sharks circling and taking hits. They were obviously deceased. Then we saw the third guy was waving; we got him and brought him back," said Cavallo who was hoisted down to rescue the man. "We sent in Coast Guard small boat crews to pick up the bodies. They had been through a catastrophic crash, so the bodies were not in the best shape and then the sea creatures were taking their turn on them. So those guys [the rescuers] went through critical incident stress counseling but not with us."

Cavallo and those affected by the traumatic event were provided assistance dealing with their stress or adverse psychological reactions, which can accompany a disaster response. Counselors helped them normalize their experience as part of a Coast Guard–wide program called Critical Incident Stress Management (CISM).

"They put us through these demobilizations, basically where the air-crews got together and each told a part of the story that we knew to be true . . . I did this, this is how I felt, I saw this, smelled this," Cavallo said. "We go around the group and everyone does that; you are able to piece a whole story together in your brain and in some ways put it to rest. Or if you have questions or you might always be wondering what happened here or there, you are able to now get some kind of closure."

Immediately following Hurricane Katrina's massive rescue and response, CISM counselors were on scene to help rescuers cope. Cavallo, a trained CISM counselor, was close to retirement, working as a marine inspector in New Orleans. He agreed to go behind the scenes with other CISM-trained rescue swimmers including Lieutenant Mike Odom, who debriefed Cavallo after he worked on the Pacific Ocean C-130 crash in 1996.

"You are able to off-load the information, and that is a part of the healing process," said Cavallo. "Rescue swimmers or firefighters are usu-ally macho, type A personalities. The last thing they want to do is admit to someone that they need some help." Cavallo said they've found that peers—folks that have been there, done that, have picked up the bodies—are the best folks to talk to these people. "If you've been around rescue swimmers, you know there is a brotherhood, a kind of a tightness. To pen-etrate that circle as a mental health worker or as a psychologist, it is not going to work. They are not going to want to talk to you," Cavallo said.

Cavallo has found acceptance as a CISM counselor throughout his career by starting off by talking about his own experiences as a rescue swimmer, stationed at five air stations and as a chief at Air Station Ko-diak. "The next thing you know they are telling you their life stories; it's great because you really see it work." The program also works the same way for the flight mechanics, pilots, and copilots.

Right after an event, counselors informally talk with rescuers one on one to hear and understand what they went through, which is called de-mobilization. "We slip in that it is normal to feel that way, you went through an abnormal event, you picked up some bodies, saw some gory stuff," Cavallo said. "You try to normalize the situation for them, so they don't feel like a wimp or not adequate because they can't sleep at night."

Cavallo advises those he talks with to spend some of their time off with family, and he also encourages exercise.

"We've been working with Master Chief Scott Dyer, the head rescue swimmer, to come up with a game plan on how we're going to talk with a lot of these swimmers. At one point he had sixty rescue swimmers working for him in New Orleans," said Cavallo.

Counselors try to match their interventions, or debriefs, with people they know would feel comfortable talking with them, for example, setting up senior officers and senior enlisted with senior people and vice versa.

Five months after Katrina, a CISM team of rescue swimmers' counselors returned to New Orleans to debrief, or "defuse," rescuers who still needed assistance processing their experience and were having trouble sleeping. "After that if they need help, they will probably be referred to an Employee Assistance Program. As a peer you can only do so much," said Cavallo.

The rescue environment following Hurricane Katrina was diverse and unusual. The sheer volume of cases over an extended period of days caused stress to build up with little room for release. Everyone involved in saving lives was dealing with a catastrophic event, a new environment where people had lost everything; each day was uncommon to behold. The culmination of it all led to instances of post-traumatic stress disorder.

"A lot of rescue swimmers were affected by the kids. [A helicopter] would lower a swimmer down and fly off, which is very unusual, usually the helicopter never leaves," said Cavallo. "They would fly off so the rescue swimmer could hear the yells for help. It was dark and they could not see where the people were, so they'd listen. Then [the swimmers] called the helicopter back, got picked up, and [would] go over to the house they heard the cries coming from. They were able to help some, but they would have to leave when the helicopter was full. That meant there was never closure. Rescuers asked, 'Did all those people get saved?'"

In another case, a flight mechanic aboard one of the first helicopters involved with rescues after Katrina stormed ashore was exhausted. She had been hoisting all day long. "We did a debriefing with her," Cavallo said. "She was very concerned about hurting or putting the rescue swimmer in danger because she was so fatigued."

Cavallo was aware that a lot of pilots were having trouble sleeping. In another situation, a rescue swimmer was lowered to search inside a darkened hospital for survivors. "He came around the corner and was faced with four guys with shotguns," said Cavallo. "Earlier that same day people were firing at helicopters. It turned out they were security guards, but [the swimmer] didn't know that at the time." Swimmers were essentially unarmed during the operation. They did carry an ax to help chop into roofs. "You don't want to bring an ax to a gunfight," Cavallo said. "Some of the people in hospitals were in there trying to get drugs. They had to bring Seal teams in to storm the Convention Center to take it back. There were gangsters in there with guns who were mad they had not been rescued from there and after a while were shooting at helicopters.

"Of course that's on everybody's mind. That's not the thing you're used to. Usually people are very excited to see us and rescue them and now you're dealing with the possibility of getting shot at, and that's not good.

"Any rescue swimmer will tell you that it is the whole crew, they can't stress that enough, the whole crew has to be cohesive and work together to adjust and overcome the situations they find themselves in, like in Tristan's case," stated Cavallo, referring to rescue swimmer Tristan Heaton, profiled in chapter 5.

THREE YEARS AFTER THE ENTIRE COAST GUARD aircrew died in the Air Station Humboldt Bay crash, another tragedy would befall Air Station Humboldt Bay. Cavallo, still the AST shop supervisor and AST1, was six months away from transferring to another air station.

It was June 8, 1997. ASM3 James G. Caines jumped with excitement aboard the HH-65A Dolphin helicopter, tail number 6549. It was his first search and rescue case. Pilots Lieutenant Jeffrey F. Crane and Lieutenant Junior Grade Charles W. Thigpen, along with Aviation Machinist Mate Third Class Richard L. Hughes were the other members of the aircrew. They were responding to a floundering thirty-seven-foot sailing vessel's call for help. The disabled vessel, with five people on board, was approximately fifty-seven miles west of Cape Mendocino. Buffeted by high winds and heavy seas, it was hardly afloat.

A Dolphin helicopter aircrew flew out twice to circle the boat. The crew dropped a radio to establish communications with the sailors and convince them to abandon ship. "They wouldn't. Then another aircrew assembled, and I flew out with them," Cavallo said. "We spoke to [the people on the boat] on the radio and tried to convince them to get off during the daylight hours, and they said no." Cavallo and his aircrew returned to the air station, close to being "bagged" with too many hours to continue flying. Phone calls were made to bring in a third team.

Meanwhile, the Coast Guard had dispatched an eighty-two-foot patrol boat to the sailing vessel's location to tow it in. A Coast Guard C-130 was circling overhead to help coordinate communications and monitor the unfolding case.

"I was walking across the hangar deck after cleaning the aircraft and here comes Jamie," said Cavallo. "He said, 'Let me take the duty; in case this goes down, I want to take the rescue.'" ASM3 "Jamie" Caines, twenty-four, had qualified as a rescue swimmer two days before. "He was a sharp kid, really driving hard, and we marveled at how he qualified in record time," Cavallo said.

Cavallo tried to convince him that the case was over and would be handled by the patrol boat. He told the younger man to go home, be with his family and young son. Caines was not deterred, saying to Cavallo, "I've trained so hard, worked so hard over the last five months, and I really want to put it all together."

Cavallo, who believed the case was in fact over, said, "All right, if you really want it that bad, you can have it."

"He reached over and hugged me on the hangar deck and said, 'Thanks, I really want to do this,'" recalled Cavallo, very surprised by the affection. "It was just weird, like he was waiting all his life to have this case."

Cavallo went home and had dinner with his wife before going to bed. His phone rang around 11:20 P.M. that night waking him out of a deep sleep.

IT WAS KEITH YOUNG, a flight mechanic performing the duties of the air station watch captain that night.

"He said, in a really monotone, depressed tone I'll never forget, 'I've been trying to call the '49. We lost comms with the '49 for over a half hour.'"

"It still didn't dawn on me. I said, 'The '49? Is it on another rescue?'"

"No, they went back out," said Young. "That sailing boat took a bad wave, and it blew out a couple of windows. They took on a little bit of water. The 82er came in and tried to remove the people off the deck. The seas were too rough. It was determined that a helicopter needed to come out and hoist everybody off the vessel."

Cavallo replied, "I'll be right in." He hung up the phone and told his wife they had lost communication with the Coast Guard helicopter, tail number 6549. "I ran out the door and drove to the air station at light speed and went into the communications center." He was informed that they were launching another helicopter to go look for CG 6549. It was now forty-five minutes to an hour after they had lost communications with their fellow airmen.

Cavallo's wife was very alarmed and called his brother-in-law, another rescue swimmer, who in turn informed other swimmers assigned to the air station who all raced over.

Cavallo got his gear. "I got all dressed up except for my harness. I went out on the tarmac and laid my harness down to step into it. I was pretty frazzled trying to put on my harness." His brother-in-law, ASM1 Mike Steinbach, and another rescue swimmer, ASM2 Rick Flemming, walked over and helped him get dressed. "We didn't say a word to each other. The pilots came out. We were all professional, talked about where we were going, what we were going to do."

The aircrew got into the helicopter and launched into the darkness. "About that time we knew they didn't have enough fuel to get back so we were all thinking the worst," said Cavallo. They had been briefed about what had happened on scene. "The eighty-two-foot motor lifeboat had put its small boat [a rigid hull inflatable], back in the water again. It took them a while, but they were able to get everybody off the vessel. The sailboat was bobbing up and down so badly that it would land on the rigid hull inflatable and bounce off. It was bad conditions, and they were able to pull it off somehow. They had a really rough time."

Cavallo's helicopter arrived on scene, and the aircrew searched until they exhausted all their fuel and had just enough to make it home and land with their normal reserve.

"That was the hardest thing I've ever done in my whole life, my whole Coast Guard career. It was like searching for family or searching for your own. It was very emotional for all of us," Cavallo said. Inside the helicopter it was silent, except for the crew maintaining their professionalism, flying and doing the jobs they had to do. "Everybody was glued to every window, looking for a flare, looking for a guy in the water waving, anything. We could not fathom that the whole crew would be lost."

"While maneuvering to pick up the sailors, the 6549 and its four-person crew disappeared from contact and was lost," wrote George Cavallo in his summary of the accident. He believes the aircraft hit the water while making an approach to the sailing vessel.

"By this time, every air station along the Pacific Coast had sent a helicopter, and every ship within a thousand miles had been diverted. The Coast Guard is a small service. Everyone and their brother were coming in to look for their fellow Coastie."

The captain of the air station grounded Cavallo and the entire aircrew once they landed because they were too close to the situation. There was an abundance of other aircrews and helicopters to continue the search they had started.

The tail of CG 6549 was located later on that afternoon. It would be months before the helicopter was recovered from the deep. There were no survivors. Only the flight mechanic's body was recovered.

"Three rescue swimmers threw their wings on my desk and said they were never flying again," said Cavallo, who was the one to support and lead the swimmers in the shop through the emotional stress and tragic loss. Other air station swimmers were called in to assist. "I left their wings on my desk and as soon as I got permission to stand duty I was the first person to stand duty. Three or four days later they all started standing duty again. They all went on to fly and have great careers . . . The initial shock was over."

Cavallo says he has a good support system and credits his wife, a psychiatric nurse, with helping him. She also assisted many Coast Guard families as a CISM counselor in Kodiak. "One month later, for about three days, I could not get off the couch, and my wife said to me, 'You know, you are going through depression?'"

The two Air Station Humboldt Bay helicopter crashes and resulting loss of precious life in an attempt to help "so others may live" have a significant place in the history of Coast Guard aviation. Neither rescue swimmer was actively deployed when he died. The loss of each man, each member of the aircrew, resonates throughout the Coast Guard to this day.

GALLERY OF RESCUE SWIMMERS

Rescue strop is lowered by a HH-60J helicopter to a rescue swimmer in the immense surf of the Pacific Ocean.
GLENN GROSSMAN

Master Chief Butch Flythe, life support and equipment manager for Coast Guard Aviation and one of the First Five.
McCLEARY COLLECTION

"Top Fin" ASMCM Darell Gelakoska was in charge of the rescue swimmer STAN team in the early 1990s and founded the Advanced Rescue Swimmer School in Astoria, Oregon.
GELAKOSKA COLLECTION

Rescue swimmer Jeff Tunks (fourth from left) stands with the rest of the Coast Guard Air Station Sitka HH-3F pilots and crew he flew with to rescue the father and son (pictured) from their sinking fishing boat on December 10, 1987.
ALLEN SKORA PHOTO

Master Chief George Waters, AST School Branch Chief and Master Chief Scott Dyer, Rescue Swimmer Program Manager next to banners created by each graduating rescue swimmer class from the Elizabeth City, North Carolina "A" School. AUTHOR PHOTO

Kelly Mogk was the first woman to qualify as a rescue swimmer in the Coast Guard and in all of the military services. LARSON COLLECTION

ASM2 Daniel W. Edwards beat what appeared to be insurmountable odds during the March 1993 "Storm of the Century." McCLEARY COLLECTION

Rescue Swimmer Mario Vittone holds the life jacket worn by the four-month-old boy he rescued along with his mother, sister, and father from the sailing vessel Marine Flower II on November 17, 1994. AUTHOR PHOTO

ASM2 Tristan Heaton saved a teenager from certain death inside an Oregon cave on April 4, 1993. The pilots and crew aboard the Dolphin helicopter maneuvered the aircraft into the cave to lower lines to Heaton and the drowning individual. HEATON COLLECTION

Rescue swimmer Eric Mueller (second from right) descended from the helicopter to help save a suicidal veteran straddling a rock just yards from Niagara Falls' 176-foot drop. With assistance from flight mechanic Sean Lott and pilots Lieutenant Eric Hollinger and Lieutenant Commander Richard Hinchion they recovered the man. MUELLER COLLECTION

Rescue swimmer Mike Thomas, who has served over eighteen years in the profession, rescued survivors in Madison County, Virginia, from floodwaters that ravaged everything in its path on June 27, 1995. McCLEARY COLLECTION

Front row (left to right): Rescue swimmer John Green, flight mechanic Mike Bouchard. Back row (left to right): Lieutenant Troy Beshears, and Lieutenant Commander Brian Moore helped evacuate survivors from an exploding and burning oil rig off the Louisiana coast. GREEN COLLECTION

Rescue swimmer and critical incident stress counselor George Cavallo. CAVALLO COLLECTION

Rescue swimmer Mutt Laub assisted with search and rescue operations following Hurricane Katrina along with more than 5,000 Coast Guard personnel, who also helped with rescues, waterway reconsitution, and environmental assessment operations throughout Mississippi, Alabama, and Louisana. LAUB COLLECTION

Rescue swimmers (left to right) and avid mountain climbers Jason Bunch and Bob Watson enjoyed living in Alaska. BUNCH COLLECTION

Rescue swimmer Chris Monville was aboard one of the first helicopters on scene to assist in Hurricane Katrina search and rescues. He carries an ax, not normally a part of an aircrew's rescue equipment.

USCG/MONVILLE COLLECTION

AST1 Jason Bunch, an instructor at the Advanced Rescue Swimmer School in Elizabeth City, North Carolina, assisted Bob Watson, a highly decorated rescue swimmer and friend, during the difficult recovery of two women from a Cessna 180 crash into a remote Alaskan mountainside.

BUNCH COLLECTION

Captain (retired) Dana Goward was instrumental in developing the initial proposal for the Coast Guard's rescue swimmer program in 1983.

GOWARD COLLECTION

Rescue swimmer and retired Master Chief Larry Farmer spearheaded the rescue swimmer program for over thirteen years as the STAN Team senior enlisted manager and the program manager until 1997. FARMER COLLECTION

APPENDIX:
LIST OF ABBREVIATIONS

Aviation Electrician's Mate (AE)

AE3	Third Class Aviation Electrician's Mate
AE2	Second Class Aviation Electrician's Mate
AE1	First Class Aviation Electrician's Mate

Aviation Electronics Technician (AT)

AT3	Third Class Aviation Electronics Technician
AT2	Second Class Aviation Electronics Technician
AT1	First Class Aviation Electronics Technician
ATC	Chief Aviation Electronics Technician
ATCS	Senior Chief Aviation Electronics Technician
ATCM	Master Chief Aviation Electronics Technician

Aviation Survivalman (ASM)

ASM3	Third Class Aviation Survivalman
ASM2	Second Class Aviation Survivalman
ASM1	First Class Aviation Survivalman
ASMC	Chief Aviation Survivalman
ASMCS	Senior Chief Aviation Survivalman
ASMCM	Master Chief Aviation Survivalman

AD2	Second Class Aviation Machinist Mate

EMT	Emergency Medical Technician
EPIRB	Emergency Position Indicator Radio Beacons
ICS	Internal Communication System
RRC	Rescue Coordination Center
SAR	Search and Rescue
STAN	Rescue Swimmer Standarization Team

INDEX

Italicized page numbers indicate photographs.